A Journey Through Sabbaths Lost

If God Intended the Sabbath,
Why Did He Create Home Ownership?

Ronald Citron

ISBN: 979-8-88640-451-7 (sc)
ISBN: 979-8-88640-452-4 (hc)
ISBN: 979-8-88640-453-1 (e)

THE EWINGS PUBLISHING

One Galleria Blvd., Suite 1900, Metairie, LA 70001
1-888-421-2397

I dedicate this book to my loving wife, Judy,
and my two lovely children,
David and Amy

CONTENTS

CHAPTER ONE

In the Beginning

Idyllic.

We all know what that word means even if we can't define it. I can't define it either, but I am staring at a photo that sings out "idyllic"!

The photo, taken on a gentle, beautiful late spring day, is of me, swinging lazily in a hammock: one of those great weave hammocks you just sink into. One end is tied to a mammoth oak tree and the other fastened to a steel post. There is a table next to me – a foldable TV tray table – with a large glass of soft drink. The sky is blue with streaks of clouds and haze. Everything is just softly whispering "lazy" ... Idyllic.

Oh, did I forget the birds? They aren't in the picture, but I can still hear them just the same. And the wonderful smell of newly blooming flowers and freshly mowed grass.

Mmmmmm. The world was carefree. Yes, so carefree.

Oh, sorry. I just got lost in the moment.

"Ah," you are probably saying. "What's the catch?" As in the movies there is always a catch. "That day didn't happen. The photo is a fake."

Nope! It happened just as I described.

"A storm was brewing and the photo op was staged before the skies opened up." Wrong again.

"The hammock broke five minutes after the picture was taken."

Get real!

The catch? Okay, I must make a confession. I was only eleven and it could never have occurred to me how fleeting this time of wonder would be.

Oh, by the way, my mom took the picture. Where was my dad? I don't recall what he was doing at that moment; but my memories of those carefree days show him performing some type of surgery or another on the house, on the lawn, on the trees, and on the driveway.

My mom did the family things. You know, driving my brother and me to piano practice, taking me to the dentist, making nutritious lunches – or at least that was her excuse for why they tasted soooo bad.

But to Dear Old Dad fell the duty of "bringing home the bacon," as he so often reminded us. We were always short of money and when I was little I wondered if we would have done better if he brought home some other type of meat. How the amount of bacon affected our ability to take vacations or buy toys was very confusing to my very young mind.

I do remember wondering about the place to which he traveled five and sometimes six days per week: Work! What *was* work? Dad had little good to say about it and he sometimes described it as "a prison," where he was given "hideous tasks" to do by his "ogre of a boss."

In my early fantasy days I envisioned a medieval castle, dark and damp, with horrible vines growing over the outside walls. My dad arrived in a wagon and terrible troll guards dragged him to a dungeon where his "ogre of a boss" held him prisoner until five o'clock. For some reason that time was important. I imagined the ogre lost his power after five o'clock and had to let his prisoners go before they slew him mightily.

No matter what, Sunday was supposed to be the Day of Rest. It was for Mom, my brother and me. Somehow, Sunday had a different meaning for Dad.

On Sunday, Dad performed special tasks only he knew when and how to do. The type of task seemed to depend on the time of year. Like allergies and the flu, the house came down with its variety of malaises that needed tending.

In the spring, the screens and windows required washing. We couldn't see out of them for half of the winter, but Memorial Day weekend was magically set aside for this job. We should have called it Window Vision Day weekend.

Springtime was also when the lawn needed feeding. I have no recollection of what images came to my very young mind about *this* event. Maybe this particular loss of memory is a blessing!

Feeding the lawn made it grow. Making the lawn grow made Dad work twice as hard to keep it mowed. He mowed it so it didn't look like it had grown. So why did he make it grow in the first place? As a kid I never did get that one straight.

The summer brought on a hidden urge deep within my dad to scrape and repaint some part of the house exterior. One year it was the front porch. Another year the garage had to have a new look. Sometimes the whole outside of the house called to my dad for help. If I stayed close to him I could learn many words that were somehow never okay for *me* to say.

Summer was also when the driveway cast its mystical hold over Dad. His annual ritual consisted of going to the hardware store, buying an assortment of cleaners and sealers, buying the obligatory hard-bristle broom applicator, and then dedicating at least two Sundays to satisfying the driveway's need to be jet black and crack-free.

In the fall, the screens and windows went through another cleaning. Trees got a trimming to relieve them from unwanted dead branches and the lawn went through another feeding. Dad scoured the house inside and out to locate and seal mysterious little spaces that let air in. I always thought we needed air to get in so we could breathe. Here was my dad finding ways to stop it from getting in.

Of course, I was young when these thoughts bubbled up into my frothy, little mind. For some reason, I remember more of what happened before age six than after.

No matter what the season, the roof would somehow find ways to beckon Dad up a long ladder onto its rough-looking, gray slope. Watching Dad climb a ladder and prance over the roof surface always filled me with awe and that image still does to this day.

The roof got sick on its own schedule. It always seemed strange to me the roof chose the most inconvenient time to beckon Dad. The weather was always cold or windy and always either raining or snowing. I just didn't make the connection. I imagined the boss ogre unleashing some of his power to prove to my father he was not yet free. The quest to smite the mighty ogre was to continue another day. Of course, by the time I reached adulthood the connection between bad weather and roof repair became apparent to me.

Wintertime had its own long list of needs to fulfill. Some room needed either a new coat of paint or at least an area touch-up. Moldings needed patching, rugs needed cleaning, the heating plant needed an overhaul. Winter's jobs seemed smaller, but there were just so *many* of them!

All of the seasons had a totally different set of meanings to *me*, of course.

In the spring, I cleaned, lubricated, and softened my baseball glove.

The summer brought a treasure trove of picnics with Mom, days at the playground, summer camp at the local lake.

Fall was nasty: *school started!* Somehow, though, when I developed into a teenager and became aware of girls, school really seemed all right. I even looked forward to it. But that's a topic for another book, or two, or three.

Winter brought me the joy of sledding, skiing, snow forts and snowball fights.

Ahhhhh, when I was young each season in its own way was idyllic. Each had a certain magic for me – or so I see them in my mind's eye.

And, of course, there was the Sabbath! Yes, the Sabbath! Church, Sunday's funnies in the newspaper and Sunday's family dinner!

But I was just a kid and that was what the Sabbath meant to me.

CHAPTER TWO

The Trials of Job

We now fast-forward to the present.

I am sitting on my own front porch watching my children play in the yard.

They are a carefree boy and a worried girl: He is now eleven and she is fourteen. I will describe her someday in a chapter three times the length of the combined books of the Library of Congress. Or I could settle on a triple-spaced half-page write-up that would include everything I *understand* about her.

No matter what, my children are terrific: truly wonderful miracles. If nothing more, simply putting up with me has earned them a place of high honor in Heaven.

My son, Eric, has no cares in the world. My daughter, Elaine, is terrified the newly erupted pimple on her forehead – a tiny blemish that is barely noticeable to me – will destroy any chance she may have with Mark at the dance this coming weekend.

My wife, Carla, has gone shopping for flower bulbs and little plants that will grace our front yard and the tree beds. She has a fabulous skill with plantings and I have often wondered why she doesn't start her own business. She can make gobs of money, allowing me to retire, thereby breaking the ogre boss's evil spell on my family once and for all.

Today is the Sabbath, complete with all of my good intentions.

Instead of my going into what is in store for me, let us go back in time. The Ghost of Sabbaths past, if you will, sweeps back into memory to show how I started my fateful journey into home ownership.

High school and college pass in a flurry of events. The summer after college graduation, I go on a singles cruise and meet Carla. She is angelic: a vision of pure beauty and innocence. I immediately fall in love with her and sweep her off her feet – literally. You see, I am working on this cruise as a shipboard cleaning crew member. I am sweeping the deck near her and decide to intentionally move in a little too close and she trips back into her lounge chair.

After a series of non-too-quiet oaths Carla catches a glance of my startled and yet so apologetic look. I offer her a free drink and a special cleaning of her room. Anything to keep her attention on me. It all works and sixteen months later we are married.

As newlyweds we take on the limited responsibility of an apartment. No painting, no window cleaning, no scraping, no sealing, and no mowing. Just living there.

I have gotten a job as a slave for an ogre who wants to grind my bones to make his bread. Fortunately, he falls under the same spell as my dad's boss and his power fails at five o'clock allowing me to escape onto the roadway and head back to my beloved Carla.

Carla has taken a job as a fourth grade teacher at the nearby elementary school.

I fight an ogre and she duels with gremlins. After dinner we trade war stories. The pattern of our weekdays has become established.

A typical conversation might as well have gone like this.

"So, Carla, how did your day with the gremlins go?"

"About as expected, Honey. Today a short, thin gremlin was added to my class. He may have been smaller than the others, but his uncle runs the Gremlin Academy for Torture, where only the most aggressive students are accepted."

"So I assume he made your day pure agony?"

"Not really. Pure agony is set aside for tomorrow. Today he just stared me down, letting me know any possibility of peace in my class is over. So how did your day go?"

"About like yours. It started out okay, but my ogre of a boss brought in a new grinding machine to grind my bones to make his bread."

"But hasn't bone grinding been outlawed?"

"No. So long as the machine has the proper safety guards on it, it is allowed."

My dad's now ancient Sundays are not even an afterthought at this time. With my being an adult, the world is no longer idyllic and my worries have begun. The first serious bills have arrived: car payments, utilities, and rent.

Let me digress here because car payments can be interesting.

Being new to the world of credit I decided to pay off the car quickly. By adding an extra $150 to the payment a small fortune in interest could be saved.

One day a notice arrived warning of delinquent payments and a looming repossession of my car.

I called the finance company and with a panicked voice tried to resolve the problem. Being a large company – any company with more than one employee – difficulty arose in locating the proper person to handle the case. The actual sequence of calls has somewhat faded from memory, but the following exchange covers all such calls – for me and for everyone.

"Yes, I am Mr. John Doe and I am calling about a delinquency on my car payments."

"Yes, please hold," chimed the operator.

After twenty minutes I hung up and called in again.

"Yes, I am Mr. John Doe and I am calling about a delinquency on my car payments."

"Yes, can you please hold?"

"No, no. Last time I was on hold for twenty minutes and nobody came back."

"How may I help you?" the operator replied in a resigned voice.

"I am Mr. John Doe and I am calling about a delinquency on my car payments."

"Please wait while I transfer you."

On came the music, some sappy tune on a synthesizer that just added an extra edge to my frustration. And, of course, every fifteen seconds a recorded voice came on saying, "Please stay on the line. Your call is very important to us and someone will be with you momentarily."

I have often wondered what went through the minds of the idiots who designed this system. Does hearing the music mean I was disconnected and I needed an interruption every fifteen seconds to tell me I am still connected?

After another twenty minutes, I hung up and called in again.

"Yes, I am Mr. John Doe and I am calling about a delinquency on my car payments."

"Can you hold, please?"

And the sequence began all over, only this time somebody answered after my transfer.

"Yes, this is Shipping and Receiving, how may I help you?" a gruff voice answered.

"I am Mr. John Doe and I am calling about a delinquency on my car payments and I think my call was sent to you by mistake."

"No kidding. Hold on while I send you back to the operator," he grumbled.

After about twenty seconds of silence I hear the beeps indicating my call had been disconnected.

I called in again. This time I held the operator on the line explaining my unfolding tale of woe and will she please, please, please get me to the right party.

"Customer Service, this is Wilma. How may I help you?" a chirpy voice answered after about five minutes of sappy music and interruptions every fifteen seconds to remind me how important my call was to them.

"I am Mr. John Doe and I am calling about a delinquency on my car payments."

"Oh, I'm sorry, but you have reached the Mortgage Department. You need to contact Customer Service in Auto Financing."

"That was my intention, but so far it has been a most elusive goal."

"I apologize for the inconvenience. Let me transfer you."

After another eight minutes of sappy music and interruptions, a new voice came on the line.

"Customer Service, this is Leanne. How may I help you?"

"Yes, I am Mr. John Doe and I am calling about a delinquency on my car payments. And have I reached Auto Finance Customer Service?"

"Yes, you have. How may I help you?"

A small scream of desperation formed in my throat, but after a day on the phone I didn't want to be disconnected so I throttled the scream in its crib.

I repeated for the fortieth time, "I am Mr. John Doe and I am calling about a delinquency on my car payments."

"On the letter there is a reference number. Can you please read that to me?"

From this point events transpired smoothly. I found out one cannot just send in any amount and hope it is credited. Only exact amounts of payments will be credited. Furthermore, being a new customer first establishing credit, I must make at least three monthly payments to establish my credit.

"You mean adding an extra $150 each month doesn't prove my credit worthiness?"

"No. You need to make at least three monthly payments to establish your credit."

I was now conversing with a parrot. "Aark! You need to make at least three monthly payments." "Aark! You need to make at least three monthly payments."

At least she put the extra payments toward my principal. To this day I wonder what the blazes they did with the payments I had made. Did they just keep the money hoping nobody would notice?

The payments for utilities and rent just didn't cry out for extra money each month, but I wondered how would a utility company respond to an extra payment?

"Hey, Hal. Some Bozo just sent in his bill with an extra fifty bucks added. What should we do with it?"

"Joe, send out for pizza for the whole staff. Shouldn't let an honest mistake go to waste."

"Good idea. Should we send the customer a Thank You note?"

"That'll be sweet. Pass it around so we can all sign it."

No, we scrupulously paid what was owed to the exact penny.

I am done digressing.

Sunday belongs to Carla and me. I still read the Sunday funnies in the newspaper – old habits sometimes don't die – and Carla and I go to her or my parents' homes on alternate weekends for family dinner.

Compromise, jobs, and rent have replaced idyllic.

I still keep the Sabbath and probably don't understand a whole lot more about it than I did as a kid, but it remains a special day – a day to be honored and respected.

After three quiet months in a very nice apartment, the empty apartment upstairs swallowed a new tenant. I say "swallowed" because what was to occur over the next twenty one months did not derive from any normal origin.

We had signed a two-year lease due to the perks: one rent-free month, 50% off the security deposit and 15% off the monthly rent. Sounded like a terrific deal, right? Enter Dr. Cough Plop!

Why did Carla and I develop this non-neighborly name? Somehow by naming an unknown terror, one is allowed to get a grasp on the fear – a modicum of stability in the face of sheer chaos.

I am simply exaggerating, you feel, because people under stress make more of a situation than really exists. For my part, I do not believe the English language contains enough adjectives to even scratch the surface as to what Dr. Cough Plop was like.

Oh, Ghost of Sabbaths past let me not dwell on the visions you have placed before me. Sweep me back to the present. I need the respite of a cold beer and the soothing quiet of watching my children at play.

I must admit, my children aren't exactly *playing*. They are performing a ritual of brother-teasing-sister with sister-ignoring-brother, while she talks to her school chum, Leslie Ann, on her cell phone. No doubt she is trading stories about parties and, especially, Mark and life-threatening zits. But the scene is pure bliss to me and gives me the strength to return to my story.

The day Dr. Cough Plop arrived was one of those inexplicably cold days that occur now and then in late June. The weather trifled with drizzle and light mist all day, occasionally tossing in a hair-wrenching gust of wind. These seemed to be omens that Dr. Cough Plop's reign would not be easy on Carla and me. To complete this scene all we needed was a mind-numbing crash of lightning and thunder followed by one of those double-struck sounding deep voices cheap monster movies use when demons speak. A cackle-like laugh would have made a nice touch, too.

I am not an avid fan of horror movies, but the little watching I have done has prepared me for events like the Cough Plops. All I needed was for Dr. Cough Plop to appear hovering over my bed, lit in a sallow light to emphasize his other worldly presence. He would say nothing, just pointing at me and then Carla and finally evaporating into the darkness.

On the contrary, Dr. Cough Plop looked benign enough. He was a short middle-aged, pudgy family physician. His wife physically matched him perfectly. We seldom saw her; but when we did pass each other, she always smiled and nodded her head deeply into her copious chest while maintaining eye contact at all times. Once in a while, she would chirp out a "Helllllloooooo."

The good Doctor had sired a son named Toby – a child of mammoth proportions. He was four years old, but with the head size and body girth of someone years older – perhaps *fifty* years older. He rarely talked to us, though I never considered this non-communication a problem. What would our conversations have been like?

"So, Toby. What are you planning today to torture my wife and me?"

"I dunno. Maybe I hammer railroad spikes through the floor into your ceiling."

"That's nice. What else?"

"I dunno. Maybe I punch holes in the floor with DaDa's twelve-pound sledge hammer."

My callous memories spring from the torture we were put through by him. Really, Carla and I felt sorry for the tyke. After all he was only four – in human years, anyway. His parents were seemingly such meek and unassuming people, making any complaints by us fruitless. No landlord or police officer would have ever believed our stories. No judge would have convicted. No, we were in the Valley of the Shadow of Cough Plop and we definitely knew fear.

For brevity, let's call them Dr. and Mrs. CP.

Dr. CP opened his practice at 7:00 AM six days per week. This daily grand opening required a series of prelude operations that began at 5:00

AM and grew in intensity leading up to the inevitable ferocious door slam at 6:40. Luckily he was punctual so we didn't have to anticipate this slam, the way an edgy track star has to anticipate the starter's pistol.

First, Dr. CP seemed to literally roll out of bed the way a log rolls out: *wham!* Over the twenty one months this ritual occurred, Carla and I never ceased having a near catatonic fit from his bed exit.

Dr. CP often went into a coughing spasm at the ringing of the alarm clock. His wife explained her husband was a mouth breather while sleeping, leaving his throat dry and itchy upon awakening – hence the coughing spasm. I suggested he keep a glass of water by the bed as a preventative. She just smiled, tucked her chin deeply into her chest, maintained eye contact, and then suddenly swirled around and walked away from us.

So, there you have our initiation: a series of floor rumbling coughs followed by a nerve-shattering plop onto the floor.

Dr. CP's awakening activated Toby who rushed into the bedroom screaming "DaDa." His stomping was akin to a 370-pound tap dancer wearing four-inch square taps.

We really didn't suffer from Garden Apartment Syndrome, wherein a neighbor whispering two apartments away could be heard as though he or she were sitting in your living room. No. These apartments were heavy wood construction with concrete firewalls between apartment groups. Wall-to-wall carpeting existed throughout. Except, of course, in the CP apartment.

Anyway, Carla and I went into suspended animation from 5:00 to 6:40 AM every day – six days a week – for twenty one months. After the tromping and slamming finished, we arose to capture what was left of our sanity. An ogre and a classroom of gremlins began to seem very stabilizing after just a few weeks with the CP family.

Luckily the nerve fraying antics of Dr. CP and Toby didn't pass onto Carla and me. In fact, we grew to comfort each other more. We didn't let these escapades come between us. After all, nobody could have predicted this situation, not even the most astute psychic who had a 99% prediction rate.

"Oh great and wondrous spirit, I am Madam Zazoots and Carla and her husband have asked me to predict their future."

"Yes, Madam Zazoots, my husband and I want to know what our future in our new apartment holds for us. We want to be prepared for the worst possible events."

"Let me hold your hands. Hmmmmm ... I see horrible events coming your way."

"Wh-wh-what e-e-events," I screamed at her.

"There will be a rabid dog blocking your way in for at least a month. You will have to climb up the side of the building to get into your apartment."

"That's horrible. Anything else? Carla and I hate rabid dogs."

"Yesssss ... I see a catastrophic pipe break where the water soaks your house and furniture beyond repair."

"A-a-anything else?"

And Madam Zazoots rattles off another six items of pure terror that will befall us, including my car going out of control, driving up the steps and crashing into the kitchen table.

One month after the Dr. and Mrs. CP and Toby entered our lives we updated Madam Zazoots on our adventures.

"Everything you said came true, except one thing: Dr. and Mrs. Cough Plop and their son Toby," I explained to her.

Her face grew ashen with a look of horror. "The Cough Plops! I could not have predicted such a horror. You are doomed, I say. Doomed! Doomed! Doomed!"

A real life Madam Zazoots would have run off, screaming in terror, hoping to ward off the curse of the Cough Plops.

We got no relief from our reticent landlord who promised endlessly to place rugs in the CP family's apartment, but never delivered. By shifting schedules to an earlier bedtime, we controlled our sleep deprivation.

Luckily we weren't home for most of the day and we judiciously found ways to escape on weekends. The time we did spend at home subjected us to the occasional indoor road races Toby staged or the earth-chastening tantrums he threw when he was denied something, such as the right to dismember his cat, Wootsie.

Wootsie was a pleasant tabby, with big eyes and a petrified smile – or at least the frozen expression appeared to be a smile. When leaving the apartment, I often shot a glance upstairs from the parking lot. Wootsie normally sat on a table near the window, seeming to contemplate whether cats really do land on their feet should he make the leap.

My dad had his pat answer to the neighbor problem: "Buy a house. When you own a house you don't have problems like this."

His advice sounded reasonable – with no upstairs apartment there can be no noise from upstairs. The seeds were planted.

While the Cough Plops were wending their way through our life and our nervous systems, a new neighbor replaced Mrs. Connor downstairs. Mrs. Connor was the stereotypical wonderful old lady, complete with the pillbox hat with the lace veil.

Why was she wonderful? Did she attempt to solve world hunger, or deliver fantastically delicious pastries to us, or tell us spellbinding stories about the century that just passed?

No. Mrs. Connor was wonderful because *we didn't know that she was there!*

At least she had no impact on our lives until she moved! She departed to live with a friend in another state, so the landlord informed us, and left a deep vacuum in Apartment A51. The apartment number was soon to have special significance.

Sci-Fi conspiracy addicts love to believe that Area 51 – Roswell, if you will – is the storehouse of aliens from outer space who came to earth only to be captured by our Government, stuffed into cages, examined by teams of surgeons and mad scientists, and then forced to make three meals a day for the earthlings.

Whether I believed in alien invasions or not depended on what make-up and clothes my boss's, uh, *ogre's,* first secretary was wearing on any given day.

Back to apartment A51. The vacuum left by Mrs. Connor's departure sucked in a set of creeps who loved the most acidic of acid rock. There were four of them including, as best as Carla and I could guess, a frumpy mother of about 50, but going on thirteen, twin teenage daughters with matching multi-colored punk hair styles, and a younger brother of about ten. There was no father; no doubt he was evaporated by a ray gun.

Two weeks later we met the brother, Tommy, and because he found Carla and me to be an oasis of sanity in his life, his visits became a daily ritual. He turned out to be an interesting conversationalist. Tommy was quite mature for his tender age. I guess he faced a choice between growing up quickly and curling up in a fetal position on the floor, sucking his thumb in between helpless babblings.

A Madam Zazoots would have jettisoned herself into outer space to escape the double curse Carla and I were now going to suffer.

Some of the horror movies I saw spoke of a malevolent spirit attracting an even more malevolent spirit once some kind of portal had been opened. In our case, there were only two possible apartments from which torture could occur and both had been filled.

Now, back to the twins. They were named ... Oh, I don't remember their names. No doubt my brain has been desperately trying to sever the cells holding that memory. I'll call them Punk 1 and Punk 2. But since they always worked together, I'll reduce them to 1P2.

On their first full night in A51, just as the Cough Plops were plopping down for the night, the Creeps from Beyond cranked up the volume. The assault lasted about as long as the average air raid in World War II and probably as noisy! Because their speakers were set wrong, at least the walls and some portion of our nerves were spared.

The next afternoon, Carla had a discussion with 1P2. After a long series of "yeeeah's" and "uhhh huhhh's," the result was the assaults began earlier, lasted longer, but terminated simultaneously with the Cough Plop's final plop for the day.

Of course there were numerous incidents of food preparation that left us wondering whether Mother Creep had learned how to release the nutritional value of charred hockey pucks.

The bathroom vents created a small inter-apartment air leak. Apparently, the vents were a daisy chain of ducts and when a strong odor emanated from A51 on windy days it got drawn into our apartment. We learned to defeat it by turning on our bathroom fan, but success was dependent on quick reflexes.

There was a type of pie Mother Creep manufactured that seemed to require burning as though it were created strictly for sacrificial purposes. The odor was a cross between burnt coffee and burnt prunes with a touch of rotten apples. Grown men, tough men who had seen combat throughout the bowels of our planet, were known to collapse in place and whimper for mercy, when the aroma wafted over them.

Mrs. Creep sometimes baked this wondrous pie creation beyond the point of value for even the sacrifice. She broke those failures into many small pieces and spread them around the grass for nature's unsuspecting victims to find.

Squirrels and birds may seem to be basic creatures to humans, but luckily nature has equipped them with innate warning alarms. Carla and I watched with amazement as squirrels, chattering with excitement, darted around and over the morsels without actually touching them. Birds, on the other hand, clawed at them, scattering them about. Once in a while a brave bird grasped a morsel in its beak and seemingly flung it as far as its little beak could.

"What are these things and why do they seem to resist rain, snow, sun?" one of the birds may have said to his friend. "And why do the ants seem to avoid them?"

"I don't know," his friend would have responded, "I have seen newspapers flying around in the wind and from time to time there are articles about horrible new weapons that can destroy all life."

"You mean this may be one of those weapons?"

"Probably. What other explanation can there be?"

Eventually rain, sunshine and air pollution combined to degrade the pie to the point where it could no longer pose a danger.

On hot days, 1P2 sunned themselves on the lawn below our small patio. The quantity of metal attached to their bodies cast them in an eerie glow on sunny days: dazzling sparkles reflecting from over a dozen places on each girl. Carla reasoned the array of metal was arranged in a specific pattern designed to contact their home planet. I felt we should alert NASA. No doubt decoding this pattern could advance our extraterrestrial contact program several hundred years.

"Yes, this is Doctor Mazzarazza, Head of NASA's Department of Extraterrestrial Hoohah. What is this call about?"

"Well, Doc, my wife and I have caught sight of two beings that may have escaped from Area 51 and thought you may be interested. They have actually taken up residence in the apartment below us."

"Hmmm … Do they speak English?"

"Sorry, Doc, they don't. But they have at times produced guttural grunts and moans similar to rudimentary language."

"Have you been able to decipher anything meaningful from these utterances?" doctor Mazzarazza continued.

"No. But their bodies are adorned with metallic symbols that can only originate from some distant galaxy. On sunny days the objects flash in a pattern not unlike Morse Code."

"Have you been able to translate any of the code?"

"Yes, Doc. They are saying 'Wow is this sun hot.'"

"Let me look this one up. NASA just so happens to have a statement cross reference chart. Let me see. Yes, here it is. 'Wow is this sun hot' cross references to 'Man are we getting a sunburn' from the galaxy TX23. Thank you so much, sir. By locating these beings from outer space you may have just saved us several hundred years of watching the skies for messages from distant stars."

"Doc? Do you think you folks can send over a wagon of some sort to collect these beings? And sooner rather than later?"

Alas, we never called NASA or the military at Area 51. We would have loved to have asked the military if they had accidentally left a steel cage or two open, allowing the contents to escape. Nor did we try to find out if the Government had offered a reward for the recapture of 1P2.

Despite the antics of 1P2 and Mrs. Creep, there was still Tommy, the eloquent ten-year old. Tommy may have believed we were his oasis of sanity, but he was *ours*.

The CP/1P2 circus lasted about eight months before we ended it by purchasing our first home.

What iced the decision? One day Carla's Dad, who was an accountant, gave us the run through of how much we could save in taxes and how much we could gain in equity and how blah blah we can blah blah blah blah if we bought a house. To us what mattered most was we could escape from being a neighbor sandwich! And he would loan us $25,000 to get started.

CHAPTER THREE

Exodus

"Moses led the Israelites through the desert for 40 years before he found them a home. He would have done much better if he had used a realtor," a great rabbi friend of my dad told me.

He found Carla and me a realtor: Mrs. Eschermann.

We told Mrs. Eschermann we had a bit of a deadline: our lease and nerves were to expire in five months.

"You have come to the right person," she chimed. "We have plenty of time and I'll have you sitting in front of your TV, sipping piña coladas by then. No problem, Sweeties."

She said two of the most dangerous words in the English language: no problem.

The problems started when we specified our desires. We wanted a single three bedroom two-story with central air, two car garage, two baths or a bath and a half, a mud entrance, and in a development or neighborhood near schools and shopping.

The first place we visited took us twenty minutes out of town to a development of four houses next to rows of farms. This twenty minute drive pulled us thirty five minutes from the nearest school and strip mall. The house was a quaint split ranch with two bedrooms, two baths and a carport.

"It's expandable," Mrs. Eschermann crowed. "And just look at the carpentry: hardwood floors and oak moldings."

Carla whispered in my ear, "I don't think she gets it."

The next weekend we traveled to a series of townhouses in the city center. These were nice townhouses and only five years old. They did have three bedrooms and two baths, but a single car garage underneath.

We also had directly connected neighbors on each side. Carla and I wondered how much less annoying 1P2 and Cough Plop would be next door rather than above and below.

We were getting closer, or so we thought.

Oh, did I forget to mention these housing jaunts took place on a Sunday? For some reason real estate offices all closed on a Sunday, but house hunting reached its peak on that day. We were beginning to wonder if Mrs. Eschermann may have been less dangerous inside an office rather than on the road.

Two weeks passed and then she came through with a five-house junket that would surely land us in our home.

"I have picked some nice peaches for you. I'm sure you'll be happy with what you are going to see," she cooed. The smile on her face was a bit reminiscent of Wootsie's look of frozen fear.

Mrs. Eschermann had now replaced two of the most dangerous words with *the* two most dangerous words in the English language: I'm sure.

"Don't worry, sir. I'm sure your insurance will cover that," the insurance agent said before you shelled out thousands for storm damage for which you had no coverage.

"I wouldn't be concerned. I'm sure this skin cream will not cause an allergy," the cosmetics counter sales girl said before your skin began to peel.

"Oh, I wouldn't concern myself with that knocking noise in your engine. I'm sure it is really nothing," the garage mechanic said before you became stranded fifty miles from the nearest anything.

Now, Wootsie's look of frozen fear was justified. We visited a two-bedroom ranch, a three story Victorian with twelve-foot high ceilings, two more ranches with three bedrooms, but only one bath and a one-car garage each, and finally a fixer-upper.

When Carla saw the fixer-upper from the front, it was the third time I had witnessed Wootsie's frozen fear expression. She went in, I believe, out of a sense of macabre curiosity. The smell of ever-present dampness permeated the entire house. The walls needed serious patching and the rugs were so discolored if the staining had continued for perhaps another six months they would have been a uniform color again.

When we entered the kitchen, Mrs. Eschermann's eyes widened as she moved quickly over to the cabinets. "Look at that. Real cherry wood."

In her defense the house did have three bedrooms, two baths, central air and a two-car garage. It was just they were hard to recognize through the rubble.

We then bid Mrs. Eschermann goodbye.

The next few weekends we scoured the housing section of the Sunday paper and visited likely candidates. Somehow it appeared every house seller and realtor had become Mrs. Eschermann. The match-up between description written in the ads and reality bore the marks of her inspiration.

One of my favorite items often appeared as CT&T, meaning ceramic tub and tile. The term loosely meant something of value. After all, a tiled tub area exuded a nice clean look of gleaming tiles to accent a lovely tub – or at least that was the image so often displayed in home centers and stores dedicated to bathrooms and kitchens.

The reality proved quite different in every case. We also began to notice a connection between the condition of the bathroom and the overall repair situation of the house. Someone who let the bathroom go to seed – algae and mildew dominating every crevice and grout line – also seemed to let the rest of the house go into disrepair.

One owner even tried to convince us of the benefit of the grouting.

"You see," he went on, "grout is so easy to clean. All you do is use a mild bleach solution and a scrub brush. Not like wallpaper that stains and you can't get those stains out."

A little work on the Internet showed just the opposite. In fact, both Carla's and my parents had plastic-coated wallpaper in the tub areas, because their previous tile and grouting had stained so badly it couldn't be cleaned. A nice wipe down with a sponge and bathroom cleaner kept the wallpaper clean.

In our apartment, the tub and surrounding wall was one unit. Strangely, we weren't seeing this assembly in any of the houses we visited.

Another favorite line in the ads was one declaring three bedrooms and two-and-a-half baths.

The third bedroom was invariably an eight-foot by nine-foot room that would not fit anything bigger than a sewing machine and a small cabinet for sewing supplies. Sometimes, the fourth bedroom really comprised just a large alcove with no door.

The half bathroom in at least four of the houses was either a converted closet or a shower stall in the basement. One house even had a free standing toilet in the basement – one that was not even hooked up to the sewer or water.

I suppose with a little imagination one could take a make believe shower, become make believe clean, and then make believe all the sour looks cast on us by people with whom we made contact were really looks of approval. I'm sure that would work.

Home buying is really a very emotional experience. One will buy a house needing some repairs over one in perfect condition if the emotional tug to the former is much stronger.

Carla almost fell for a nice house that reminded her so much of her childhood home. She had had a very happy childhood. For this house, distance, poor neighborhood and a poor school system finally ruled the day, but her emotions were running high on that one.

This emotional connection leads me to wonder why anyone would so deceive potential buyers by lying about features of the house. The shock at seeing some of these fabrications would either put the prospective buyer off enough to just walk away or to offer a much lower price.

Curb appeal is another feature. When Carla and I arrived at a house whose front yard served as a depository for junk, weeds, and uncut grass – sometimes adorned with a broken fence – the house would have to be a veritable palace to break even against the image of the yard.

How does someone let his yard go into such disrepair? What does this say about the maintenance in general? The view approaching the house can intensify one's perspective walking around inside, allowing defects that might otherwise go unnoticed to show up exaggerated.

Time was getting close. There were only three months until the lease expired and we knew we faced at least a six-week loan approval cycle. As for our apartment, if we didn't sign a new lease within thirty days the lease could be renewed only if there were no potential tenants in waiting. With the reign of the Cough Plops and the Creeps from Beyond, re-signing was definitely not an option.

I tried to imagine a discussion with the landlord.

"Sir, Carla and I really want to renew our lease, except there are a few problems we want you to fix."

"What problems. My apartments are perfect. My tenants are perfect, except for those louts who say my apartments aren't perfect."

"Well, you see there is the issue of no rugs in the upstairs apartment."

"Oh, the Cough Plops? They are perfect. So what about the rugs?"

"I was hoping you could put a few thousand clickers on the floor to amplify their walking. We really enjoy their walking."

"Okay. Done. What's next?"

"Carla and I can't enjoy the cooking odors from downstairs. We want you to install a vent fan that blows inward into our apartment so we can enjoy it more."

"Done. Anything else?"

"Can you supply rabid dogs to guard the downstairs door?"

Our house hunting intensified. Carla and I now spent weekdays as well as entire weekends meeting realtors, scouring newspapers, visiting the physical representations of the advertised lies.

The next six weeks were a blur. A whirlwind of structures containing a tortuous assembly of rooms that sometimes added up to three bedrooms if definitions could be stretched. Getting a fourth bedroom – four full-sized bedrooms – would have been easier for us to find, but the price range was out of our reach unless we moved far from town. Just getting three full-sized bedrooms became a more and more distant hope.

One realtor with the obnoxiously fitting name of Mr. Houseman, showed us a new two bedroom creation with an oversized master bedroom closet. "This closet is so big," Mr. Houseman chirped, "that with a little imagination it could be converted into a den or even a third bedroom." At least the two-and-a-half baths were real.

Based on Mr. Houseman's view he could have declared the large cement birdbath in the back yard as a half bath.

A few houses were offered by the owner with the declaration we could save realtor fees by buying direct. After romping through a number of houses and neighborhoods, I easily got a feeling for how much a house should cost and these buy-through-the-owner deals simply got priced as though a realtor offered them.

Worse, the owner-sellers learned to lie in their ads the way the realtors did.

Okay, "lie" is too strong a word. Let's just leave it there were some overstatements that stretched the truth until you could hear it start to rip.

This realtor experience was beginning to make the Plops and Creeps tolerable by comparison. It was probably just such an odyssey that converted Dr. Cough Plop into the seemingly mindless, oblivious creature we knew.

Due to time constraints, Carla and I had begun being afraid we would have to settle for something much less than we wanted. A possible conversation may have gone as follows.

"Honey, look at that cabinetry. It is real cherry wood."

"But, Carla. The kitchen is in rubble. The floors ride the waves. The walls have splatterings from a thousand dinners."

"But, Honey, look at those cherry wood cabinets."

"If we were to redo these floors, the room height would shrink six inches."

"But, Honey, look at those cherry wood cabinets."

"But, Carla, we have to compromise on room space. This is what I feared: an alcove claimed to be a third bedroom."

"Oh, Honey. Don't be so negative. We can squeeze a cot and a makeshift dresser in there and, for privacy, a rolling curtain will do fine."

"This place is so brutally dirty even the most corrupt health department of the most corrupt government – one that approves living on dung piles – would condemn it."

"But, Honey, think of the benefit. This place is so bad even bacteria can't live here. We'll never get sick."

It was definitely time to bring house hunting to an end!

We were down to five weeks to doomsday when unexpectedly we received a call from Mrs. Eschermann.

"Uh, yeah?" I stuttered, after she had introduced herself. "Hold it for a moment," I continued.

"Uh ... Carla? Want to get on the extension?"

"Why?"

"Please, just get on the extension."

I had forgotten to use the mute button. Now we were in for it!

Instead she was amazingly contrite. I don't know whether overhearing my beckoning to Carla humbled her or she had simply gained wisdom on her own, but she was definitely a changed person.

"Look. You were such darling people and I know I didn't do right by you. But believe me, I have one I know you two lovely people will fall in love with."

Somehow her plea didn't seem so farfetched. After all, at least she had never tried to convince us to convert a closet into a bedroom.

We met her at the sample home in a sprawling development. Carla's eyes were wide, only this time they were filled with sparkles of delight. The development was nearly finished and the landscaping was beautiful. The houses were on half-acre lots giving us plenty of distance from any potential Creeps.

"All of the houses have two-car garages," Mrs. Eschermann bubbled, "and maintenance-free siding."

Maintenance-free! The words resonated as beautiful music in my ears. No maintenance meant no scraping, no patching, and no oaths. Dad would be proud.

Upon driving into the development, I hadn't noticed the array of neat, green, near perfect lawns and weed-free mulch beds. I would soon find out the more perfect the lawn and the more weed-free the mulch beds, the more their maintenance will bite into the Sabbath.

The lawn perfection is something inherited from kings and nobles, whose rambling estates always had perfect lawns, even hundreds of years before lawnmowers were invented.

How did those noblemen keep such huge magnificent grounds? A flock of carefully eating sheep? Lots of people with lots of scissors?

Today, we poorer folk can imitate the ultra-wealthy by at least having great lawns. Of course, it just doesn't seem to occur to anyone the ultra-wealthy never touch a lawnmower or hedge trimmer or any rake or shovel. They have staffs for that purpose or they hire upscale yard services. The rest of us gather up our claim to yard perfection by borrowing time – too often from the Sabbath.

Lawns and their effect on the Sabbath were not the order of our business today. This day we dedicated our effort to the escape from the dismal Cough Plop Creepdom.

"So, do you want to go in?"

"Of course," Carla and I sang at once.

Inside, the house was bright and cheery with wall-to-wall carpeting, central vacuum cleaner, and deep-set soffit lighting in the two baths and a half – yes, *two* baths and a half – and in the kitchen.

The kitchen. Oh, the kitchen. Carla simply beamed. Mrs. Eschermann told us it was a forty-handle kitchen which meant nothing to us. Maybe that many handles would make it easier to carry it somewhere.

All Carla saw was the center island with its combined counter and grill, the expanse of countertops and cabinets, and the oversized double sink with additional silverware soak tank. If Heaven could have been transferred to earth, for Carla it would look just like this kitchen. The built-in dual oven and built-in microwave were sweeteners.

"So what do you think?" Mrs. Eschermann beamed at us.

"You came through. You most certainly came through. Carla? What do you think?"

Carla didn't immediately answer; she had yet to descend back to the floor. I took her speechlessness as a "yes" and we followed Mrs. Eschermann to the office in the sample home.

A slippery looking fellow introduced himself as Corey, or Corty. It didn't matter so long as it wasn't Plop or Creep. He informed us if we decided today we would get a free twenty-two cubic foot side-by-side refrigerator. Carla was still imagining the kitchen and I am not sure it would have mattered had he said by signing today we would have to buy *him* the refrigerator.

Mrs. Eschermann guided us through the next steps and both she and CoreyCorty were very sympathetic to our deadline: five weeks and counting. As one could have guessed, the developer happened to be partial to a bank that coincidently had a representative on site from 8:00 AM to 3:00 PM daily. We signed over a check for ten percent of the cost to secure the property and bounded to our car for the joyous ride home.

Joyous ride home? Knowing our battle had been won cast a warm glow over both of us. Now when I looked at Wootsie, he seemed to plead for me to take him with us.

That night the Creeps gave us a rare double performance, breaking only for dinner, and Toby gave tirades with world-class tantrums. Once again we were the meat in this sandwich of chaos. Carla smiled, leaned to me for a kiss and whispered, “Soon.”

The money my boss paid me for the right to grind my bones to make his bread and Carla’s gremlin combat pay were more than enough to secure the loan. With my father-in-law’s $25,000 for the down payment, we passed the financing hurdles with ease.

Most people have financing horror stories to tell. There are the inevitable misplacement of the down payment check, surprises from the inspections, deed glitches, unaccountable delays in processing. We finished in four and a half weeks, the interest rate was competitive, and there were no surprises. Don’t worry, though: we still had moving day ahead of us.

But for now, the house was new and even came with a one-year warranty. Everything was in good shape and the exterior was maintenance free. My dad’s experience would not be my own: I was going to enjoy the Sabbath. Yes! Enjoy the Sabbath, the grandest day of the week.

CHAPTER FOUR

Entering the Promised Land

Into everyone's life a little rain must fall. In our case, it was the Steve Rain Moving Company.

Steve Rain was one of those gruff individuals whose appearance cried out "moving man." When Carla and I went to his office he came out from the back of his building wearing a soiled Tee shirt with the obligatory holes. His large belly and bulbous nose spoke of beers past, present and future. His hair was sparse, but wooly. He had the powerful hands of a laborer and the deep-set eyes that exuded "gotcha!"

Why did we go to Mr. Rain? He was a personal friend of Carla's Dad's boss and came with the highest recommendation. Carla felt the recommendation went something like this: "Ya' kid's gonna use Steve Rain *or ya' fired!*"

In any event, Steve's quote was reasonable – so the articles we had read had indicated – and he offered a comprehensive damage insurance package. Isn't it the more comprehensive the insurance is, the more likely we are to need it?

The Rain van line arrived at 8:00 AM sharp on Friday, just forty hours before our lease expired. Four large men bounded off the truck and into the apartment.

Wootsie stared down at us from his den of horror, seeming to plead even harder for us to find a shipping box for him to jump into and go with us.

"Sorry, fella," I called up to Wootsie, "we just can't take you. You will have to apply for asylum first."

My words were heard by Toby who pulled Wootsie out of the window. I could have sworn Toby's eyes suddenly glowed red for a moment. My mind briefly drifted to the fate of the hapless people who will replace us, but that will be their story. Our story has ended with the great escape.

The moving whirlwind began. One man directed the activity, one man assembled cartons and wardrobe boxes, and the other two began gathering the items to wrap. The toaster oven, microwave, and computer were unplugged, placed into boxes, and moved out to the sidewalk. The dishes seemed to sail into the cartons, gathering a coating of wrapping paper while in flight.

The refrigerator hopped onto its own dolly and drove itself out the door and up the truck ramp into the truck. The television sprang up on its tiny legs and pulled blankets around itself and waited to be carried into the truck. Chairs, couch, and end tables all stood at attention waiting their turn for a place of honor in Steve Rain's coach. Even our king-sized bed gave up with a whimper to the muscled bodies of the moving crew.

Carla and I stood out of the way and watched the ongoing show with amazement. The efficiency of the operation settled us into a false sense of security.

By noon the truck had been packed and was ready to roll to our new home. Our New Home! The words had such magic to them. Carla and I kissed, then hopped into the car to follow them.

We arrived at 246 Oakridge Lane. The address had suddenly acquired a musical rhythm. Carla darted to the door ahead of me and rushed into the foyer bouncing up and down off her toes like a little child on Christmas morning. I rushed in, grabbed her by the waist and swirled her around.

A low gruff voice broke the moment. "Where do you want this stuff?" The men were holding the couch and two arm chairs. The furniture was coming to claim its rightful place in our home.

The unloading passed without a glitch. The men plugged in the appliances and assembled the bed. We were giddy. By 4:30 the Rain Moving Company was on its way back to the station and we were opening the boxes spread out in the appropriate rooms. One box contained several broken pieces from a set of China. Carla looked aghast and a small tear welled up in her right eye.

I said, "Don't worry. We have the insurance."

She shot a cold look at me. "How *could* you! This china has been in my family for three generations."

"Let's calm down, dear and take stock of everything we have."

She frantically looked around the house. "Where is the wardrobe box with my dresses?"

I joined the search. Indeed, the dresses were nowhere to be found. We had not looked at the truck during either the packing or unpacking.

"How can they not notice a six-foot tall, two-foot wide box?" Carla cried.

Luckily we had not yet turned in the apartment keys. We drove back to the apartment and were greeted by not one but two wardrobe boxes. I called Steve Rain, but reached his answering service. Our first long weekend had started.

Carla and I took apart the wardrobe boxes and transported the clothing in two trips.

We worked to about 4:00 AM opening boxes and checking the contents. We managed to put everything away and had the house organized with the damaged items placed in the living room for handling the next day.

Totally exhausted, we slept to nearly 1:00 PM. Neither of us had slept past noon in years. After showers and breakfast the job of accounting for breakage began.

The claim form was nowhere to be found. "Aren't they supposed to give us one ahead of time?" Carla asked me.

"I suppose so. Let me call them again." I reached Steve. He informed me it was impossible for his men to have done any damage and *we* must have done it after opening the boxes. After a brief back and forth I wimped out and hung up the phone.

I told Carla and she initially began to cry, but her tears rapidly turned to anger. She grabbed the phone and reached Steve Rain's answering service. She leaned against me and started sobbing.

I felt terrible and helpless. Here was the start of something wonderful; instead, we had a fight on our hands.

Over Sunday dinner at her family's house, Carla spilled the story to her dad. He was sympathetic but felt he could do nothing. "Where does your boss live?" she snarled.

"Honey? Let's stay calm," I said firmly.

"Never mind calm. I put up with plops, bangs, burnt sacrifices, acid rock, an invasion of space aliens, but I'll *not* put up with this!"

The way she said it made me laugh. Her mom and dad also began to chuckle. But, Carla was definitely not amused.

"Someone's going to learn that into every Rain a Carla sometimes falls with two fists. And I'm going to ..."

"Hold it, young lady," her dad cut in. I'll talk to Jim (his boss) on Monday and get this straightened out." Carla's eyes were burning and the fire was growing.

"Monday? Monday? I will *not* wait until Monday. I want action now. Where .. does .. your .. boss .. live?" Carla's staccato delivery reflected her anger.

"Look, Dad," she cried, "you've worked for this man for over fifteen years. You and Mom have gone to parties at his house. You've played poker, gone bowling with him. He is the one who recommended this moving company and he is going to get this settled *now*."

Carla and her dad kept a distance for the next month. She was bitter that he did not intercede on her behalf. She just didn't know how corporations work. A boss can be a friend until you press him. Her dad knew the limits of his relationship; Carla couldn't understand it.

Monday came and went and nothing happened. Steve Rain did not return our calls. We got the China set appraised – it held a value of $1,200 if intact – and called the main office of the company Steve represented. His was a franchise, but he was still under the authority of the national company.

After two weeks of our trying, the national company finally responded and sent a representative, Mr. Caulder, to examine the damage.

The major damage was to the China. The microwave had a crack on one side and there were a few nicks on tables and couch legs.

Mr. Caulder carefully observed the boxes and the damage. We had foolishly not thrown the boxes out. He looked at the box marked "Dishes/ Kitchen" and saw no dents or visible damage.

"I'm sorry to tell you, but the box is not damaged in any way. Therefore neither my company nor Steve Rain is responsible. We'll send a furniture repair man to fix the mars and we will give you twenty five dollars for the crack on the microwave."

Carla was livid. I had known her for three years and had roused her dark side from time to time. I had never seen *this* expression.

"Twenty five dollars? Twenty five dollars?" She snarled that line over and over, getting steadily louder. She then moved close to Mr. Caulder and placed her extended index finger a few inches from his face and seethed with a deep hiss, "Look, Mr. Caulder, you had better do a whole lot better than *that*. Tomorrow I will be on the phone with your boss or the president of the company, if I have to, but .. I .. will .. get .. satisfaction."

The staccato this time spewed such anger and venom Mr. Caulder took a step backwards.

Carla never blinked while she fixed her eyes on his – a deep, burning look that caused a flush to come over Mr. Caulder's face.

They stood there for what must have been seconds to Carla, but two full eternities to Caulder.

Even the Gremlins who dragged me to work for my daily bone grinding would have collectively taken a step back. My ogre boss would have taken a step back. Carla was not to be trifled with.

"Here is what I can do," he said with a tremor, "I will authorize a check for $500 to be sent to you."

"And the furniture and microwave?" Carla knew she had his jugular vein in her teeth. I was never so proud of my wife.

Caulder's voice had a low tremor to it and he swallowed audibly before continuing. "The furniture repair man will be out this week and we will offer to buy you a new microwave." He reached into his briefcase and began to assemble the necessary documents. After filling in the appropriate spaces, he, Carla and I signed, locking in the agreement.

"Thank you. Mr. Caulder." With the cold way Carla spoke, poor Mr. Caulder realized he had better leave before he had to offer us his first born, $100,000, and a rookie to be named later.

"Honey. Uh, where did all of *that* come from?" I was still amazed at her Academy Award performance.

"You wimped out on me with Steve Rain. I was definitely not going to let you botch this up with Caulder." Carla was obviously not pleased with me. She went upstairs and stayed away from me for the rest of the night.

The furniture repair man did his job; a new microwave arrived as did the check for $500. Carla felt a sense of accomplishment, but she still held me accountable for my outward display of whimpery.

A few weeks passed and all seemed forgotten. Our husband/wife role reverted to what it had been before the onset of Rain and Caulder. Carla and her dad were laughing and hugging again. He had also gained a new respect for his daughter's negotiating prowess.

We were home. Yes, Home! The very sound of it filled us with warmth and hope for the future.

Sunday's were unusually quiet now and we could stay home. Ah, Home! Instead of traveling to our families we could entertain them at our home. We no longer heard a 370 pounder's impromptu tap dances. We no longer enjoyed day-long concerts by Ripping Gizzards or whatever obnoxious group 1P2 was into at any given time.

During these early months Carla became pregnant and gained that soft glow that happy pregnant women get. Her face shown with love and tenderness. And we still had the Sabbath.

We had the most fantastic start to home ownership in the entire history of the modern and ancient world.

Idyllic? Possibly. Wonderful? Most surely.

CHAPTER FIVE

The Plagues – Part One

During the first two months, 246 Oakridge Lane was blessed with much rain with interludes of sunshine, causing the lawn to grow in nicely. In its recent history, this development had been a farm. The land was unforgiving to farming and produced enough to entice the owners into believing prosperity was possible, but failed often enough to drive them into bankruptcy.

As any shrewd developer knows, spent farmland carries no premium and can be purchased at rates far below other properties in more populated areas. So it was with our development. Very cheap land led to affordable housing which in turn led to quick growth. In total the development contained 230 homes with empty lots for nineteen more.

Our home was built as one of four spec homes to jumpstart further sales after a selling lull had set in. Part of the problem was the reputation of the land: poor drainage, rocky, and poor for planting. The builder compensated by spreading loam to about a ten-inch depth and fertilizing with the seeding. This tactic gave the seeds something to grab onto with food to grow once they had become established.

My dad had given us a mulching lawnmower as a housewarming gift. His attached note lovingly stated, "The greatest of success to the greatest of couples." He may have more appropriately written, "With this I doth end thy Sabbath."

After about five weeks I yanked the lawnmower out of the garage and christened my yard with its first mowing. I didn't think anything about this event occurring on a Sunday. I simply responded to habit. My dad often mowed on a Sunday and, in fact, preferred that day.

It was to be an overcast Sunday that brought the first true Sabbath busting event into Carla's and my life as homeowners.

"Honnneyyyyyyyy! Come quick. Something is happening to our lawn." I rushed to see why Carla was panicking. There were long, low mounds of dirt crisscrossing over the lawn surface. The grass was withering over these mounds.

My eyes darted up and down and back and forth across the yard. In disbelief I purveyed an underground highway crisscrossing swathes of my yard.

Before taking any action, I wanted to go to the County Records Office and see if a permit had been issued to small critters to build an underground roadway.

"I demand to see the Roads Supervisor," I would say to the desk clerk as I entered the building.

"Sorry, Mr. Roadworthy is out of the office."

"Well, when do you expect him to return?"

"Sometime after you leave."

"Where do I see the permits issued for underground road construction?"

"Only Mr. Roadworthy can show you those and, as I said, he won't be back until right after you leave."

"What if I stay here for four days?"

"In that case he will be back in four days and five minutes."

I returned to reality.

"My lawn! Carla, do we have a lawn guide book or something?"

"No we don't."

"We have to go to the store to get one. I need your common sense."

Carla joined me as we drove to our local home megacenter. In the lawn care section, rows of "How To" books peddled everything from how to build a rock garden to how to build a gazebo/deck combo over an artificial pond. But where were the books on lawn problems?

"Here they are, Hon," Carla beckoned me to her collection. I was amazed at the number of books on lawn problems. Had we been aware of just how many problems a lawn can have, we might have opted for green concrete.

"Good grief, Carla. There must be close to fifty books here. Here's one on exotic lawn pests. I didn't know lawn pests *could* be exotic. Moreover what would make them exotic?"

Carla commented, "Maybe the little buggers wear grass skirts."

Carla didn't joke around much, but when she did she always made me laugh.

She and I divided the books between us and spent the next forty five minutes hunting for a photograph or a diagram that matched the pattern on our lawn.

"Here are several books on common lawn problems." Carla said after looking through the book offerings.

"Ahhh! Here we go," I said back, "a book on common pests and their signs. I didn't know little buggers could carry signs." Somehow my joke only elicited a groan from Carla.

"Look! Look! Here it is." Carla was excited in an agitated sort of way. "We have moles."

"Moles?"

"Yes, moles. Here's a picture of them."

I said to her, "Man, if they are that ugly, I won't mind bumping them off."

Carla snapped back, "We are not doing any killing. I didn't by a house to become a murderer. We are going to read how to *drive* them away." I remember thinking, "Yeah, let's drive them to the Cough Plops."

Now the thought of being a murderer by killing pests never occurred to me. I had thoughts of the police surrounding my house as the Chief of Police got on his megaphone and called out, "Okay, buster! Come out! We have you surrounded."

"What did I do, officer?"

"You certainly know what you did. You have been bumping off little critters."

"I never knew bumping off little critters was a crime."

"That will be for the judge and jury to decide," the Chief cackled back. "Now get out of here or we'll be forced to fumigate and bug spray you – fit punishment for a deranged miscreant like yourself."

With my head hanging low I slowly came out of the house, dragging my feet along the ground, tears welling up in my eyes. Thousands of little critters came running out, carrying signs that read "Hang Him" and "Down with Critter Killers" and "Show No Mercy."

The judge was completely unsympathetic to me. He even instructed the jury to reach a guilty verdict, keeping the time to less than fifteen minutes in order to allow for a long lunch break.

"No need to break for consultation," the jury foreman called out. "I wrote a note saying he was guilty, pass it on. We did pass the note on and everyone signed it."

"Fine," the judge said in a gruff voice, "Let's pass sentence. All those in favor of the death penalty say so by cheerfully waving your hands in the air."

The breeze from twenty four hands waving frantically in the air blew my hair back. The gallery was full of little critters screaming, "Spray him! Spray him! Spray him!"

"Will you get over here and look over this book with me?" Carla scolded me, snapping me back to reality.

She took a notepad and pen out of her purse. Men love to chide women on the contents of their purses, but how many men can deliver a notepad and pen on the spot the way Carla had just done?

We found two books describing the mole habitat in depth. The books also illustrated lawn repair methods, once the moles were gone. Carla scribbled ideas from several books and we settled on two to buy.

Interestingly, the home megacenter had all of the items we needed. There were the necessary miscues. For example, the aisle clerk in Insecticides guided us towards Hardware for lawn rollers. And the aisle clerk in Home and Garden – where lawn rollers reside – guided us to Sporting Goods for the smoke bombs that would comprise the front lines of our offense.

Lawn rollers are curious devices. They are a small horizontal water tank with Y-shaped prongs coming from the sides and joining together to form the handle used to push and pull it around. The tank is filled with water, adding sufficient weight to push flat newly harrowed sections of lawns.

Lawn rollers look like the offspring of steam rollers. Just as Elaine and Eric used small lawn brooms to imitate my sweeping up leaves with my big adult-sized lawn broom, lawn rollers run around lawns to imitate their parents' work on driveways and streets.

My father's lawn roller had shown me the wonders of these machines. After a light sprinkling the roller pushed the lawn flat with amazing ease. While growing up, Dad and I tried to fix a small insect-eaten section of our lawn by jumping up and down on it after seeding. Not only did that effort leave the lawn lumpy and uneven, it left us with mud-caked shoes.

No, modern technology – dating from the Jurassic period – saved the day for Dad and me and history would be repeated today.

Finally we gathered all the items to assault the sick lawn, bringing it back to the accepted level of lawns in our neighborhood.

My father's feeding and mowing syndrome had now gripped me. The grass must be knitted tightly together. The grass must be green. The grass must be fed to make it grow. Making the grass grow added mowing cycles, which led to more feedings, weedings and, sometimes, breedings – in this case, moles.

In total we spent $179 on the books and all of the materials needed for driving the little pests away and fixing the lawn afterwards.

"Let's see. Moles are tunnelers, but can come out in the open during foraging. If I get a shovel, perhaps I can smack a few of them on the head. That should send a message to the rest of them."

Carla just glared at me. "I repeat: We are *not* going to kill them. Understand?" Her stare was vaguely reminiscent of the look presented to Mr. Caulder. I quickly and wisely decided to drop that approach.

The first step required locating the main runways and the nest. I slowly measured the total length of the surface runs: thirty-three feet. What did that mean? Nothing. This ploy was buying time until Carla went inside so I could smack the moles with a shovel.

Mystically, Carla seemed to read my mind. She handed me an eighteen-inch long spike and a steel handled hammer. Apparently she had read ahead in the books before we bought them, leading her to purchase the hammer and the spike.

She continued with her mistrusting stare. "You know what to do with these," she said in a low, gruff voice. She handed me one of the books opened to the proper page.

The illustrations and guides were simple enough, but executing the task took much longer than was implied – a total of six hours.

By carefully using the spike and hammer, the main runway was mapped. The nest couldn't be located, but knowing the runway pattern allowed for the placement of five small smoke bombs.

I began setting the smoke bombs into position, packing dirt over them. Dusk was rapidly descending, forcing me to hasten my campaign. Interestingly, the continually fading light provided a good backdrop to see the smoke exits. Small hazy puffs emitted from various locations.

There was no screaming and no appearance of moles rushing out carrying little suitcases. In fact, the healing of the grass over the coming week and the lack of any new sub-surface runs were the only evidence they had left at all.

From Monday through Friday we busily prepared for the new baby, buying decorations for the house and dealing with ogres and gremlins. Saturday was a shopping day, leaving Sunday for the final lawn repair.

I took out a package of coated seeds – the type used for difficult patching – and the rake and lawn roller purchased the previous Sunday. After a long afternoon of raking, rolling, raking, seeding, and watering, the lawn repair was finished – and so was Sunday.

Had someone with great wisdom taken me by the hand, led me into his inner sanctum and explained the events of the previous two Sundays, I might have become aware of the rapid erosion of the Sabbath. As it was, the only words I received from Carla's Dad were "You got rid of moles using smoke bombs? And on the first try? Amazing. Simply amazing." My dad spoke more resolutely. "Well, son. Well done."

The two mothers chose to avoid the subject. Over the years they had heard many heroic stories about lawns and house repairs and a simple battle against moles didn't make it into their top ten Sabbath busters.

The moles had gone their way quickly returning lawn mowing as the Sunday ritual. Unless rain was heavy, I could sneak a mowing in between downpours. Someone motoring through the neighborhood on a rainy summer Sunday might come upon the curious specter of home owners yanking lawnmowers in and out of garages or whirling the machines erratically around their yards to trim down precious sections of grass before the next cloudburst.

Though the moles had departed, hopefully with one-way tickets to another neighborhood, it was necessary to remove their food source to prevent their return. Close the restaurant and the moles will not return home. My restaurant had healthy servings of insects to whet the most discriminating mole pallet.

Insects weren't the only problem to handle. Weeds were sprouting up across the lawn.

The question was which products of mass destruction should be applied. I wanted boxes packed with tiny F-16 fighter jets that would bomb, shoot and strafe the lawn into submission. I wanted boxes with pictures of lines of weeds and insects marching away on their little roots and feet.

I delved into the two books on lawn care. Carla found a contemporary volume on natural lawn care involving the total rejection of commercial insecticides, weed killers, and fertilizers.

I enjoyed the idea of brute force. Somehow the word "natural" sounded wimpier than I had been with Steve Rain. I enjoyed packages that proudly declared "kills unwanted pests on contact" or "destroys weeds in days."

"Kill" and "destroy." These are macho words, declaring war on the problem at hand. "Natural" is such a flabby word. I imagined people dressed like woodland sprites petting their weeds to death and playing flutes to draw happy-faced insects to their peaceful new home in the woods.

One company even had the foresight to show pictures of dead insects – all curled up – demonstrating the superiority of their product. After seeing my expression, Carla shook her head. She said nothing. She didn't have to.

Carla had a simple and loving view towards all life. I learned to respect her reverence for the word "natural." I also learned "natural" came at a much higher price than "kill" or "destroy." We paid over $200 for the right to pet our weeds to death and dance our little pests to a better homeland.

The next Sunday I spent the day naturalizing the lawn. First, I raked up stones and dead grass. Next, stinky organic mixtures and bacterial solutions were applied evenly across the entire yard. Finally, out came the sprinklers.

Carla helped me set the sprinklers and during the process she received several direct water hits. The giggling and playfulness that followed reminded me of the day we first entered our new home. My old Carla had returned and for the moment the world outside could be tamed. The coming week of ogre abuse and rush hour traffic would not dent my spirits.

The week contained many small trials with their coincidental tribulations. The defining moment came on Tuesday: My ogre's stapler came up missing. Office operations ceased while he arranged a scavenger hunt to locate the errant stapler.

A study into ogre lore would have discovered the importance of staplers and apparently this particular item had come from ogre royalty. It had passed through several generations until reaching my boss's hands as an object to be venerated.

A casual visitor would have cowered behind the supply cabinet for fear a major assault by armed disgruntled employees was underway. My mind momentarily flashed to an image of Carla spreading some of her natural pest treatment over his desk, driving the stapler to newer and more fertile grounds.

My luck changed that day: I found the lost icon in the copy room. My boss had brought it there to assemble several documents he had prepared on Monday night for an upcoming board meeting. Apparently, ogre brains do not have the tracking capability necessary to maintain control over lower life forms, such as staplers.

There was a look of relief on Mr. Jorgensen's face – naming him now elevated his status from ogre to human being. From that Jorgensen's Day forward, Old Jorgey flashed me a friendly smile and sometimes a hello as we passed in the hallways.

In the fable, Androcles befriends a lion by removing a thorn from the suffering beast's paw. In my real life fable, I befriended an ogre with a much lesser, though probably not much less dangerous, task.

Somehow Carla did not find the story compelling or even the slightest bit amusing. To her sense of logic, all Mr. Jorgensen did was to once again proffer his image as an idiot. My dad roared with delight. He then went into a litany of stories about his past bosses, though none of the recalled events could top the silliness of my currying such favor by simply locating a beloved – excuse me, venerated – stapler.

Within three months my job title changed to Assistant Manager with the obligatory ten percent pay increase. Carla's opinion hadn't changed, except she now viewed Mr. Jorgensen as a generous idiot.

All too often in society one is evaluated based on his or her job. We laugh at the people who work menial jobs and look longingly at those lucky enough to garner high level positions in corporations. We are dazzled by those in the entertainment business – movies, radio, TV, and music – who in addition to public recognition scoop up vast quantities of money, often making more in a year than even some of the better-heeled of us can make in a lifetime.

So it went with my job. As a lowly clerk I slouched through the hallways smiling at my coworkers as I slithered up to my desk and squeezed out a day's work. Now as an assistant manager, just one beat away from manager of the whole department, my coworkers thought I could slice through the bureaucracy for them and somehow get them an assistant manager position or at least a better raise.

Mr. Jorgensen is the manager and I am his assistant. The pecking order in corporations, large and small, is well-defined. One manager has one assistant and dozens of wannabees. Once someone escaped the masses there were no more possibilities until either the manager or the assistant moved on, was fired, or died in office.

At least for the present, my position within the corporation sparked envy among some of my coworkers. And all for the want of a stapler.

Within the hallowed halls of the animal world I wonder how closely mole society maps ours. If a manager mole had a stapler to which he was attached, would he have obliged me and moved on if I found it and returned it to his waiting paws?

CHAPTER SIX

The Plagues – Part Two

Sung to the tune of "When Johnny Comes Marching Home Again":
The ants go marching one-by-one, Hurrah! Hurrah!
The ants go marching one-by-one, Hurrah! Hurrah!
The ants go marching one-by-one,
The little one stopped to suck his thumb.
And they all go marching down to the ground to get out of the rain.
Boom Boom Boom Boom Boom Boom Boom

The song was an early elementary school effort my classmates and I learned at summer camp and sang before school started. We thought it was funny; our teachers thought it was cute. Our parents? Well, they didn't want to think about it at all – no doubt a condition inspired from bad experiences.

We had miraculously traveled the entire length of the fall and winter without any serious events. The snow stayed on the outside of the house. The inside stayed dry despite hailstorms and wind-driven rain in the fall, and sweeping blizzards in the winter. To me, a dry house fell into the category of things that were just supposed to be.

Spring arrived with the required rituals: defeating the impending crab grass, fertilizing the lawn, and mulching the shrub beds. The Sabbath had become a dear part of our lives during the fall and winter, with Sundays mostly free until the onset of spring. The magic of the season of renewal came with a price – the retreat of the Sabbath onto the shelf of good intentions.

"Honnneyyyyyyyy! Come quick." Carla's beckoning had by now become a clarion call; a demand something beyond her control needed immediate attention. It was a call that reminded me of my scream from many years earlier. I would cry "Maaaaaaaaa," when something intruded into my safe world. A large spider was enough to launch the golden tones and living on a semi-wooded property afforded a parade of spiders of different types and sizes to keep my vocal chords well trained.

This particular day it was not spiders that aroused Carla's response; it was ants. She was not bothered by spiders, anyway, seeing them as an asset in the fight against unwanted insects. Besides, spiders didn't come in by the hundreds.

Ants had a different approach. They would send their reconnaissance troops forward on foraging expeditions. When a scrumptious site was located, the forward guard had some amazing ability to bring in all of the ants of the same kind who were within a one-week steady march away.

Carla exclaimed, "You know what this means, don't you? We'll be infested in a couple of days if we don't act now." I knew she was right.

Of course, the day was a Sunday and an event like this couldn't wait until Monday night.

"By Monday night I'll be sleeping over at my parent's house. I'll not sleep in a house full of ants." Carla always overreacted to ants. I suspected her psyche had been scarred by too many ruined picnics.

"Okay. Okay." My grumbling continued all the way to the home megacenter.

The aisles were now committed to memory. Hoses, aisle seven, along with hose connections, hose reels, and sprinklers. Concrete blocks, outside garden area, along with fertilizers, lawn furniture, and patio umbrellas. Insecticides, aisle nine.

Insecticides had nearly a whole dedicated aisle. This time Carla had no interest in natural insect control. She headed directly to the nuke section: sevin, malathion, products containing lambda-cyhalothrin, d-cis-trans allethrin and a host of other ingredients that didn't roll off your tongue but rolled your tongue up.

I believe if under the glow of a full moon, I said the ingredients in the right order while wearing the appropriate cape and pointy hat with stars on it, the insects wouldn't have to be sprayed. They would stand up and march away with glassy eyes and trembling legs.

The names sounded military. The ant command forward was going to face all of the might from aisle nine. I imagined the forward sergeant barking cadence. "Hup toop threep forp, hup, toop ... hold it, men! Don the masks. It's *malathion!*"

Malathion. The name just exuded "kill," the macho word of all macho words in the world of insecticides. After all, wasn't "mal" a prefix meaning bad or harmful, or *deadly?*

"Carla? Let's get malathion."

"Hold it. I want to read the precautions."

"Precautions? Precautions? Who cares? We have ants and you want them gone."

Carla started reading, murmuring an assortment of minor warnings, such as skin irritation and keep away from pets. Then her voice rose in volume as she hit the meat and potatoes.

"Aha, headaches, nausea, cramps, dizziness, weakness, diarrhea, excessive sweating, blurred vision, increased heart rate ..."

I cut her off. "Carla, these are all of the things the ants get. We'll be fine."

She glared at me. "I am p-r-e-g-n-a-n-t." In an instant she had transformed into my mother. "You will eat your v-e-g-e-t-a-b-l-e-s or you will not play with your friends." Somehow, letters carried just the right impact, a power that transcended anything the whole word could deliver.

Imagine how the Allies would have fought in World War II, had a general simply imitated his mother. "Make no mistake about it, men. We are s-o-l-d-i-e-r-s. We will fight to v-i-c-t-o-r-y."

"Sir, we will win this one for Mom," the troops called back in unison, "or we will not get any dessert."

I saw Carla slip back over to the natural products. They carried warnings such as, "causes excess happiness, makes one dizzy with glee, heart will race with joy." The ant sergeant had his troops on alert. "They have gone to the megacenter, men. For our sake, for the sake of the environment, and for all of antdom, let us hope they do the honorable thing and go natural. I repeat, n-a-t-u-r-a-l."

"I'll tell you what, Honey. I'll get the malathion for the outside and you can get the giddy soaps for inside."

"Here is what we need," she said firmly, "ant traps."

"Ant traps?" I immediately imagined rows of tiny mousetrap devices baited with sugar. "How do we set them?" Carla was not amused. She slowly shook her head and picked up a package that looked like a collection of small hockey pucks. I was confused, but kept my ignorance quiet.

Home ownership had already broadened my learning to topics I never knew existed: blocked eaves troughs, cutworms, lawn pH, nitrogen balance, tree trunk girdling, and red thread fungus. Why would Carla think ant traps should come as common knowledge? I viewed them as just one more item that somehow required a Sunday deployment to work.

Back on the home front, the ants had multiplied their presence to several dozen members and lines began to form, indicating their successful locating of sumptuous delights. They formed the ant counterpart of the bucket brigade.

Carla put on rubber gloves, quickly tore open the ant trap packages, and started placing ant traps strategically around the house: by the rear atrium door, under the cabinets by the sink, and inside the cabinet under the sink.

I walked around the back. "Malathion," I mumbled. "Ants! You are in for it. I am the new bad boy on the block."

I took in the landscape, established my beach head, and then headed out to confront the enemy. They were small, but had the advantage of numbers – really *big* numbers.

Ant societies and human societies are often compared in cartoons and science projects. I can see the resemblance, but sometimes the analogy is carried too far. Ants don't protest or unionize. Ants don't vote in leadership or Gerrymander their districts. Ants don't play sports or give concerts. And ants don't seem to enjoy leisure time. No vacations and no weekends.

Though I have to admit many bosses I and my father have known would love to have their underlings work like ants.

Social strata are followed without question. Sacrifices come from instinct and not from a sense of duty. One trait among ants does carry through to humans: size differences. All one has to do is watch a gymnastics event followed by a pro-football and then a pro-basketball game and marvel at how variable human size can be.

From where I stood the route of penetration could not be seen. "Sneaky, buggers," I thought. Squirts of malathion went around the bottom of the atrium door and under the kitchen window.

Husband and wife retired for the evening, comforted by the knowledge that come morning the ant army would face fusillades from malathion. Those ants penetrating the defenses had no chance against the traps.

Carla normally got up first. Her mornings required extra time to assemble face and hair. I couldn't complain, since the final product was always so lovely. This particular morning Carla trotted back into the bedroom and shrieked, "They're gone! The ants are gone!"

We didn't check the contents of the traps to determine casualty rates. I assumed the little buggers' legs would be sticking out from the little holes in the trap. Okay. I didn't know how the trap worked.

After a quick glance around, we tossed the traps away, had breakfast and went on our way to work.

Mr. Jorgensen faced no further traumas needing my steady hand and stewardship. It didn't matter. Conquering the stapler had placed me on the fast track. My second raise came early. He wanted to encourage me to continue with my excellent work. Strangely, my work quality and output had not changed; he had only just decided to take notice.

Carla's and my day went smoothly – too smoothly, as it turned out. Luckily we had one car, requiring our riding together. In this way we arrived home together, allowing us to face any surprises with mutual support. She entered the house first and went directly to the kitchen to plan dinner.

"Oh, no! Honnneyyyyyyyy!"

If this were a game of twenty questions, I would have set a record by guessing on the first try: "Is it ants?"

When I arrived in the kitchen Carla's face had a scrunched expression – her eyebrows and chin seemed an inch apart. A cursory glance at the floor demonstrated the enemy's renewed strength. There were now literally hundreds of ants scurrying in different directions.

I know exactly what happened. The ants had exercised one more human trait: cleaning up. No doubt my malathion spraying caused them distress. How will they get back into the house to continue foraging? They formed a bucket and mop brigade and commenced mopping up the malathion, clearing away an entrance for themselves.

If I took a magnifying glass and carefully scouted the lawn I would likely find little empty boxes of detergent, a tiny garden hose and some discarded buckets and mops.

Sneaky buggers. Ants have their own home megacenter. All I had to do was find the hollowed out log where their mall was located.

This scenario answered why there were no ants in the morning. Ants diverge from humans in another aspect: Ants don't work a third shift.

We darted to the megacenter to get some insecticide mega-power. Instead of the prepared solution in a squirt bottle, this time I bought the malathion concentrate. The aisle clerk said, "You'll need a pressure tank dispenser to use that." A pressure tank dispenser? He moved us toward the back of the aisle to where the pressure tanks stood at attention, ready to join the battle.

He explained the operation. The model I chose sported a strap that allowed me to sling it over my shoulder and carry the unit on my back, freeing my hands to administer maximum firepower. Firepower seemed an appropriate term: the tank/hose assembly resembled a flame thrower.

"You'll also need goggles and gloves for protection," the clerk said as we started to leave. Goggles and gloves. Now this meant we were in control of some serious anti-ant weapons. Goggles and gloves, flamethrower, and malathion.

In my mind Carla, the clerk and I huddled and checked the landscape for enemy agents. We synchronized our watches and made the appropriate death pact, wherein the survivor promised to spread the story of our gallant stand against the ant world.

"You coming?" Carla's voice sprung me out of the momentary day dream. "Let's go, it's getting dark and we have to spread the insecticide tonight."

Back home I prepared malathion solution directly in the tank. After the cover was secured, I pumped the tank until the backpressure prevented any more filling. Great swaths of malathion began covering the length of the back of the house. I imagined the poisonous mist spreading across the ground out over the fields and into the woods, scattering ants of all races in its wake. The toll increased: thousands, millions, billions of vanquished ants.

Those ants unable to outrun the wave either perished or grabbed tiny surfboards to ride the wave. No doubt the ant megacenter had a surfboard section. With trillions of ants world-wide ant surfboard sales would be immense.

My dear wife had watched my display and was smiling with the kind of smile that indicated she loved me despite my silliness – or perhaps because of it.

After I had cleaned up she said, "Here, help me place the rest of these traps." She continued smiling, while gently shaking her head at me. We hugged, kissed and went to bed, comforted by the knowledge that come morning, the ant army would be no more.

In the morning Carla rushed into the bedroom, shook me hard, grabbed my hand and dragged me into the kitchen. I flew behind her like a pennant in the wind!

Ants were now *everywhere!* I could see her tears of frustration welling up. She got the vacuum cleaner and whooshed over the entire kitchen, pantry and dining room floors. She replaced the floor tool with the crevice tool and whizzed along the moldings, under the sink, and in all the cabinets closest to the floor. After the assault, the vacuum cleaner bag came into my possession. "You know what to do with this," Carla said in a low monotone.

I took the bag into the back yard and soaked it with the prepared malathion solution we had first purchased. The bag was then placed into a garbage bag which in turn was taped tightly closed. Here stood a tomb to a thousand brave ant soldiers. After the obligatory twenty-one gun salute and internment in the ant war veterans' cemetery, I returned to the war zone.

Back in the kitchen, stragglers that had escaped the whirlwind were moving hither and yon from various places. There was no more to accomplish at this hour – a friendly boss and carnivorous gremlins awaited us. During the ride to work we said little to each other. My thoughts focused on ants and what to do about them.

I worked late. Carla got a ride from a co-worker. She didn't call me either at work or on the cell phone, so I assumed the ant situation had not escalated since the morning.

At home Carla sat motionless in the kitchen. A small wave of ants moved erratically around her. The site was something out of a cheap knock-off of an Alfred Hitchcock movie. Why didn't Hitchcock use ants instead of birds? Birds are difficult to train and clean up after, but these ants acted on cue and at night left no trace they had ever been here. Morning: come in, spread out, and make our blood boil. Evening: go home, make us go to the megacenter, and ruin our sleep. Repeat endlessly.

Carla vacuumed again, but the ant population was building rapidly, even with evening setting in. "They must have a clone production line in our basement," I exclaimed.

"Basement! That's *it*," Carla shouted. "The little creeps aren't coming in the back at all. Let's look over the basement."

Armed with flashlights, we descended to the basement. The coarse floor still had mud stains from the construction days. The floor, having never been washed or painted, also bore patches of gray powder from the construction, making ant spotting difficult.

There was only one light down there. Our having only this light and the flashlights left the advantage to the ants. We searched for about an hour and found nothing. Well, nearly nothing. There were some dead ants in various places – clearly stragglers who got lost and perished. But their presence meant we were on the right track.

After one more vacuuming, I said tiredly, "Let's go to bed. The ants retreat to their hill in the evening and it is now well into the night. Let's renew our search tomorrow afternoon." We yawned, weakly locked eyes, and then slowly stumbled upstairs.

That night we went to bed discomforted by the knowledge that come morning the ant army would be out in force. And they were.

Carla and I said very little to each other. We both looked and felt tired, but went out into the world in our weakened state. Her gremlins were first-rate predators and would sense her condition, much the way lions know which members of the herd to bring down. I felt sorry for my lovely wife. At least I no longer faced an ogre – just office pests. These pests could normally be ignored and there weren't thousands of them, though sometimes it sounded like it in the hallways and lunchroom.

Through weary eyes I performed an honest day's work, whatever that meant.

I guess doing an "honest day's work" means nothing remains attached to me as I leave for the day – such as erasers, pencils, pens, sticky pads, notepads, blotters, desk chairs, desks, and refrigerators.

At one point I actually saw a small line of ants bend around the inside corner of my cubicle. After I rubbed my eyes they evaporated. That was *it!* The basement was going to be raided until the ant highway was discovered and destroyed.

Late that afternoon, Carla and I readied ourselves. I barked the details. If it was war they wanted, then war it was going to be!

"Gloves."

"Check."

"Indoor bug spray cans."

"Check."

"Goggles."

"Check."

"Flashlights."

"Check."

"Extra batteries."

"Check."

"Okay, sergeant. Let's move out and remember, soldier: If we don't come back, I always loved you."

Carla couldn't hold back anymore and burst out laughing.

"Shhhhh, you'll scare the ants away," I said quietly.

With giggles intact, we stalked down the stairs into the basement. Thinking back I am not sure whether we were actually happy, assuming victory would soon be ours, or whether we were simply reacting to the frustration.

Down in the basement the battle was joined. A small column of ants was double-time marching on the floor next to the wall behind the furnace. The flashlights did nothing to deflect their determined travel.

"What the ... Where are they entering?" I said softly. "Let's follow them, Honey. You move back toward the hot water heater and I'll see where this column is going."

Ants proved to be worse than water. Water leaks are famous for appearing some distance from their source. But water doesn't come in one place, go downhill for awhile, move straight for another distance, climb back up, and start spurting in all directions.

"Look here, Hon," she called excitedly. "Found them!"

Our illustrious builder had delivered a fairly decent home – comfortable and well-sealed. Or so we thought. Carla shined her flashlight along what appeared to be a strip of land between the bottom of the foyer floor and the top of the basement wall. I fetched a step ladder and moved in for a closer look.

The foyer area formed a nice combination entrance and mudroom. It was built about four inches above the rest of the house – the flooring was stepped and beveled to flow off into the adjoining rooms. The effect was quite beautiful.

The developer's voice seeped into my head, "This is a design you only see on houses costing two to three times as much." Fine. But I bet *those* houses didn't have an open access to the lawn under the foyer.

The light from the flashlight glistened off the small, black ant bodies as they steadily trickled into the basement. The little creeps had built a large nest next to the shrub by the front entrance. The shrub position and the shadows hid them from view, allowing their housing development unimpeded progress.

Apparently, as the nest grew it broke into the basement. Sections of tunnels were now visible giving us an ant farm view. The marching path from the nest created a very interesting pattern that would have challenged General Patton at his best.

From the nest, the ants crawled along the top of the basement wall for about fourteen feet to the end, took a left and continued on the wall for about another twelve feet. There, through some fantastic sense of insect wisdom, they trailed along the main support beam, grabbed onto a double joist section, and moved along until they hit the sink drain pipe support. Once on the drain pipe the ants moved straight upward under the sink cabinet and spread out from the baseboards through a zillion locations.

What was the column on the floor? A rearguard assault? Another nest joining the fray? We never found out. Once the main source was blocked, the ant assault ceased.

Years later this trek still fascinates me. What could have possibly intrigued them to go into our kitchen in the first place? Once there, what determined the final trail? Did they use maps? Did our builder sell us out and supply the enemy with the building plans?

"What do we do now?" Carla asked. Her eyes were now wide and her forehead had a series of horizontal creases. But she and I were relieved. The battle – no, the war – was about to be won!

"We revisit our friendly home center," I answered, my eyes squinted, reflecting my determination.

Carla remained behind to continue with the vacuuming. I returned with a pail of hydraulic cement and a bag of plasticized sealing cement. A five-gallon drywall pail confiscated from the dumpster during the house construction was now pressed into service.

The instructions were simple. Add water, mix until smooth and apply with a trough. Sounded a bit like the way my great aunt made her pastries – only the cement was going to be softer.

The open section above the wall placed a nice challenge before me. Each time I scraped away some dirt, more fell into place. The little warriors still had the upper hand.

I found some cardboard, cut it to the exact size of the opening and firmly hammered it into place with a rubber mallet. The soil compressed nicely exposing about seven inches on top of the wall. After applying a cycle of wire brushing and rinsing with wet sponges, I was ready to apply the hydraulic cement.

Carla pulled up a lawn chair to watch the action in comfort. "This is better than television," she quipped and watched, but wisely offered no advice. She knew me too well. Any advice she proffered at a time like this would only draw the standard husband reply: "If you think you know so much about it, why don't *you* do it?"

The cardboard made a firm backdrop for the hydraulic cement to compact against. I filled the space with the cement, feathering the edges to assure a tight seal all around. To prevent cracking, the cement surface needed misting every hour or two. Carla and I took turns traveling to the construction site, water-filled squirt bottle in hand.

On the weekend – Sunday, in fact – I sealed the hydraulic cement with a healthy helping of plasticized moisture blocking cement. This mixing procedure was infinitely more complex: add water, mix until smooth, add acrylic emulsion, mix until smooth, and apply with a trough.

The acrylic emulsion. Too bad my great aunt didn't know about this. It may have allowed her biscuits to pass *all* the way through my digestive system. Sometimes, Carla would pop me on the belly and exclaim, "Wow! So hard." Little did she know how much of that rigidity was owed to the continuing presence of my great aunt's biscuits.

As a finishing touch I remounted my malathion "flame thrower" and decimated the nest out front by the shrub. One can never be too secure. One never knows when an evolutionary urge may set in, allowing the ants to develop pneumatic hammers and break through the newly placed cement barricade. I was intent on saving mankind from this potential tragedy.

What I found most strange from this whole ordeal was why no water had ever leaked through this space. I remember from my youth, leaving my bedroom window open only one one-thousandth of an inch during a rain storm. When I came back to my room, I was swept back against the closet door by a raging three-foot high tidal wave. Yet here was a four-inch high by four-foot long open invitation to water and none came in.

Ants, like water, find their way, so I wondered how many other crevices existed allowing pests of varying types access to our house.

This time Carla joined me in her rare traverse into fantasy.

"Whoa! Look at that, Carla. A one-inch by two-inch hole in the attic giving passage to an array of spiders."

"Honey, we had better fill the hole before we are overrun by spiders."

"Yow! Look at this spot on the other side of the attic – a half-inch round hole giving passage to silverfish by the hundreds."

"So that's where they are coming from, Honey. All along I thought *you* were eating the bindings of our books."

"Good grief! Here is a quarter-inch high by one-inch long slit between the garage and house giving passage to centipedes by the dozens."

"I wonder, why don't the spiders eat the silverfish and the centipedes eat the spiders, Honey?"

"Oh, noooo! Here is a hole in our screen letting in scores of mosquitos."

"And all along, Honey, I thought you were biting me in my sleep."

Of course, the only real transgression we had was the ant invasion. I may never answer why water didn't come in, since it can easily seep through tiny cracks and holes.

My wife comforted me. "Don't worry, Honey. If you ever explain the Cough Plops, this answer will come easy."

CHAPTER SEVEN

The Story of Noah – Part One

This same spring, several neighbors began trapping us into conversations about water leaks and house settlement. The previous summer and fall we were too occupied establishing ourselves indoors to discover the wonders of our new neighborhood.

Our first forays out of 246 Oakridge Lane only drew looks – the kind of inquiring gazes reserved for odd-looking people one sees lurking outside of malls. When making eye contact, we were greeted with a brief smile, then a sudden turning away of the head. These smiles suggested the presenters suffered from some form of bowel distress or, perhaps, alien possession. "I think we should call this place Wuthering Heights," Carla offered.

After a few more jaunts passed their houses, we began to see smiles bearing a semblance of friendliness. Wuthering Heights was beginning the transformation to Sunnybrook Farm; except I was married to Carla and not Rebecca.

The first conversations we encountered were the standard ones strangers have when they try to size each other up. Had our heads born antlers, instead of conversation we would have pawed the ground with our feet and circled around each other, always maintaining eye contact, puffing snorts of superiority from our noses.

As humans, our posturing reduced to simple proclamations:

"Hello, I'm Joe. Joe Mathews and this is my wife, Ellen."

"Hi, we live at 246 Oakridge Lane, that house over there."

"Hello, we seen you working on the lawn. I'm Frank."

"Hi, we live at 246 Oakridge Lane, that house over there."

"Hey, I see you're new in the neighborhood. I'm Helen"

"Hi, we live at 246 Oakridge Lane, that house over there."

The passage from proclamation to cries of distress occurred suddenly.

"So, you folks got any leaks? Leanne and I have been fighting with the builder for nearly a year now. He is soooo 'busy' you know," said one distraught neighbor.

Another neighbor declared outright frustration. "How's your basement? Got any water down there? Try and get it fixed. My wife got Brock, the site foreman, out here twice. It didn't do any good. This builder is one for the books. Nothing fits right. I'm surprised the whole house doesn't fill with water."

A third neighbor gave us a mini-dissertation. "Speaking of barbecues, my husband is having one Sunday; you're invited. We can't eat in the family room, though. We had to have the rug pulled up. It was starting to rot from water underneath. You'd think the jerk would have put a small crawl space under the slab. My husband says that's the only *right* way to build on *this* type of soil."

Our reactions became the occasional "Yeah" or "Man" or "Whoaaa," applied at the appropriate breaks in their speech.

As I noted earlier in this book, part of the problem was the reputation of the land: poor drainage. Poor drainage allows water to puddle and when water has nowhere to go, it seeks the most expedient path. That path is usually the basement wall or the space where the basement floor meets the walls.

The builder used a variety of subcontractors, some good, some fair, some poor and some who just didn't know what they were doing. I was too soon to become a victim of that last group.

Now, back to the conversations with our neighbors.

Conversations are a two-way confluence of thoughts where each party contributes. Our interactions reduced to a storm of words on one side with responsive grunts from us. The grunts signified we knew something was being said; although, because the content held no value for us, we had no interaction.

I have heard it said for every person who praises a builder's work there are ten who complain. This adage follows across all aspects of industry – restaurant food, appliances, home entertainment products, and on and on.

Of course I am generalizing, but in our travels through our neighborhood we only heard perhaps two compliments for the builder. Complaints, however, rolled off their tongues with ease.

Carla and I tried finding alternate walking routes, but to no avail. One neighbor or another would accost us about the developer's dereliction, much as the Ancient Mariner accosted the wedding guest in Samuel Coleridge's famous poem.

The Ancient Mariner railed on about an albatross, shrinking boards, undrinkable water, but not house leaks. The binding similarities between neighbor and Mariner were the line segment in the poem, "Water, water everywhere ..." and the need to seize someone, holding on with great tenacity until the tale of woe had been revealed.

I wondered at times how this tact would work with my boss.

"Ohhh, Mr. Jorgensen," I would say as I grasped his shoulders firmly, "the Dolleranty Report. A travesty of mental carnage. How can we manage as a company when that is the level of performance we can expect? What kind of jerk would write such a report and what worse jerk would approve it?" Mr. Jorgensen could only nod his head in agreement. "Go forth, my grand assistant. Go forth and spread the word about the Dolleranty Report."

And go forth I would, hanging onto every hapless soul who crossed my path, beseeching him or her to go forth and spread the word. Soon the whole world would know about the travesty known as the Dolleranty Report.

Would the report be repaired or revised or demolished? Of course not. It would continue on through the ranks of the company until it either was filed or became law, but no remedial action would be required of me. Instead, in reality, I would have endless nights repairing the Dolleranty Report.

Complaining about the builder came a bit late for us, our having completely settled into the fabric of the neighborhood. Complaints wouldn't cause us to move and they wouldn't lead our neighbors to move.

My great uncle once told me it's human nature to complain. "Nobody wants to fix anything – too much work," he told me many times. "They would rather complain. Kind of soothes the soul, I suppose. Won't fix anything. Just feels good."

Carla and I paid little attention to the neighbors when they complained until fate changed our situation.

One day we joined the chorus of complainers: the Day of the Flood.

That infamous Saturday brought its own version of Noah's storm. The skies darkened and continued to darken throughout the morning. Though the winds were still, by noon the streetlights had been fooled into believing nightfall had settled in. The eerie cloud flow pattern was a smear of various dark shades of gray with jet blacks.

Ghost-like puffs of clouds seemed to hover just above the treetops. Blurred lightning flashes stretched through the dense billows. The lack of thunder indicated whatever was to come had not yet arrived – and we were probably in for it!

Carla flashed me a nervous look. "Let's go down to the basement," she pleaded. She scurried indoors and collected candles, matches, and a lantern inherited from her grandmother. I moved to the front porch, where I stood, frozen by the amazing site forming around me.

Neighbors scurried around, bringing in lawn furniture and related sundries before heading indoors. The sky was now nearly pitch black. The wind, mild up to now, began rapidly accelerating, swirling chaotically, making an ominous whooshing sound that increased to a roar.

"Tornado!" The scream leaped from my mouth, surprising my next door neighbor. After shooting a frightened look in my direction, he whirled around and ran into his house.

"Carla! We're having a tornado. A *tornado!*"

Carla looked at me with the look only mothers give. The kindly, soothing look meant to comfort a frightened child. "We're not having a tornado. Just a really bad thunderstorm. Now come inside."

"Then, if it's not a tornado, why go into the basement?"

"Precaution, Hon. Did you see the lightning show coming this way? There must be two to three flashes a second. We shouldn't be near windows and the basement is the safest place to be." I went inside.

The lightning show was now upon us, arriving with the rain. I stood slack-jawed by the bay window – staring and only rarely blinking. Lightning strikes, bright glares through the raindrops, grilled the fields behind the houses across the street. Flash … Bang! Sometimes the time between flash and thunder was too fast to measure. The storm stood mightily over us, challenging every nerve in my body.

The rain front was horrendous. Torrents of water flowed like an angry river, driven by tree-snapping gusts of wind. The house trembled with the gusts. The house trembled with the thunder claps.

Growing up, my mother had a deathly fear of spiders and lightning. Since she was always home when either one came calling, her fears transferred to me. To this day I have a fear of both.

I know a fear of spiders is irrational, except for maybe the ones that have a leg spread which can fill the palm of your hand. Any spider that can be ridden with or without a saddle also must be feared.

Now a spider hitting you on the head can be very annoying, but it can never carry the impact of a lightning bolt bopping you on the head. Fear of thunderstorms can be healthy if it makes one get out of them. I had my fear reinforced when I was a teenager.

I remember in high school being with a group of friends at the beach, when a thunderstorm rose over the horizon and started racing towards us. The lifeguards hopped on four-wheelers, rode around alerting everyone to get off the beach, and then scooted off to safety themselves.

Where I live we normally go to lakes and getting out of the way of storms calls for a short run from the waterfront. In this trip, I and my friends were in Florida as guests of the aunt of my closest friend. She had a beach house and offered us a two-week stay for fun and frolic on a white sand Florida beach.

The main problem in Florida is storms in summer can come up very quickly and chase down unsuspecting victims. These are near tropical storms with ferocious lightning strikes, strong winds, and blinding rain. They often end quickly as well, but the effect is both horrifying and mesmerizing.

This particular storm seemed more ominous than usual for Florida. I had already seen a few while at my friend's aunt's house. This event was my first, outdoors on the beach.

The run from the waterfront seemed to be something on the order of twelve miles. Normally it was a couple of thousand feet, but with the storm closing in fast the distance just seemed to grow and time for me was slowing to a crawl. Every minute of my time translated to a few seconds for the storm.

My friends and I just made it to the cabanas when the storm caught us. We still had about a hundred feet to go before we could get shelter under the awnings on the buildings on the boardwalk.

The lightning was mostly cloud-to-cloud but a couple of bolts hit the ground close enough to cause a small crackle in my ears before they hit. The sound outdoors of the thunderclaps shattered my already fraying nerves. The surge of dread in my body outstripped any emotional reactions my mother could declare. If she had been here with me we both would have collapsed into blubbering heaps.

As the years have passed, anyone who tried to talk me out of my fear of thunderstorms found a most unwilling audience.

"Do not talk to me of storms and gales and winds that beach whales. Do not dare belittle my fear, for I swear I do not care." I actually said this ditty to Carla who could not reply and simply sat down on the couch in bewilderment. She just smiled at me for she knew my Florida beach story and my mother's fears.

So when this current storm hit, I strangely found myself truly horrified, but also mesmerized by the spectacle dancing around me. It was a most macabre dance, but the power of this storm firmly gripped me.

The storm slammed us for a full forty days and forty nights! The newspaper later erroneously declared "... a violent twenty-minute storm wracked the area yesterday afternoon." By my math, that reporter undercounted by 57,580 minutes!

As the storm passed, the low lying cloud puffs became light puffs of mist and finally just a soft haze. Street lights turned off as nighttime faded back to afternoon. In the distance, a soft, giant rainbow spread its colors, seeming to rise from the houses at the end of the block.

Carla and I stepped out onto the porch. Though the temperature had dropped about fifteen degrees, the air was incredibly heavy. We moved to the street, greeting the neighbors who were slowly emerging from their houses. Their hesitating, jerky motions reminded me of coyotes in nature shows coming out of their caves after a storm.

At least the conversations weren't about how bad the builder was. Nature's fury had provided, if briefly, a respite.

We joined a group of nine – husbands, wives and children – and ambled off with them on a walk through the neighborhood, examining how successfully the houses had survived.

"Look. There's a missing shingle," exclaimed one.

"And two shutters flew off that one," another cried out.

"Wow! Half that pear tree just snapped off," a third person shouted.

"Mommy, I'm thirsty," a little girl of about six called out.

"Let's go back," Carla whispered to me. "I've had enough of this."

I walked around the house, cutting as wide a circle as possible in order to see the roof and siding from all angles. Everything that was supposed to be there was there. Relieved, I went inside.

Evening had crept upon us and the television waited in the family room to provide us an array of mind-numbing programs to span the hours before bedtime. The vegetating finally wore us out and we gathered ourselves together for the slow trek to the bedroom.

"Oh, no!" The words fell from our mouths simultaneously. Long streaks of water had flowed down the bedroom wall. A large dark half-circle spread onto the ceiling from the corner out over the streaks. The image was of an extraterrestrial jelly fish.

We were sickened. Inspection showed one other water breach: The ceiling above the main bathroom doorway had a much smaller version of the jelly fish.

"Tomorrow's Sunday," Carla moaned. "We'll never get anyone to look at this. Honey?"

"I know," I said, cutting her off. "I'll get up on the roof first thing tomorrow morning."

The weather forecast gave the foreboding more rain was on the way for Sunday night into Monday. Another Sabbath was about to evaporate.

That night my dreams focused on storms and roof leaks. In one dream I was climbing a ladder while carrying a basket of very large sponges. Two of the neighbors came out of their houses and walked to edge of my property. With arms folded across their chests, they asked together, "We suppose you want to hear about our leaks? We got 'em solved. Know how to deal with the builder." I stopped, looked back at them, and pleaded, "How did you do it?" "*Now* you wanna know? You were too good for us before, politely giving us lip service. Sorry, Mr. Big Shot, you'll hafta figure it out yourself." They turned and walked back to their houses, laughing all the way.

On awakening, Carla went downstairs to prepare breakfast. She was only a couple of weeks away from delivering our first baby and could only offer me minimum help.

I made a list of needed supplies: ladder, flashlight, bucket, sponges, towels, and brush. I briefly thought of tennis balls to ping off the neighbors, should my dream come true.

"Hon, I need some leak detector solution and some roof patch. I'll be back soon. Sure you'll be okay?"

"I'm only having a baby. You've got a roof ahead of you. I'll be fine."

I had grown more and more protective as the due day crouched ever closer. My imagination showed Carla calling for me as her water broke. I was wearily slouching around the home center's endless aisles, trying to locate leak detecting solution and a bucket of roof patch, while she lay helpless on the floor, crying for help. I had to move faster.

At the megacenter I collared a clerk and asked him where the leak detection solution was. "We are all out of leak detection solution," the clerk informed me. "Besides, how do you expect to use it?"

"I don't know. My roof has a leak and the solution is made to find leaks."

"It is meant to find air leaks or gas leaks from pipes or fittings," he corrected me.

"Oh. Then how do I find a roof leak?"

"Got a garden hose?"

"Yeah."

"Bring it up to the roof with you and spray – don't use a hard jet – but spray water over a small section of the roof for about ten minutes. Wait about ten minutes and see if any water has come in. Start at the bottom of the roof and work your way up, a section at a time."

"Does that usually work?" I asked him.

"For leaks as big as yours? Sure. Your best bet is to have someone in the attic with a light. He might spot where the water is coming in."

This advice was all good. A plan of action was taking shape. Furthermore, the hose would provide me with an assault weapon, should neighbors arrive to heckle me.

I was relieved to find Carla sitting comfortably on the couch, reading the Sunday paper. After hearing me describe my fears, she retorted, "Wives are a lot tougher than that. If my water broke and you weren't here, I'd either call 911 or have Gladys drive me."

Gladys was the wife of the neighbor I frightened with my shout of "tornado." He and I had never formally met, but she and Carla were fourth grade teachers at different schools. No doubt they shared war stories about gallant, fateful battles against gremlins. They may have even exposed their shrapnel wounds to each other. "Oh my," Gladys cried, "how did you ever survive *that?*" "Believe it or not, I dragged myself back to my desk and before blacking out, forced order in the classroom, holding back the ravenous beasts until reinforcements arrived." Yes, my wife was strong, resilient.

The test of my resilience was unfolding before me.

Memories carry comfort or fear, depending on the current event sparking them. My memory of my father's bounding over the roof flashed before me. Could I perform with the same poise and grace? Did mountain goat tendencies pass on from generation to generation? In my case, the answer was "no!"

The raising of the ladder was the first task. The ladder needed to reach over twenty feet, the height of the eaves trough. My dad had convinced me to buy a wooden ladder. "They don't spring on you half way up," he said, "the way aluminum ladders do. Scared the bajeevers out of me the first time that happened. Thought I was going to be launched into the bushes."

So, wooden ladders do not spring when you climb to the halfway point. That's the good news. The bad news? They weigh six hundred times as much as aluminum ladders!

I wrestled the ladder out of the garage, found the middle and hauled it to the action spot. The roof had three adjacent gables jutting from the front. Two of the gables contained the master bedroom windows and the third the main bathroom window. The section of the roof containing the gables projected forward six feet. The leak was likely involving this configuration of roof shapes.

After a few Herculean thrusts, combined with obligatory grunts, I propelled the ladder into position. The extended tips stood a dizzying twenty two feet in the air – dizzying to me, the ladder took it all in stride.

I am not particularly acrophobic. I can ride external glass-walled elevators and four-hundred foot Ferris wheels. I can stand at the edge of cliffs, overlooking a panoramic view.

Ferris wheels are grounded firmly and are unlikely to roll away. Cliffs that have existed for millions of years are unlikely to choose the day of my visit to crumble. Outdoor Elevators? Well, they may be different. The ones I have ridden do work my nerves a little.

My ladder freely stood and, it seems, on its own terms. Sticking a small board at the ladder's feet held it firmly in place. At least, this technique worked for my father. For me the ladder wanted to use the board as a springboard. Once I was more than halfway up, the ladder would make its move, hop over the board and walk away in a jutting fashion trying to shake me off.

My ascent began with pail, sponges and hose in hand. After reaching the first 12,000 feet, I rested, intending to camp for the night.

Carla came outside to offer encouragement. "What are you doing? Why are you sitting on the ladder?"

"Oh, was I?" My voice telegraphed fear and concern.

"If you are nervous, call someone to do this." Carla did not exude reassurance.

"I'll be fine, don't worry."

"Hey, neighbor. Got a roof problem?" Larry had arrived and offered a hand. Larry was one of the few neighbors who could hold a conversation without introducing jabs at the builder. He had problems with his house, but leaks were not among them. I didn't have to fear his heckling.

"Here, I'll hold the ladder to stabilize it." His help filled me with confidence. I was going to be king of the roof! At least that was how I felt for a full ten seconds.

Arriving at the top still didn't place me *on* the roof. Fear and nervousness began welling up again. "Stay low. That's it." Larry's voice slowly instilled some of the confidence that had so quickly deserted me. "Keep your hands on the ladder as you place your foot on the roof. That's it." The rest was a blur punctuated with a number of that's-its from Larry.

"Tell you what. Let me in your house and I'll go into your attic and see where the water's coming in."

His offer rang through my head like a carillon's beautiful tones. Inside my head a quiet voice proclaimed, "You are saved." Without Larry, I would have had to make the trip up and down the ladder however many times it took to find the leak.

"Here's a flashlight. Come in." Carla overheard the conversation and sprang into action. Within minutes Larry had slipped upward through the ceiling opening in the bedroom closet and had taken up a strategic position in the attic under the middle roof gable. Carla opened the window beneath the same gable. She moved over the chair from near the bed and sat within earshot of the ceiling opening into the attic. She was at the ready to relay information between Larry and me.

She later confided how she had marveled at Larry's ability to so nimbly pass through the closet ceiling opening. The builder had placed the opening close to the front corner of the closet by the doorway, putting Larry in an awkward position as he moved his large bulk through it. He never admitted to his statistics, but Carla estimated his height at six feet seven inches and weight at over three hundred pounds.

I began the spraying operation over the gable above the bathroom window.

"Anything yet?" I shouted. "See anything, Larry?" Carla relayed. Larry shot back a bellowing "No." Before Carla had a chance to relay, I shouted to her, "I heard him." Had he been a singer, he would have challenged the tuba for low notes and sound volume.

After about twenty minutes, the bathroom gable proved sound. I moved on to the middle gable.

After only five minutes of spraying Carla shouted out to me, "He found something. Keep on spraying."

I kept up the torrent for another five minutes. Larry invited me to join him in the attic. Without anyone's guidance, I seeped over the roof edge and onto the ladder. I found it strange how secure a ladder felt in comparison to a roof. The ceiling attic access welcomed me far more easily than it had Larry. Once in the attic, he beckoned me over.

"Look, here's your problem." As he shined the flashlight over the rafters, hanging water drops glistened like little points of light. The water's pathway imitated that of the ants – in ingenuity, anyway. In fact, the trail of droplets reminded me of a trail of ants, much to my discomfort.

The water came in through a space at the back of the gable and spread out in two directions – left and right. There was a support structure shaped like an "A" around the gable. This support had two smaller triangles at the bottom for reinforcement. The water had followed these supports until hitting the roof truss's bottom chord, the horizontal member that holds the ceiling. The landing points were just above the main bathroom doorway and over the edge of the bedroom ceiling.

"See that?" Larry pointed with his pen into a soft spot at the back of the gable. "Whoever put this together didn't bring the plywood back far enough to the back of the gable here." He shined the flashlight closely and I could see his pen tip pressing out water droplets from the gap.

"All you have here is tar paper and shingle," Larry continued. "The heavy winds must've separated the shingles because there is no direct wood support here to nail the shingle to. You probably have a tear in the paper."

I now had my own war story to fire back at my self-absorbed neighbors. "Hey, pal. Do ya' have any water leaks?" "Do I," would come my retort. "*Do* I. Man, sit down while I tell you a story. No, while I unfold my saga of woe before thee." I could then wrap them with images of fire bolts crashing around me, while I fought my way to the roof. There, under the unrelenting force of nature's fury I discovered the idiot builder didn't fit the gable correctly.

Larry and I examined the other two gables and found them to be properly constructed.

He followed me back up the ladder, armed with the can of roof patch and a trowel.

He lifted back two shingles, exposing the tear in the paper. "Ah ha," he exclaimed with a grin. "Got'cha! Got some time today?" His question presumed somehow my Sunday's had been designated for more pressing matters – like, breathing, smiling.

"Yes," I whimpered. "What do you have in mind?"

"We're gonna fix this leak."

Larry went into his basement and came back up with a small sheet of plywood, a few roofing nails, a hammer, some drywall screws, a screwdriver, a caulking gun loaded with construction adhesive, a tube of silicone caulk, ruler, pencil, and a circular saw. If I had done the fetching, only the plywood would have arrived on the first trip. The second trip: screws and pencil. Third trip: ruler and saw. And so forth until nighttime fell, stopping any further progress.

But my contribution was the most important: extension cords to plug the saw into a bedroom wall socket. Larry could only carry so much and was about to make a return trip to his house to collect his extension cord.

My father's imagined words of wisdom washed over me – words passed down through thirty generations of roof repairs. "Son, whatever you do in life, make sure of three things and these three things will propel through a life of great and lasting success. Make sure you have a twenty-two foot wooden ladder, a fifty-foot and fifteen-amp capacity outdoor grade extension cord and a neighbor who can do your work for you."

"B-b-but D-d-dad … what if all I can get is an indoor extension cord, like those for lamps?"

"Don't let me down, son. Don't settle for anything but an outdoor extension cord. Heed my words: an outdoor extension cord and nothing less."

And so it came to pass. I bought an outside extension cord to meet the needs of a future neighbor like Larry.

Sorry to make so much out of an extension cord, but even small victories are significant victories, when the job before you swells beyond your best efforts.

Back in the attic, Larry cut two triangular pieces of plywood to fill the gap at the back of the gable. They nearly fit perfectly. He then cut two rectangular sections and glued them to the triangular pieces, securing them.

"I'm gonna caulk around the filler pieces with the silicone. I'll use the construction adhesive to form a water-tight seal and hold the sections up. Here, hold them in place while I fasten 'em with screws."

I was back in high school – in shop class. Mr. Tilden replaced Larry. Here was Mr. Tilden in all of his glory, schooling me on the principles of butting edges and securing sections of wood together.

Mr. Tilden knew every conceivable way to assemble two pieces of wood so they would remain locked in marriage for centuries – thousands of centuries.

"If you polished the surface. No good. The glue won't stick the right way." My classmates and I had gloried in the beauty attained by rubbing one piece of wood against another, creating a silky smooth, shiny finish. The "polished" wood felt so velvety. Mr. Tilden frowned on this practice. "So how ya' gonna get the pieces to glue proper? How ya gonna get the stain to take? You closed the pores in the wood."

Wood working shop was a mixed time for me. I enjoyed working with wood, even loving the smell of newly sawed wood. It was just that I couldn't color inside the lines with crayons when in the first grade. Sawing within the pattern lines drawn on a piece of wood proved much more difficult than coloring within the lines.

After several attempts at sawing the perimeter of my pattern, always cutting off an edge inside the pattern, Mr. Tilden showed me a trick: cut the outside larger than the pattern and use a file to bring the size into compliance.

While the other students were cutting and sanding away, making beautiful gate-leg tables, end tables, couches, ornate monuments the envy of Michelangelo, four-poster beds making King Louis the Fourteenth jealous, and full-wall entertainment centers selling for several thousand dollars at the finest furniture stores, I settled for a two-piece door stop.

Talent in woodworking proved an elusive trait for me. Larry's presence extended beyond luck; he was a vital necessity.

I rejected asking Larry if he knew Mr. Tilden. If the answer were "yes," we would have remained in the attic for days passing Tilden stories back and forth. A "no" answer would have had the same final result. Once the Tilden story barge launched, there was no stopping it. "Tell me more, more, more," Larry would have pleaded as the days passed effortlessly.

No, Larry was not Mr. Tilden. Mr. Tilden would have talked the roof to death. Larry had a wonderful ratio of words to deeds. It took him just over an hour to secure the gable from underneath. His technique and approach were amazing, making the hour pass quickly.

We made one more trip to the roof where he sealed the tar paper with roof patch. He applied the patch to the front underside of the shingles for security and nailed them fast.

"That'll do ya," Larry beamed with pride. The image of my father's free-wheeling roof jaunts had now been joined with this wonderful image of Larry, standing erect on the roof, and broadly smiling with the satisfaction of helping a neighbor.

Blessedly, Carla never queried me as to how I would have accomplished the repair without Larry.

How would I have done it? The short answer: no way! The long answer: Noooooooooo Wayyyyyyyyy. Of course, one must never discount the confluence of sheer madness and a huge supply of luck. With both of these traits I might have succeeded.

During this entire ordeal I had to resist falling between the trusses and through the bedroom ceiling, an action confirming to Carla to never allow me to rise more than one inch from a large, flat, secure surface.

Buried somewhere in the "Manual of Husbandly Required Duties" is a warning ahead of the chapter on prancing on roofs and crawling across trusses, stating, "No husband should attempt any house repair that is likely to cause thinking, physical action, and panic to occur simultaneously." Of course, this warning excluded adventurers like Larry.

Larry illustrated a true master workman's instinct and control. He measured and marked, but then creatively cut the boards while crouched in the attic space – a space barely able to accommodate his large size, let alone him with tools and plywood.

Again, I may have arrived at the solution after several tries and a great many hours, but at the expense of my sanity. Larry finished the inside repair in about an hour, while retaining his warm smile and soft demeanor.

All of this activity amazed me then and still does. Here was somebody who could measure, cut and assemble, and everything fit just right. No second attempts. Just once and done.

My mind darted back to my weeks-long effort to construct a two-piece door stop in Mr. Tilden's class. The two pieces were a marvel of construction: a horizontal wedge shape to fit under the door to secure it and a vertical member with a flower design on it to make the wedge a meaningful item to fit in a living room.

Now, the wedge had two ways to be attached: the right way and the wrong way.

The right way had the wedge flat on the floor looking like a ramp. In the wrong assembly the wedge stuck up with the ramp on the underside. Now the latter is how *I* assembled it.

"No, no, no … You place the pieces together to see how they fit and *then* you nail them," Mr. Tilden cried to me in frustration.

Pulling the pieces apart left some marks on the design allowing me to learn another lesson: applying wood fill and painting to match the background.

No, this level of talent would never allow the fitting of a connecting piece to repair a defective dormer. Maybe my son will acquire this inexplicable talent. My father had it. I don't. Maybe this talent is a genetic trait that skips a generation, like green eyes or the ability to bowl without hitting the gutter.

Carla's time proximity to the birth of Elaine prevented her witnessing Larry's expertise. The climb into the attic was now well beyond her capabilities. She relied on my glowing report, much the way husbands crowed about their feats to their families in early civilization.

"Gather around me, my family. It is time to tell you of my exploits." With eyes widened and mouths slightly agape, the warrior's children and wife and the family elders formed a circle around the fire.

"Today, your husband, father, son and nephew faced grave danger against the roof of ancient legend."

With "oooooo's" and "ahhhhhhh's," the children's eyes widened more and their jaws dropped fully open.

"Tell us more," they called in unison, visions of fanged roofs flowing through their heads. "Did it breathe fire?"

"No, my children. The gods of the North came upon us and dropped great floods of water upon it, quenching its fire."

"What happened next?" his dutiful wife called out with apprehension.

"I appealed to the gods of the saws and ladders and with mighty thrusts, putting my very essence at risk, I brought the roof mightily down. I met its every slash and gnash with all of my power."

"You touched in the head or something?" It was his great aunt's grating voice punching through his words.

"The roof is real. Real, I tell you. *Real!*"

"I still think you're touched in the head," she grunted as she turned her back on him.

"Go on. Tell us more," his wife cried out. Several members of the tribe joined the circle, chanting in unison, "Tell us more. Tell us more. Tell us more."

"With only my wits and small weapons I fought the roof. Gray fangs and black claws slashed at me. With no help and seeing the god of death rising over the hills, I fought on. The roof was vanquished."

"That's not how it happened at all." The deep, assertive voice of Larry the Craft Maker caught everyone's attention. "No, that's not how it happened at all," Larry repeated as I slid away from the circle and headed back to my cave. There I carved and painted my version of the story on the walls. My legend would live on! Archeologists of some distant time will display wonder at how a leaky roof predated written recorded history – and the development of roofs.

"Why are you staring at the wall?" Carla's question rocked me back to reality.

"Oh, nothing, Hon. I was just thinking about how great it is to have a neighbor like Larry."

Yes, how great it was.

In time Carla and I learned more about Larry's kindnesses to other neighbors. The leak stories turned from screechy complaints about the builder's incompetence to how wonderful it was to have Larry around.

He never asked for anything in return. We offered dinner – either at home or at a restaurant – but he demurred. "You don't owe me anything. I enjoy helping people."

That was it. So simple. He just enjoyed helping people, no strings attached. Any repayment insulted him.

The roof never did leak again from the gables. Larry happened by from time to time, lending knowledge and muscle to some of my more critical house problems. Having Larry around relieved some of the burden of the lost Sabbaths. Knowing him made some of those early losses tolerable.

Eight years later a job change beckoned him to a far corner of the country. We maintained contact through holiday cards for a few years more, but soon, through the mystery of human neglect, that little contact faded. Though Larry was gone, he was still never to be forgotten.

CHAPTER EIGHT

And the Earth Opened its Mouth and Swallowed Them

I do not intend to be prescient about this great moment in the Bible. Living in an area prone to sinkholes, however, may proffer Biblical meanings not intended in Sunday school. Before discussing the Earth's attempt at having me as an appetizer, let me go back to the time just prior to this momentous occasion.

Our first blessed event, Elaine, came upon us more quickly than the doctor's had predicted – nine days more quickly. Carla and I did not complain about having nine more days to enjoy our child or, as Elaine countered many years later after enduring our cooing recollection of her birth, nine more days to torture her. We just wanted more preparation. As many first-time parents may recall, the doctor's timing has a built-in inviolability, permitting last-minute preparations – buying infant clothing, crib, bottles, diapers, and rubber room for the parents. We still had nine days to perform our duties. The crib was on order – one of those nice little combination crib/youth beds with an ingenious bassinet insert – and we had told the salesman he had plenty of time, nearly three weeks.

Before continuing, let me state one of the great, unbreakable rules of life: All events requiring immediate attention occur after all businesses close on Friday, guaranteeing maximum fretting time.

Let me repeat this law: All events requiring immediate attention occur after all businesses close on Friday, guaranteeing maximum fretting time.

They never occur mid-day Thursday, for example. That would be unfair to the evil gremlins from the Land of Bother. Solving a problem during the day and having Friday evening or the entire weekend free? No, that would never do.

The gremlins from Bother had to have their way. The chaos must occur Friday night.

There must have been some contractual agreement Adam and Eve signed before being expelled from the Garden of Eden. This agreement was somehow deleted from all record.

God had called to Adam, "Oh, by the way, Adam. All of your descendants and all of their descendants into time *ad nauseam* will suffer from the Friday Night Effect."

"The Friday Night Effect, Lord? What's that?"

"That is for your descendants to discover, Adam. Now scat."

Out into the wilderness Adam and Eve wandered. The Bible recalls vividly how Cain slew his brother Abel. What is never discussed, either in print or through oral tradition, is the true reason. I know this reason and will share it with you.

As time passed Abel invented the wheel and opened a wheel sales and repair shop. His brother, Cain, bought the first model off the assembly line. Being the first descendant of Adam, Cain was the first to discover the Friday Night Effect.

One Friday Cain rolled his wheel out into the countryside to his garden patch. As dusk settled in, his vision became clouded and he rolled into a small crevice – a type of ground opening that was to garner the name "pothole" many generations later.

"Oh, no!" Cain cried out. He gathered up the broken wheel pieces into a net he constructed out of vines.

"I'm in luck. My brother's shop is barely a lizard's short gallop from here." He dragged the damaged product back to Abel's Wheel & Deal shop.

"Abel, ol' Buddy. I need a quick repair on my wheel. I kinda need it to roll flat some new seeded spots in my garden. If I don't do it tonight, the seeds will be washed away by the rain."

"Sorry, Bro', but can't you see my sign? It's after five o'clock and I'm closed. Come back Monday."

"Wha' th'? Monday? You crazy? I can't wait all weekend, fighting with my garden and worrying about my plants. I got my mouth to feed, man."

"Sorry again, Bro'. But I'm closed." Abel turned his back on Cain and walked away.

The rest is Biblical History.

What Cain could not have known was the contract his father had signed was kicking in for the first time, establishing its prominence in human existence for all eternity. Even after the final battle of Good and Evil, the residents of the Golden City of Jerusalem will have an idyllic life, except after five o'clock on Friday night.

So it was with Elaine. Carla had been experiencing small cramp eruptions for about two days now. Nothing spectacular. Nothing regular. Just an occasional wave, enough to remind us our child was getting bored and restless.

Dinner came and went uneventfully. Carla had gathered up a few dishes and was heading to the sink, when Elaine decided enough was enough. With one great convulsion, Carla's water spilled freely over the floor. She collapsed into a writhing, throbbing heap.

"Quick! Call an ambulance. Our baby is coming!"

My first call went to 911 and help was dispatched. But traffic and the gremlins from the Land of Bother surely had plans to divert the ambulance to some distant town or place endless lines of cars in the way, adding to the time.

Time was surely on the side of the gremlins. Like any nervous father-to-be I needed another plan set in motion.

My next call went to the Doctor's office. After 22,223,911 rings the answering service picked up.

"Dr. Fenton's answering service. Please hold"

Hold? That was exactly what Carla could *not* do. We were way beyond holding. Images from Hollywood movies flashed through my mind: spectacular appendectomies performed out at sea by an ensign sailor following descriptive orders barked to him by a surgeon on land, a thousand miles away.

Dr. Fenton was only five miles away, if I could reach him. Instead, his answering service was requesting I hold. Perhaps the local library had birthing books. I could rush over there, find a book, rush back and deliver our child.

The fantasy didn't matter; the time was 6:23. Events like this burn time into your brain. It was not about 6:30. It was 6:23. Libraries and doctors' offices had closed!

After a few minutes the receptionist came on and promptly disconnected me. I pounded out the numbers, forgetting to use redial. Thinking clearly was not on my agenda that night. Adam's secret agreement with God had reached overdrive along with my nerve endings.

"Dr. Fenton's answering service. Please ..."

"I cannot hold!" I shouted into the phone before she could finish.

"How can I help you?" she chirped, as though I were calling about a vacation time share offer.

"My wife is delivering our baby here on the kitchen floor. The water is everywhere. I need to reach Dr. Fenton."

"Well, I'm sorry. Dr. Fenton is gone for the weekend. Dr. Friesport is on call. I can pass your message on to him, if you like."

Pass my message on to him? What was this? One of those pass the message games kids play in elementary school?

"Billy has a crush on Suzy. Pass it on."

"Billy is crushing Suzy. Pass it on."

"Billy got crushed and it's a doozy. Pass it on."

No doubt my message would pass among the receptionists and arrive several hours later at Dr. Friesport's ears: "Carla had a baby and is cooking it in the kitchen."

"Is she fricasseeing it? I heard they go good with turnips."

My fantasy sarcasm had apparently played out audibly, inspiring the receptionist to grunt a loud, "Uhhh," and hang up on me.

Losing out on the opportunity to be served by Dr. Friesport mattered little to me. We had never met him, but the city hospital had a top-quality neonatal ward.

Declaring victory to the Friday Night Effect, I dropped to the floor and held Carla until the ambulance arrived.

The medics scooped her up onto a gurney and swooshed her into the ambulance. I jumped inside, taking up my husbandly position next to her, dutifully holding her hand. There was nothing else I could do anyway. How could someone so helpless against lawns suddenly rise to the occasion during the delivery of a baby?

At the hospital Carla remained on the gurney until orderlies located an open waiting room. The Friday Night Effect had apparently sprung onto a broad, unsuspecting populace. The city's population was going to experience a surge this night.

A nurse ambled into our room, seemingly unflustered by the scene of pandemonium raging through the ward.

"Let me get a read on your wife's dilation. Hi, Honey. I'm a Carla, too. So just relax, this'll only take a moment."

Why did she offer the information she was also a Carla? Were we now going to get preferential treatment? Would she feel a special empathy with my Carla? Silly questions like these must have special meaning during times of stress, for they seem to stick in memory.

The centimeters of dilation at this first measurement apparently had lesser meaning, for I recall nothing Carla the nurse said. My Carla was in too much pain to pay attention.

Soon Nurse Carla became a fixture. She instructed my woeful wife on breathing, on positioning for the next dilation measurement, and on positioning to best help the baby along.

"She's at eight centimeters. We're getting close," Carla the nurse bellowed.

My Carla's memories were only of the pain and the now sequential waves of convulsive spasms.

Nurse Carla summoned a Doctor Edmunds. He was to deliver our baby and never be seen again. Dr. Friesport would collect the spoils of war the next day, replacing Doctor Edmunds as our care giver.

To us, at that moment, Doctor Edmunds stood a full seven feet tall, with flowing golden hair and a giant shining sword. His actual countenance mattered little to us. Carla had undergone nearly seven hours of stubborn dilation and short-lived waves of spasms signaling only disappointment. Our baby was hanging on, seemingly refusing to leave the warm, friendly, safe womb.

Ultrasound had broken the news months earlier our first child was a girl, but at this moment, in this place, the words "our baby" held a calming resonance. "Our baby" would soon become "our little girl," but for now I clung to the soothing words: our baby.

Had a parade of parents marched through our house during the preceding months, warning us of the traumas, worries, confrontations, expenses we would face over the years, we would still not have been deflected from the wonder of this moment.

An orderly wheeled Carla into the birthing room. Dr. Edmunds told me to gown up and don gloves in order to accompany my wife.

The gown's clasps didn't line up and it took two full unsnappings and resnappings to get it assembled. I put on gloves, but had forgotten to wash my hands. Washed hands matter under gloves? Off came the gloves, on went the antiseptic soap. I rubbed my hands together, rinsed, dried and hunted up another pair of gloves.

"You had better hurry, sir. Your baby's coming," Doctor Edmunds called to me.

I frantically pulled a fresh pair of gloves over my trembling hands and rushed into the room. Elaine slid out only a few moments later.

Carla released a long moan of relief. I clasped her hands in mine and she squeezed my hands briefly and then sank deeply into the bed.

Elaine was given the obligatory slap to spur her breathing. She cried out in all of her glory, though sometimes I believe after crying, she swung her head towards me, stared into my eyes, and growled, "Just wait. You're in for it, Buster!"

Carla stayed overnight and was released the next day by the elusive Doctor Friesport. I hoped his answering service had not passed on my sarcastic message. I waited for him to say, "I've got some fresh turnips in my car."

Nothing of the sort happened, of course. Carla, Elaine and I quietly journeyed home.

Now, let me make a plug for mothers-in-law. Despite an occasional pothole in life's road, Carla's mom, Ruth, and I get along fabulously. She even likes the way I treat her daughter! Imagine that? I am a hero for a son-in-law.

Ruth's value as a relative reached mountain-top heights that Saturday. She greeted us at the door, when we arrived home.

Carla's old bassinet served as Elaine's early nesting ground and Ruth had prepared it immaculately.

"Now you rest, I have some shopping to do." She darted out to her car and whizzed out of the neighborhood.

My mom and dad were due later. Mom wanted to give us a little recovery time before descending upon us.

About three hours later Ruth and her neighbor, Mrs. Carlton, arrived with bundles of groceries and supplies, including diapers, formula, bottles, bottle sterilizer, and baby clothes. In fact, Ruth's supply list mapped the most comprehensive baby survival guide item-for-item.

Mrs. Carlton was a true dear of a lady. Having reached the tender age of sixty six, she beamed warmth and friendship and genuine caring. Widowed four years earlier, she had turned her life to helping others.

"My Gregory treated me like a queen," she cooed. "I miss him dearly, but he left me financially comfortable and I can think of nothing better to do with my time and money than helping people."

As it turned out, Mrs. Carlton selected and paid for much of the merchandise. Despite a kindly exterior, she sported a strong will and personality. Ruth took me aside and whispered, "Don't fight her. She wanted to do this. She never had any children of her own. Let her have her way."

Over the years Mrs. Carlton became an infrequent, but most welcome guest. Elaine knew her as Auntie Jean. We were grateful for the experience of knowing her.

The weekend brought both Elaine and a heavy rain storm. The storm hit before dusk on Saturday. The local newspaper reported over four inches of rain fell in just under two hours. This deluge came after two weeks of on and off rain that had already accumulated six inches.

The events of the previous two days deflected my attention from the yard. Away from my watchful eyes, the yard wreaked its havoc. A gaping hole had opened up on the front lawn about ten feet from the street.

It wasn't until late Sunday afternoon I noticed the yawn in my lawn. My dad and I took a tape measure and strolled over to see who or what was trying to escape. My first thought was Mrs. Creep and her two punk daughters had burrowed their way here from apartment A51.

"Surprise! My daughters want to play you Grizzly Remains' latest hit on their 4,000 watt boombox."

"Sorry, Momma, we're getting a signal on our body rings that we need to return to our home planet."

My dad was right: Home ownership had its appeal. At times of high stress, when fighting the latest house assault, my thoughts sometimes race back to those turbulent days of the Cough Plops and The Creeps. Those thoughts keep me stable while my next grand fixit project takes shape.

"Watch your step," my mom called after us as we crept closer to the crater, "the edge could be weak."

"Son, this thing's gaping. I think it's getting bigger as we stand here."

We worked the tape measure across the widest point.

"It's six feet wide here, Dad. Seems to be about three feet deep."

The shape was an odd crescent with one end a lot rounder than the other. I had heard of sinkholes, but this was my first direct experience with one.

Carla was still too tired and sore to care about the encroaching sinkhole. For once I could do nothing because it was Sunday. My and Carla's parents passed through our doors like shoppers in a mall. One set came with goodies, while the other set went foraging for their offerings. The loot built up through the day: baby bootees, baby food, blankets, clothes, and a car seat. Carla received cards, candy and two bouquets of flowers.

I took the Sabbath as a Sabbath for once and let the house fend for itself for a day.

On Monday, Ruth came over to care for Elaine and entertain Carla. I traveled the long route to work, winding around nearby developments in search of other sinkholes. None were to be found.

How lucky I felt. A good day to play the lottery. After all, don't good things come in three's? Elaine, the sinkhole, win the lottery – all life-changing events and coming in sequence. Unfortunately, today my sarcastic thoughts gave me no comfort. Ants, moles, roof leaks all had terminal points. But sinkholes played to a folk lore all their own. City blocks can fall prey to their avarice.

A call to my insurance company confirmed, luckily, I had taken a sinkhole rider on my home plan and any damage would be covered.

My next call was to the city engineer, Mr. Tom Orson. He sounded sympathetic to my circumstances.

"Yes, sinkholes are a real problem in some parts of this county."

"My part in particular?"

"Yes, your part in particular."

His parroting did little to raise my confidence. The earth was setting up to swallow my house and all I could get from my city's engineering official was "Awk, your area in particular. Awk, your area in particular. Awk!"

Mr. Orson drove to the sinkhole on Tuesday and was already examining the cavity, when I arrived after work.

"She sure is a big one. Was it this big on Sunday?"

We gawked at the size of the opening. The crevice now took on an oval shape with the center nearly six feet deep.

Within a short passage of time it went from a sinkhole to an awesome gape in the ground: nineteen feet long from end-to-end and six feet across the center. All of this growth happened in just two days. The heavy rain both started and deflected attention away from the hole during its formative stage.

"I'll have the police cordon this area off. A city crew will be over the day after tomorrow to get started," Tom Orson said with authority.

"What do they intend to do? Feed it a virgin? Perform an animal sacrifice?"

"You're funny, you know that? We'll have to dig into a few places to see if it breaks through anywhere else."

He angled around the perimeter for a minute and then said, "An assessment will be made how to treat this. Gotta stop it before it swallows the whole neighborhood."

Tom Orson gave a disquieting laugh, got into his car and went on his way, leaving me to contemplate how many days my mailbox had to live. At least the hole seemed to be moving *away* from the house.

Thursday, the police arrived along with a city maintenance crew. Yellow safety horses with red stripes ringed the opening. Warning flags poked their sinister heads upward, telling all who dared venture near to come no closer. Flashing yellow lights positioned on the horses declared 246 Oakridge Lane a tourist site.

Some neighbors took up a pool, making bets on how wide and how deep the hole would grow. First prize? No doubt an all-expenses paid trip to the Grand Canyon, soon to be a minor attraction when compared to my front yard.

More rain arrived for the weekend with a dense thunderstorm adding two inches of rain in only forty-five minutes. Rivulets coursed through the street.

On Sunday morning Carla and I peered out onto a strange site: an open cavern sprawled through the middle of the sinkhole. With our mouths wide open we carefully walked to the perimeter. Some of the safety horses had been swallowed along with our mailbox. The center opening bore a black, ominous appearance.

The Sabbath was now unknowingly turning into monster watching day. It seemed as soon as Elaine dozed off, I sauntered nervously to the perimeter of the Gape – a name several neighbors and I had given to the ground opening. Somehow giving a name to the enemy seemed to offer us a modicum of control over the situation.

The events near 246 Oakridge Lane had elevated our little house to a cult status in the development. The conversations no longer centered on whose basement sweated the most or whose rugs got the dampest. Nope. Having the Gape for a buddy put Carla, Elaine and me on the map. Or maybe *into* the map.

The Sabbath was no longer a day of rest; a day to honor God and family and a day to recharge the batteries in order to successfully face another week of prattling coworkers and disappearing office appliances. What the Sabbath now held in store for me were vigils over the Gape, planning escape routes, studying what to do if our water, sewer and electric services failed. And, of course, there were the endless streams of neighbors who collared me for insight into this new phenomenon as soon as I made a showing.

I could imagine the neighbors peering out of their windows or through the tiny slits allowed by doors held only slightly open.

"Denise, I think I see a door opening over there. Yup, the husband is peeking out just a little. He thinks the coast is clear. Ha ha ha ha haaaa."

"Harold, should we make a break for the Gape?"

"No, Denise. Might scare him back into the house."

"Ellen. I can see movement over at 246. The lights are out, but I see a shadow moving toward the hole."

"You sure, Joe? Last time we scared him so much he didn't come out for a week."

"Frank. Frank. Come quick. I think their door is opening."

I make my break, tossing stones and clothes in different directions to throw my neighbors off the scent. But all is in vain as people slither from doorways, windows, out of chimneys, and out from under crawlspaces.

Soon I am surrounded by thousands of people. News crews bound around me and hang from utility cranes to get a precious photo of me with the Gape that will show up on the evening news.

"Yes, listeners. Our KRUD news crew caught this image of the home owner standing guard over his sinkhole. We go live to Stan Stanson who has the home owner shackled to a pipe. Stan?"

"Thanks, Bo. I am here with what looks like 31,000 people trying to jostle and push their way for a peek at what the local neighbors have fondly named 'The Gape.'"

"No, Stan," I chime in. "It named itself. One night low guttural noises started coming from deep inside the hole and ..."

"Back to you, Bo."

Carla's not so gentle shove snapped me back to reality.

"Oh! I didn't know you were standing there. How long have you been here?"

"Long enough to make out your under-the-breath mumblings." Her mouth was straight across, matching her eyebrows – a look I have long known to say, "Okay, time to come back to reality."

"How deep do you think that is, Hon?" Carla asked in a low, worried voice.

"To China?" I responded. Carla was in no mood for humor.

"This is serious, very serious. Something has to be done and soon." Her voice, now firm, conveyed her concern.

On Monday the city crew arrived in force: three trucks, a fire truck, and eleven men. Jackhammers, fire suits, hip boots, and chain ladders complemented them.

I was warned there was now a danger for a gas line to rupture and the fire chief expressed his fear the local neighborhood might have to be evacuated. Evacuated? Evacuated? The word ricocheted around my head. The seriousness now sunk in.

A large crowd assembled forcing the lone policeman to bring in reinforcements to keep everyone back. We were all warned there was a very real possibility of the sides collapsing. Apparently the now monstrous gape beveled under the surface. Nobody knew how much larger the hole expanded underground.

Over the next several days, workmen buzzed all around the site, taking measurements, and boring test holes around the perimeter to determine soft spots. By Friday the Gape's yawn had grown to fifty five feet long, thirty one feet wide, and twenty six feet at the deepest point, closing Oakridge Lane to traffic.

Late on Friday Mr. Orson called an impromptu meeting, gathering Carla and me, the neighbors on each side of us, and the three counterpart sets of neighbors from across the street.

"I've called you folks together to tell you won't have to be evacuated. The natural gas line spur ends just beyond your houses, so we have capped the line before it gets to the hole."

Thoughts whirled through my head: was this *good* news? Was it good news for the folks east of us six and bad news for us?

"You're probably wondering the impact of all of this," Tom continued.

Aha! Now the other shoe was dropping. This was shaping up into a classic good-news-bad-news joke. I could hear Tom's voice in my head. "I've got good news and bad news for all of you. The good news is you won't have to move. The bad news is your houses will be unlivable." Then, swirling around to us and locking his eyes with mine, "And since it's late Friday, you folks in particular are in for it!"

Tom Orson's summary was not far from that of my imagination.

"Without gas, some of you won't be able to use your stoves or get hot water."

"What about the electric and water," Gladys chimed in. "My house is all electric. How'll this affect me?"

"You'll be fine," Tom answered. The gas line could blow up and we are required to shut it down. The water and electric lines are on opposite sides of the street and the feeds to this side cross the street about a block up from here. All the electric lines have been supported by cables. The city Board of Supervisors, counsel, and the Electric Company are letting us keep them supplied."

Of the six affected houses, five had all electric service and one – just one of the six, a mere 16% of the affected houses – had been outfitted for gas.

Imagine that. Just *one* household would be affected. Years later great, great grandchildren of the current residents would repeat the story.

"A hundred houses were in danger of being swallowed by the dragon sinkhole and only *one* house actually fell into a toothy demise. Imagine that! Just one in a hundred. Just 1%. And can any of you guess whose it was? Can ya'? Can ya'?"

When Mrs. Eschermann had brought us to our promised land, she and CoreyCorty read off a litany of benefits of gas over electric. The house under consideration was set up for gas, of course, so the praises of gas now seemed a natural part of the sales pitch.

On that fateful day if only a lurking dark figure had come out of the shadows as Carla and I were leaving and cautioned us. "Beware the Ides of March. Hold it. Wrong warning. Beware! Beware! Beware! Sinkholes and gas lines do not mix. Remember the Friday Night Effect, the Curse of Adam and Eve."

After the figure slipped back into the shadows, Carla and I would have returned to the office and demanded all electric service, smiling with the knowledge at least one evil prophecy had been thwarted.

Alas, our fate was sealed. We could read, watch television, wash with cold water; but we could not take warm showers or cook our food. The air conditioning still worked, of course, so Carla and I could stew in our juices in comfort.

After the crews departed for the evening, Carla and I stood with about a dozen of our neighbors staring blankly at the spectacle. Our closer approach brought us a bizarre site. The underground piping hung from a crane, exposed like a museum exhibition showing a cutaway view of a city street.

We could trace sewer lines, water pipes, electric cables and the gas lines. Cables had been tethered to all of the lines to prevent their breaking free. The cables joined to a large crane suspended over the edge of the hole.

The damage to my property consisted of a digested mailbox, a chunk of caved in lawn, and a missing front section of my driveway. The city owned an eleven foot easement onto my property, leaving me responsible for filling in a seven-foot length of lawn. A shudder suddenly rippled across my upper back. Though the insurance rider covered the damage beyond the easement, how would I coordinate repair crews – the city's and my own? And the driveway. Did the city own the front eleven feet?

The usual images flowed over my brain. Fights erupting between city crew members and my own. The inability to reach agreement leaving my yard with a three-foot wide no man's land each crew claimed was the other's responsibility. Mr. Orson ordering me to avoid driving on the front eleven feet of my driveway.

"But, Mr. Orson. How do you expect me to get to my garage?"

"Not my problem. Just stay away from the front eleven feet of your property. Any violation will force us to grab another eleven feet."

For now, any repairs waited until the main sinkhole was tamed.

With the gas shut off, Carla took Elaine and moved in temporarily with her mother and father. Elaine required diaper changes and frequent cleanups, often without advance notice. I didn't want to close the house down, anticipating a fairly short battle between city and nature, and stayed at home most nights. The neighborhood seemed safe, but my suspicious mind wouldn't let me abandon the house completely. Images of mice, spiders, and wild orgies assuming control of my clearly empty house prevented my leaving.

By the end of the following week, test holes located no more soft spots and giant steam shovels arrived to pull away and round out the edges. More rain headed toward us Friday night and continued steadily until Sunday morning, producing another one and a half inches.

During the entire next week the hole showed no further growth. Our monster had gaped too wide and now suffered from locked jaws. The sinkhole was only marginally larger and all of the underground piping had been secured with more tethers. A honeycomb of cables and chains glistened in the morning sun, creating an eerie sight.

The neighbors and I played paparazzi all that week and the next, shooting pictures of the hole from all angles and shooting candid pictures of workmen in action. At one point six of the men gathered together and mugged while we street urchins fired away, catching their muscular images and broad smiles.

At the start of the fifth week fire hoses were attached to the two closest hydrants and water began pouring into the hole. Mr. Orson supervised this operation and explained he wanted to be sure the hole had maximized its run and held no further surprises in store.

After five days of soaking, the hoses were removed. A new road crew arrived to begin the repair work. For three days, trucks hauled necessary equipment to the site – front end loaders, a backhoe, two pile drivers, and ponderous steel I-beams.

As a child I played with construction sets. Some included small plastic pipe sections that could be snapped together to form a piping network. One of my favorite sets had a crank-handled crane capable of lifting beams and pipes into place. I assembled small buildings complete with piping feeds. In my little child's wondrous imagination, the two-foot by three-foot scene transformed itself into a full sized construction site. I could imagine the sound of diesel engines, the hissing of water jets, and the raucous retorts from pile drivers and jackhammers.

Here I stood many years later and the fascination from my youth sprung from me with the same magic. I took my lunch at odd times just to be around the activity. The resolution of this sinkhole intrigued me no less than my childhood building of skyscrapers.

I am reminded of a comedian who once said a man must marry because events take place that he cannot blame on the government. Normally, government ineptitude presents easy targets for irate citizens and the citizens living along Oakridge Lane certainly presented an angry front. The city management, however, did a spectacular job in containing and repairing the sinkhole. They did not push towards a speedy fix that might not work, creating more sinkhole damage over time. No, the city fathers protected their brood on Oakridge Lane. The attending crews had their orders: win this one and win it big.

"Gentlemen, we are workmen for this fine city, but most of all we are soldiers," Mr. Orson might have declared as his charges stood at attention.

"We have met the enemy and we will prevail. Do you understand, men? We will p-r-e-v-a-i-l."

"Sir, yes sir!" the crew shouted as they cleaned and readied their formidable weapons.

Some six weeks had passed since the fateful day I had inspired Tom Orson to speak like a parrot. My mood of dismay and sarcasm had now fallen into awe and amazement at the quantity and efficiency of the work performed by his loyal crew. They worked double shifts for seven days.

First, a large pile driver slammed vertical beams deep into the sinkhole, peering out about two feet from the bottom. Next, thick concrete footings were poured into the bottom of the hole, smoothing out the base. Then, a bridgework of cross beams were dug deep into the side walls and bolted to vertical beams. Finally, cranes lowered heavy steel mesh sections over the bridgework.

By the following week the assembly was ready to receive cement layers. Cement mixer trucks paraded in and out of the neighborhood for the next few days, building up a thick foundation.

The crew allowed the cement to set for two weeks. The cement trucks then gave way to large dump trucks filled with soil.

Paparazzi neighbors stayed with the project, though crew members now ignored them. One photographer traveled daily from the next town to create an album record of the forming and demise of the Gape. I never questioned his motive, assuming his hobby was chasing and recording monsters.

Workmen interspersed loads of stone and gravel with loads of soil to allow drainage. Tethered pipes remained secured with cables until steadied by the newly laid ground.

"Quite an event, huh?" Gladys from next door stood next to me. "Caused quite a commotion. I guess this boring place needed a little excitement," she continued.

Boring place? Want to discuss ants, roof leaks, and babies? A wife and new child in retreat in a foreign land! Boring was certainly not currently on my list of words used to describe my existence.

For a few more days fire hoses again soaked the ground, settling it. When the ground dried, a large steamroller compressed the fill. More fill was added, rolled and soaked. This process continued until Mr. Orson satisfied himself the surface could now receive blacktop.

The ordeal had taken place over ten weeks, leaving us with a gleaming new road as a reward for our patience.

Through this time period Elaine started walking, learned to play the trumpet, finished reading "War and Peace" and said her first word, "Waaaaahhhhh." Of course, only the last part was true, though at times the sinkhole project seemed long enough to allow the first three to occur as well.

What caused the beast to yawn? Could it happen again? Tom Orson felt sure the current hole would not reopen in our lifetimes, but more could spring up.

He explained that geologically the area, supported by a foundation of sedimentary rock, once contained a vast network of underground streams. Glacial movement, road projects, and other factors eventually diverted these streams, leaving a honeycomb of caverns behind.

The weight of nearby houses plus the turmoil caused by truck traffic and road building may have caused one of the cavern's ceilings to weaken and drop away. The very heavy rains of the current spring could then have caused the erosion precipitating the sinkhole.

"Couldn't this have been found before the development was put in?" I asked him.

"Hard to, you know. You drill a bunch of holes to test the ground structure, but hitting one of these things is a bit like finding the proverbial needle in a haystack," Tom Orson told me with a voice reflecting the authority vested in him by his job.

"But this hole was ... was so *big*. How could it be missed?"

"Think about it. The hole was what, about fifteen hundred square feet? This whole development is over 300 acres. That's nearly a million and a half square feet. Like I said: a needle in a haystack."

Tom Orson shook my hand, bid me a good day, squeezed into his car and disappeared, removing from the scene the last vestige of a foreign presence. We had reclaimed our neighborhood and the buzz about sinkholes rapidly decayed back to complaints about the builder.

In retrospect, the Sunday whirl of activities at the Gape held my attention far more than it should have. I vowed to myself if another event forced my family out of the house – such as a massive rock slide from the mountains ninety miles away or the basement floor collapsing away giving an entrance to armies of trolls from the netherworld – I would scoop up Carla and Elaine and head to safety as a family. The spiders, mice and orgies could swarm in. The Sabbath would not be sacrificed again.

With the gas back on, Carla and Elaine returned triumphantly to our home. Carla's dad had driven them and I had prepared a feast of home-cooked pot pies to honor their return. Anything more extravagant – such as requiring the boiling of water – might have led to tragedy and our being driven from the house again.

"What!" Carla might have screamed. "*You* of all people tried to *cook?*"

"How *could* you!" Ruth might have shouted, reinforcing Carla's stance.

"Dad, do something. Hit him. Choke him!" Carla screamed to her father.

"I've a better idea. Let's tie him down and force him to eat what he just made," leading all three to shout together: "Make him eat it! Make him eat it!"

I simply loved my family too much to cook more than pot pies. I wanted to prove to myself the gas was really back on. Having confirmed that a flame indeed existed, I then wanted proof it was not a prop. So the pot pies became a ritual sacrifice to the fire.

During Carla's and Elaine's absence I often traveled to Carla's parents' house to exert my visitation rights. Had we known the ordeal would span more than two months, we might have designed a more appropriate living arrangement – perhaps a motel, or perhaps exile in Tanzania. My parents' house had the room for all of us, but my mom and dad worked during the day. Ruth, on the other hand, did not work, leaving her available to help Carla during the day as well as hiring me on as a pack animal. Carla would have been alone, otherwise, trying to handle a new baby while fighting off loneliness and bouts of post-partum depression, antagonized by the family dislocation.

When visiting, Ruth had me trundling off to one store or another to buy formula, diapers, new crib sheets, rug cleaner, or aspirin. Sometimes I barely entered the house before being ordered off on an errand.

Ruth lived about an hour away in a direction opposite my normal twenty-minute trip to the office. She also lived in the part of town plagued by rush hour traffic. Something needed adjusting. I finally hatched a plan to bring Carla and Elaine back home.

One weekend I tried to rig up a propane system to heat water. Lucky for Larry he was traveling in Europe on business, or he would have been dragged into this fiasco. My idea was simple enough: assemble a propane stove in the garage and heat pots of water, storing the water in a barrel. I was missing Carla and Elaine and anything was better than their absence. Unfortunately, in addition to my family, I was missing a serious portion of my brain – the section imparting logic, reasoning, and common sense.

The home megacenter, the wonderful playground for home owners, rose to the occasion. I purchased the necessary items on Saturday, leaving the evening and all of Sunday for assembly and operation.

"Can I help you?" The voice emanated from a short, stocky fellow with a heavy beard surrounding only his mouth and short, but wild, hair that was thinning through the middle. His demeanor and deep voice filled me with the confidence I had found someone who truly understood propane stoves and storage barrels. His name tag declared "Roy." The name was the clincher. Certainly a strong name like Roy would only be given to clerks who knew about manly things such as propane fires and hot water storage.

"I am looking for a propane stove and a water storage barrel."

"That's an interesting combination. What are you trying to accomplish?"

I should have said, "I'm trying to get my wife and kid back." Instead, the words that came out were, "I want to heat water and store it in the barrel. That's why I want a stove and a barrel."

Roy scrunched his face slightly, tossed his eyes upward for a moment, and then said, "Follow me."

He deposited me in an aisle in between Sporting Goods and Housewares.

"Do you know what you want?"

"I'll know it when I see it."

Roy scrunched his face again and said, "Here you go. Knock yourself out." He then swept around the corner and disappeared, leaving me among a variety of propane stoves and storage bins.

After about an hour of my rummaging through square and round garbage cans, Roy reappeared.

"You sure you don't need help?"

"Well, you can tell me one thing. What can I use to hold boiling water?"

"Well for one thing you don't want a garbage can. They are too flabby. You need one of these plastic tanks over here. They come with their own covers."

Ahhh, I thought: came with their own covers. This situation should save me a week of searching for a cover that would fit.

"Is there anything special I need to know before I pick one out?"

"You see this symbol on the bottom? This symbol means polypropylene. You want polypropylene. The other plastics will hold, but they'll become too soft to move. Go only with the polypro."

I gathered up two polypropylene – or in the jargon of the store professional, polypro – cans. One can fit inside the other with enough room to slip a thermal blanket between them to keep the contents of the inner can hot.

A neat two-burner propane stove and an oversized spaghetti pot rounded out my equipment needs.

Sunday was dedicated to making all of this work.

I wrapped the smaller plastic can with a thermal blanket and stuffed it into the larger can. They fit snuggly, making attaching the two cans together unnecessary.

"How do I move the filled can?" I thought out loud. "Twenty gallons is sure to be heavy."

Back at the home megacenter Roy greeted me. Most likely Sunday was his day off, but the possibility of my returning to the store overwhelmed his desire to stay home.

"I see you're back," he seemed to chide. I resisted informing him he had just passed an eye test and instead answered him in kind. "I see you recognized me."

"What do you need?"

"I need a roller dolly for a round twenty-gallon plastic can."

"Hardware."

As I began to wander off, Roy couldn't resist making a correction to my terminology. "Sir, it's a tank. A tank and not a can."

I stopped for a moment, with my back towards Roy, as the words filtered through my hair and into my brain. "A tank?" The thought brought me back to the military campaigns against moles and ants. In the military one never uses a can, when a tank is available. Besides, how could I mount a 105 millimeter gun to a can? A machine gun always makes a nice touch, but no can could ever handle one.

Roy was definitely correct in setting me straight. There was a war going on in my front yard against the Gape. A can would never do. No. Roy set me straight: "You need a *tank.*"

After finishing processing Roy's words, I ambled over to hardware and discovered four types of dollies that seem to do the same thing. Had there been only three, the choice would have been easier: "This one is too expensive. This one is too cheap. But *this* one is just right."

With four came a decision process. Luckily a dapper gentleman named Cassel came to my rescue. "Cassel" sounded a bit exotic for a home megacenter clerk. Maybe he was just working in between movies. After a few prodding questions he reached onto the shelf and plucked my ideal dolly.

Back home I mounted the mated cans, I mean tanks, onto the dolly. Next came the propane stove assembly. By the time I had the stove snapped into place, the megacenter had closed. Of course, the stove came with two valve options, with neither one supplied!

A busy week ensued between working late nights and supplying the items Ruth had me procure each time I visited.

On Saturday, Carla and I carted Elaine to two different doctors: one for a checkup and one for a follow-up. The follow-up doctor wanted to determine the progress of a treatment he had prescribed for a rash Elaine had developed. Next we foraged for clothes to keep Elaine in style for the coming season. Keep those words in mind: clothes to keep Elaine in style.

The store had just under a trillion aisles with each aisle holding a specific motif. Imagine. Infants needed to be matched to a motif. What had happened to plain cotton pajamas? Elaine, a girl, meant pink didn't it? Maybe a sewn on bunny on the front was all the motif she needed.

How would Elaine manage the deep scars imprinted on her psyche if we didn't choose the correct motif? How would Carla and I afford the endless visits to psychiatrists? The shock treatments?

"Here, you two handle this one. Anything beyond blue jeans fogs my brain." Carla showed no surprise at my admission and added, "Good thinking."

Not all men are fashion blind. Many, in fact, follow trends. Some even set them. My artistic talent ended at making smiley faces: a circle, two dots and a curved line. I was heavily schooled in knowing where to place all of the components.

Back to valves.

Ah, yes. Then came Sunday and the fulfillment of my dream for a supply of hot water. Up to now I showered and shaved at a body beautiful gym next door to my work place. Their requisite three-month trial period for new members proved sufficient to keep me off the health department's list of air pollutants.

At the megacenter I was again greeted by Roy.

"Seems you like this place," he snorted.

"If your dumb stoves came with warnings on the box that certain parts needed to be bought separately, maybe you'd see less of me."

"Now, now, we love our customers."

"Oh really? I need this valve right here in the instructions – part Z-0031. Can I have it for free?"

"We don't love you *that* much." We both laughed, indicating, in my state of frustration, I was finally losing my mind.

Unbelievably, the store had the valve. It didn't have to be special ordered. "How could this *be?*" I wondered. These types of parts usually require six to eight weeks to arrive. A moment like this called for a celebration.

"Roy, in honor of having this part in stock, let me give you this crisp, new dollar."

Roy scrunched his face and tossed his eyes upward again, but he did take the dollar.

Valve, propane tank and stove all worked together.

Now came the test: the manufacture of hot water.

The stove came to life, pouring all of its BTU's of heat onto the bottom of the spaghetti pot, which bridged across both burners.

"Let's see. The pot holds twenty quarts and the tank holds twenty gallons. That's simple. There are four quarts to a gallon so it'll take four potfuls to fill the tank. We're in business."

The water resisted heating to boiling, whether or not I watched the pot. Altogether, it took nearly six hours to fill the insulated tank. By the time the last potful joined its three brothers, it met a cool reception – the insulation seemed more intent on tossing the heat out.

In years to come the greatest living minds will revise engineering textbooks to reflect my discoveries in thermodynamics.

"Students, please turn to page 40, the Chapter on 'Thermodynamics for and by Dummies.' In this chapter we will learn though it is shown a watched pot can and does boil, the heat generated in this effort must quickly return to nature, eliminating any gain."

"Professor Gimble, what do you mean by 'eliminating any gain' and why is it important?"

"Hmmm. Perpetual motion machines are impossible. When a watched pot boils, there is a tear in the fabric of the Carnot Cycle. Were this tear to remain, heat would be gained infinitely, causing the implosion of the whole universe."

"So, Professor Gimble, in order to prevent this runaway heating, the energy added to the water by the watching of the pot must immediately return to nature to bring the whole system back into balance?"

"Yes. Something like that. I really don't know. Prior to the events that fateful Sunday at 246 Oakridge Lane – the events are well documented, you know – nobody had ever witnessed the boiling of a watched pot."

Needless to say, Carla did not buy into my hot water supply system. We decided to wait out the inconvenience.

Back to the pot pies. To me their taste was incredible because they were being enjoyed in the presence of my family, finally reunited in our home. This Sabbath was going to be savored.

On Monday, with the sinkhole vanquished, the time came for my home insurance company to come to the rescue. They sent a representative, a Mr. Gotcha, to evaluate the damage. His name was not actually Gotcha. I just don't recall his name, but Gotcha just seemed appropriate when applied to some insurance agents, such as Steve Rain's cohort, Mr. Caulder.

Mr. G was formal and succinct. He spent a total of ten minutes with us. He sized up the situation, recommended a course of action, and departed. His stance, deep voice, and abrupt action reminded me of a vampire who had the ability to appear in daylight.

"You muszt file within zixty days to gedt coverage. Call zer officze if you need me. I vill appear before you in an insztant!" Whoooosh! He was gone.

Mr. Orson's crew paved up to my driveway, noting driveway repairs were my responsibility. Printed in readable and understandable text, my insurance policy confirmed Mr. Orson's information, noting my costs were covered.

Mr. G said nothing about the details. He simply asked me for an estimate. Here was an insurance company only wanting an estimate with no strings attached for the repair of my driveway. Huh?

"But Mr. G," I could have retorted. "The city owns the first eleven feet. There must be some clause somewhere saying I must do battle with your six-headed monster troll, with my burial under the driveway should I lose!"

"Sorry, sir. Sorry to disappoint you. There will be no troll match, no arguments from us. Just simple unfettered customer service."

"B-b-b-but you can't do this to me! Hit me. Break something on your way out. Insurance companies do not act in this manner. Do you realize how much therapy is going to cost me? Will *that* be covered?"

"Yes, provided you receive all counseling within the first eleven feet of your driveway." Mr. G then swept his golden cape over his shoulders and disappeared.

So insurance wasn't a problem. I needed a service to repair lawn and driveway. I knew one source to avoid: Carla's father's boss. He probably owned a private list of Steve Rain clones, with each one designed to demonstrate gross incompetence in a specific area. No. Closing my eyes and pressing my finger on the phone book would serve me better.

I perused the phone book for ideas. Harley's Construction had a meaty, full page ad. He even had sinkhole repair prominently placed in bold. Soon, 246 Oakridge Lane was to have a mini version of Tom Orson's assault.

Harley's representative had a name that has long fled from memory. I only recall his stature: a slight, friendly man with a soft but authoritative voice.

He queried me about my insurance coverage. I suppose, with insurance the repair would be one destined to last through the ages. Had I not had insurance, no doubt he would have pumped oatmeal into the hole and topped it with black cardboard for the driveway and green paper mâché for the lawn.

Tom Orson's crews had filled my lawn hole and missing driveway end level with the rest of the repair, including smoothing of the surface. Harley's Construction just needed to dig out several inches to receive gravel.

On Saturday, two trucks arrived. One brought a backhoe. One was a dumper standing ready to receive anything removed by the backhoe.

The backhoe operator was a large, surly individual. His nose reflected the results of many fights. His deep-set eyes flashed at me from time to time, while he whirled his machine to and fro, digging out shovel gulps of soil and driveway chunks. He never said a word. His flashing glares spoke all I needed to know: stand clear and don't bother him, lest I end up as landfill. I didn't know his real name so I started calling him Mr. Surly.

The backhoe zipped around for about three hours. Occasionally, the surly man dropped the stands to place the backhoe firmly in position for more aggressive digging.

A third truck arrived mid-afternoon, delivering a cute steam roller.

My yard repair covered about a thirty-four foot long by twelve foot wide swath. The site foreman ran through a few calculations and placed the order for a dumper full of gravel to arrive.

Harley's men made sure there were no unseen cavities waiting to open when I least expected it. Also, the front of the driveway had been torn away further back to allow patching the front half, giving a greater chance of blending than trying to patch a short section.

This ripping up more driveway seemed important from another perspective: It allowed Mr. Surly to vent his frustrations in a socially acceptable way.

Mr. Surly started up the little roller and filled its wheels with water, using my garden hose. His repertoire of talents began to unfold before me. Besides the ability to stare down a charging lion, he could operate a backhoe, a steam roller, and a garden hose.

Mr. Harley arrived in the flesh as though to prove he really existed. He strolled over to Mr. Surly and the two of them spoke for a few minutes. I could not hear the conversation, but it probably went something like this.

"So, did you find anymore underground cavities?"

"Unnnnhhhh ... Grunt."

"Think we can start backfilling today?"

"Unnnnhhhh ... Grunt."

"Glad we had this conversation."

The small crew, comprised of Surly and a much smaller man who seemed to do a great amount of standing, departed around 4:30. The backhoe and roller remained onsite, awaiting further orders from Surly and his cardboard cutout assistant.

Carla filled me in on Monday's events. I had a lunchtime meeting and could not break free for the festivities. Mr. Surly probably looked around for me and, not finding me, was forced to turn down his glare to dim.

When I arrived home the lawn section sat level with the surroundings. The driveway was ready for blacktop.

Tuesday and Wednesday brought heavy rains. For once rain didn't bother me. It helped settle the new ground fill.

On Thursday Harley's sent a different crew: the lawn and driveway experts. The rain had settled the ground a little, requiring a final soil and gravel topping.

While two men raked, seeded, and placed straw over the lawn repair, a group of three men rumbled over the driveway with a small asphalt machine, laying the paving flush against the existing driveway. A much kinder and gentler man than Mr. Surly operated the steam roller. He even smiled in my direction. Any smile from Surly would have come from his envisioning the roller flattening me into the pavement.

The driveway repair was amazing. The seam between the old and new sections was nearly perfect – a seam likely to mostly disappear with an application of driveway seal.

"Let the driveway set for a day before sitting your car on it," a man identifying himself as the site foremen told Carla. "Also, be sure to let it set for ninety days before applying any sealer. Most people recommend sixty, but we're having a cooler than normal summer, so I'd like to give it more time."

All Carla needed to hear was, "Blah blah blah blah ... Don't seal for ninety days … Blugg blugg blah blah ..." This meant at least one and maybe two Sabbaths would be saved. Ninety days brought us too far into the fall to apply driveway seal.

Ah, but all was not lost: the new seeding required watering. When the seedlings grew to about two inches, the straw had to be removed. Saturday brought rain and the final growth, forcing me to remove the straw on Sunday.

CHAPTER NINE

The Plagues – Part Three

I now fast forward to Elaine at age two. This is the maturation period often known as the "terrible twos." If the twos are supposed to be terrible, what words best describe 12 to 14? "Horrifyingly-frighteningly-disastrous" middle school? "In-your-face-outta-my-way-buster" pre-high school?

Had the Ghost of Sabbaths Future come along and swept me to Elaine at age 12, upon returning I would have hugged the daylights out of her at two, cherishing the simplicity and comparative ease of the "terribles." As my mother aptly said, "When your kids are small the problems are small and when they get bigger so do the problems."

The house warranty expired without requiring much from the builder. His duties encompassed replacing a dislocated window track and supplying four screens he had neglected to install. The big roof leak occurred later.

Outside of the battles I have noted, I had ones that focused on crab grass, weeds, a second ant attack, five cracked patio blocks, lawn insects, two curtain rods that collapsed and needed replacing, and a small water leak around a back window – with most events requiring some part of or all of the Sabbath.

The lawn insect malaise brought me the awareness of a creature called a mole cricket. The moles never returned, but their surrogates gave me two pitched battles, one at the start of each of our second and third summers. Their voracious appetites more than made up for their smaller size.

In nature size matters, but the size that matters is numbers of members doing the attack. If an elephant comes after you, the number is one. For ants the number can be several thousand. Bacteria? In the millions.

Still, bumping off mole crickets proved easy: My old friend malathion worked wonders. The problem was recognizing their presence before incurring serious lawn damage.

By this point, Carla had given in to my need for the big guns when facing down a serious enemy. The failure of a couple of attempts at loving the pests to death the natural organic way pushed her over to my side. Or at least, she simply left the job to me.

Elaine was into her third summer, when we noticed her lethargy. I first took notice because she would normally run to me upon my arriving home from work. This summer she began staying on the couch, watching television or sometimes curling up on the couch with her doll.

With a house replete with plenty of closet space, playing hide and seek offered us a barrel of fun. One time I hid in the hall closet where the winter coats take up residence. Because the coats had bulk and I had more bulk than needed, I was forced to hide in plain sight.

To my surprise, I won that game because Elaine opened the sliding doors, stared into the closet, saw nothing and went on her way. We had a great laugh about it later.

Today Elaine didn't even want to play one game of hide and seek. I was sad for the loss of fun with a great kid, but now worried she had contracted something bad or, worse, she had a physical problem.

When one is not a parent, stories of childhood illnesses mean less than when one is a parent. As a parent, the seriousness of conditions a child can have can drive you crazy.

Lycanthropy? Good Lord, can our child have lycanthropy? Is it serious? Could it cause lethargy?

Of course, I am being silly here, since lycanthropy is the condition of being a werewolf. But the reader can get the point. No illness is too benign for a child to have. Parenthood instills a sense of dread only a parent can know.

Carla had taken a leave of absence from teaching to be a fulltime mom and her busy days deflected her from observing our daughter's growing lethargy.

"Is something wrong with Elaine?" I asked one day.

"Why? She seems fine."

"Well, she just seems so tired when I come home."

Carla began taking notice of our daughter's activity. Soon Elaine developed a runny nose and a cough. The persistent symptoms forced a visit to Dr. Frangianelli, a pediatrician who besides having a beautifully resonant name exhibited a wonderful manner with small children.

Dr. Frangianelli popped his head around the doorway. Elaine saw him and raced over, giggling with joy. He swooped her up, swayed her back and forth a couple of times and put her back down.

Smiling, he said, "Scoot over to your mom and dad. I'll see you in a few minutes, okay?" She darted back over to us.

In the treatment room, Dr. Frangianelli scanned her from head to toe, peered down her throat, into her eyes and up her nose.

"Tell you what. She has a slight fever and a red throat. Let's put her on an antibiotic."

After a week of treatment, Elaine showed little improvement. Carla began acquiring her own set of symptoms. A revisit to Dr. Frangianelli was in order.

"What is this? A matched set?" Dr. Frangianelli quizzed us after hearing the similarities between Carla's and Elaine's conditions.

"You both have sore throats, runny noses, reddish eyes. How are you feeling, Mr. Dad?"

"I don't know. My throat has become a bit scratchy lately."

"Let's see. Hmmm. Scratchy, all right."

Carla asked, "Why are my daughter and I so *tired?*"

"Your eyes are runny. You both have conjunctivitis. This brings on tiredness. Tell you what. I want to run a blood test on all three of you. I know I am not your family doctor. Just pretend you old timers are kids again."

A week later, the good doctor called with the information all of us were suffering from allergies. Allergies? To what? Work? That would have set me apart. Plants? All *three* of us coming down with plant allergies within a few weeks of each other?

"I am afraid you likely have something in your house," Dr. Frangianelli informed us after hearing our queries. "This makes the most sense. None of you had allergies last year or over the winter. You all have lived in this area many years. Your symptoms are similar and a classic reaction to molds."

"Molds?" Carla and I chimed in together. "You mean damp rugs?"

"I can only diagnose people. I am terrible with sick houses. Tell you what. Call Tom Everssold's Environmental Services. He understands sick buildings. He even cured City Hall, if you can call that bunch up there curable."

If Everssold could cure City Hall, 246 Oakridge Lane should prove to be no challenge.

Dr. Frangianelli prescribed a small list of medicines to bring Elaine back to her happy self. We went to our family doctor and received a slightly longer list of considerably more potent medicines: decongestants, antihistamines, eye drops, nasal sprays, coats of armor, and hermetically sealed bubbles.

On a damp Thursday evening, Tom Everssold arrived in person to size up the battle ahead.

"Who said you got molds?" Tom asked us dryly.

Carla and I answered in syncopation, with one of us filling in information left out by the other.

"Our family doctor examined us and antibiotics didn't work on my wife, so ..."

"He looked at my throat and saw pustules and redness and said it was the same with my husband and it didn't look like a bacterial or viral infection. Instead ... Uh ..."

"He told Carla and me it was some kind of life-oid or something and ..."

"The only thing he felt sure about was my husband and I were suffering from the same kind of allergy, whatever it was and ..."

Both together: "Basically, he said we had a sick house."

"Symptoms are one thing," Tom inserted, "We have to uncover the problem before we can treat it."

Without knowing the details of the problem, Tom could only give us a wild guestimate of the cost. He gave us a price quote for the initial work, leaving the final shock for when he determined the extent of the damage. This initial quote only covered the discovery phase: finding out what the problem was and how pervasive it had become.

"Seems our pests are getting smaller and smaller: moles to mole crickets to ants to molds to ... To what? Proton invasion?" I groaned. Carla didn't seem to find my comment humorous.

"It just never ends, does it?" she asked with an obvious resignation in her voice.

Tom sent a crew of two armed with air samplers and sterile filter bottles. The two placed small glass plates – Petri dishes filled with something called a type of agar, we were told – in strategic locations, then roamed around the house sucking air samples into bottles and sealing them.

"We'll come back in a few days and collect the plates," one of the men informed us. "Make sure not to move them or touch them at all. Don't blow on them either."

About a week after the plates were collected Tom returned with a small group of graphs, charts and grids filled with calculations.

"You've got molds, all right." Tom stared at me blankly and then turned his head towards Carla. After a ninety-hour silence, he continued. "I couldn't pinpoint the source, but it seems there are spores all over."

"Could these cause allergies?" Carla asked quietly.

"Oh, yes," Tom replied after a shorter seventy-hour delay. I assumed if he had charged by the hour, he was going to make sure to maximize the time regardless of how little he had to say.

When I was small, my dad needed a plumber to fix a difficult leak in the upstairs bathroom. He charged by the hour and seemed to have a way of maximizing his time spent by using time extenders.

What is a time extender? It is a side effort that can be eliminated, but is used by the contractor to add time to a project. Let me give you the plumber's example.

He left his tool and fittings box in the hall while he worked on the bathtub some fifteen feet away. Each tool he needed required his rising up off his haunches, walking into the hall, picking up the appropriate tool and returning to the bathtub.

Now a novice homeowner's plumbing effort might lead to choosing the wrong sized wrench. As I recall this plumber never got the correct wrench on the first try and had to repeat the wrench retrieval effort until seemingly by pure chance he chose the particular wrench he needed.

If he required the use of a wrench and a screwdriver, he retrieved each tool separately, failing on the first try for each item. When it came time to select a replacement fitting the effort grew worse.

My dad toiled on some problem or another outside during the plumber's stay and did not become aware of the time extenders being employed. My being a little child the plumber felt safe with his secret, assuming I couldn't know what was happening.

In our modern times jobs are bid on estimates, more or less locking in what the homeowner will have to pay for a completed job.

Tom belonged in the untroubled, uncomplicated world of the Nineteenth Century American cowboy and, like this cowboy, he told you exactly what had to be done and stood by his estimate. All estimates carry the caveat should unforeseen events occur – like a giant mold spore leaping out of the wall, wrestling him to the ground – the cost of remediation would be extra.

Tom appeared in true cowboy tradition, complete with the hat. I actually expected him to talk like the American icon.

"So, Tom, I reckon you found the source of what ails Carla and me."

"Eeyup. Reckon I did."

"So, Tom, what are you fixin' to do?"

"Somethin'," and Tom slowly turned to gaze at the sunset, dallying several minutes rolling a new cigarette. "Yep. Somethin'."

Tom's short answer was followed by a long delay, another "Oh, yes," and again a long delay.

Carla broke the silence, "So, what is the source of the molds?"

"We didn't locate it. The spores are everywhere, but no location had a particularly high count."

I climbed into the conversation, "So what do you propose to do?"

"My men will come back the day after tomorrow and drill sampling holes in some of the walls. We'll draw samples and see if we can identify a source."

Sampling holes. I imagined a line of mice waiting to move in as soon as the walls had been drilled.

Tom strolled slowly to the door, having exhausted himself with his great outpouring of prose, mounted his trusty steed that looked strangely like a Chevy and road off into the night.

His posse arrived two days later and drilled half-inch holes in about twenty locations. At a half-inch, the holes proved too small to welcome the mice, so I was spared an extra infestation.

Tom came back after the weekend with the results.

"There are no hot spots behind the living room and dining room walls, but the upstairs back bedrooms have hot spots in the outside walls," Tom stated.

I was startled. "What do you mean hot spots? Little nightclubs for the tiny critters?"

Tom replied without changing his expression, "I mean there are probably mold growths behind the walls. No doubt this resulted from the wet weather when this house was built."

"Wet weather? Aren't houses built in wet weather?" I asked.

Tom then broke into a long discourse about the builder's financial plight causing his delaying finishing several of the houses. By standing exposed to the weather without a siding skin, the plywood and wafer board remained too wet for too long.

He then finished, "Probably this humid summer was the last straw and the mold count grew enough to break into the general house environment."

Carla saw several thousand one-dollar bills flying out the window, shouting out a cacophony of hideous laughs as they flew towards the horizon.

I saw a thousand more wrecked Sabbaths. Tom's crew's presence had the weekdays to work, but the repair of his work – steam cleaning the rugs, wiping down furniture from loose dust, painting, and hitting errant mold spores with a hammer – were to be relegated to the weekends.

Tom had spewed forth more words today than the total from all of his other visits and phone calls combined. He must have taken a few swigs of his prairie juice to loosen up before trekking up our walk.

"What's next?" I fearfully inquired.

"We must start the remediation."

"Involving exactly what?" Carla took her turn in our new syncopation.

"The walls in question have to be torn open, the drywall and insulation replaced," Tom said.

The questioning swung back to me, "Will that make much of a mess?"

"We will work on one room at a time, keeping the door closed while we carefully tear out the structures and seal the scrap in plastic bags before carrying it out of the house."

Plastic bags. Sealed rooms. Handling with care. This was the stuff of science fiction: 246 Oakridge Lane had to be isolated to protect the remnants of civilization in a post-apocalyptic world.

Tom promised a quote by the next day. My job was to scour my insurance policy for any glimmers of hope.

The quote arrived on schedule – all $18,500 of it! My call to the insurance company precipitated another visit by Mr. Gotcha. Actually, Mr. Gotcha was away on vacation, no doubt examining termite and storm damage in the South Pacific. His assistant, a Miss Something-or-other, came to our rescue.

Because of the proven health risks, this type of damage was covered. But we had an out-of-pocket outlay of one thousand dollars. Carla sighed with relief. "That is certainly a lot better than $18,500."

To this day I have never understood the intrigues wrapped in insurance policies. Some things expected to be covered – like a tree falling on the house – have ninety two exceptions and thirty conditions, whereas an odd circumstance – such as a wall broken by a charging elephant – simply requires filling out one form and no visit by a claims adjuster.

I certainly am not complaining about saving over $17,000. Had the walls grown black with a seven-inch thick mold growth without affecting our health that condition did not fall under our home policy.

We were spared another day with the vampiric Mr. Gotcha.

"But look at the walls. The molds have oozed through the pores of the drywall and now cover the walls to a thickness of seven inches."

"Look, my little charges, do you feel alright?"

"Well, yes, Mr. Gotcha. We feel fine, but the mold is all mucky and smelly and makes squishy noises when touched."

"I recommend you live with my little friends, pet zem in zer morning and eefening. Zey vill luff you for it."

"But what about the smell and squishy sounds?"

"Don't vorry ... don't vorry. Zey are harmless and if you love zem you can live with zem."

No doubt Carla would have felt we could expect nothing better from a vampire.

Tom Everssold's Environmental Services initiated the rescue operation at eight o'clock Monday morning. Tom was a less repressive ogre and allowed his workers to escape by 3:30 every day. Carla and I faced five weeks of their comings and goings.

With the approval of my boss, I went to work before 6:00 AM so I could take long lunches in order to keep track of their exploits.

Elaine's bedroom was first to be attacked. Four men scurried up the stairs carrying an assortment of pry bars, hammers, buckets, spray bottles of who knows what, and lots of thick, black plastic bags.

The closed door muffled the din emanating from their toil. A series of hammer blows led into cracking sounds, succeeded by more hammer blows. Muffled blows suggested the crumbling of the drywall to fit into plastic bags.

By Wednesday the crew dragged out the first group of mold-filled bags, depositing them into a small dump truck parked on the lawn.

I wandered upstairs to observe their progress. The entire outside wall had been stripped to the external plywood.

"Watch it, Buddy," a soft voice called out. A very large man with a kind expression touched my shoulder, signaling me to move aside.

"Did you find much mold?" I asked him.

"Here, take a look," and he turned over a few pieces of drywall. The backside looked gross: grayish with some dense black sections. "The insulation was worse," he added.

On Thursday the men exposed sections of the side walls, to be sure the mold had not spread there.

The kindly giant came over to me and introduced himself. He was simply Sal, the site foreman. "We see a lot of this in some of these new developments. A soft local housing market delays finishing houses causing weather overexposure. Usually the house and occupants survive. You had a bad roll of the dice."

Roll of the dice. Somehow, to Carla and me home ownership was supposed to carry less risk than a dice roll.

"Okay, place your bet, place your bet," the stickman called to me. The stickman placed my chips on the next roll of the dice at the gambling table.

"Put all my chips on no-mold," I chimed in.

I shook the dice in a little can, the rattling inside the can calling out my fate. I released the dice and they whizzed away from me with the number dots rolling over and over, blurring my vision. The dice rolled slower, seemingly in slow motion now as my fate grew closer. Would I get no-mold or black-mold?

"Alright … It is black-mold, black-mold. Call in your chips."

"Sorry, Carla. I was never any good at gambling. We lost – or, should I say, won – the mold. But it is a soft black color and will blend with our furniture."

Tom continued, "Really, most of the problem was along the lower half of the wall where the water must have collected. I think they put the insulation in way too soon, before placing the siding. It's supposed to go in just before the drywall. Probably soaked up water, holding it against the plywood."

Roll of the dice? Sounded more like Carla and I had been rolled by the builder: soaked insulation and grimy wood covered over by siding and drywall.

By Friday the men were on to the next bedroom where they found more of the same.

Midway through the following week, a short, stocky man with damp curly black hair trotted up the stairs with a pressure tank slung over his shoulder. The word "fungicide" was scrawled in red paint on the side of the tank.

I could hear the thumps of his pumping to pressurize the tank followed by the low hiss of the discharging mist.

Sal came over to us. "Don't open the doors tonight. The windows are open to vent out the mold spray. We soaked the plywood to finish off any mold there."

Here was someone else using a flame thrower to win a battle against an enemy vermin. I charged my thrower with glorious malathion. I don't remember the mold killer they used, but hopefully it had as satisfying a name as "malathion."

The little mold spores likely scattered to safety.

"They think we can be eradicated by a ... By a tank full of something called fungicide?" the mold captain crowed to his spore army. "Look, men or spores, there is a hundred billion of us. How can Mr. Malathion hope to win against these odds?"

"I can hear you, you little twerp. It's fungicide. You all are a fungus. A fungicide is to get rid of the bunch of ya'"

Captain Spore turned paler gray. "Get rid of us? I thought fungicide meant a fun cider. Run, men. Run for your ... Oh, yeah we don't got legs. Hey, fella up there? Can you turn on a fan and blow us away?"

Sal would have none of this. The stocky man with the tank soaked the walls well beyond the observable locations of the mold to assure complete coverage.

Tank man applied two applications a day apart. The odor alone should have knocked the little buggers out. Just as any spores were reviving the second treatment would have finished them off. The smell in the room could have done me in. As a nice gesture Nature gave us a break: no rain and no fog, allowing the rooms complete venting.

After the venting, Sal and his crew buzzed around the plastic film sealed room installing all of the niceties a happy wall needed. The crew installed new insulation and Sal made sure the drywall was set in properly, even feathering the drywall compound to make nice joints and seams. Images from my youth gurgled up into my mind when feathering dry wall compound meant making it look like the texture of bird feathers.

At the start of the third week Elaine reclaimed her bedroom, returning the sole domain of the master bedroom to Carla and me.

"I miss her little gurglings," Carla said about our first night without Elaine's close presence.

Tom's crew tore out eight-inch square sections from all of the upstairs walls, searching for evidence of lurking molds. All of the damage seemed confined to the back section of the house. Sal theorized the rain had driven that way or, perhaps, only that part had the insulation installed.

How did all of this impact the Sabbath? During this episode, Sundays became the day for Carla and me to clean, mop, vacuum and paint. Tom Everssold's Environmental Services generated copious swatches of new drywall begging for two coats of paint. Tom's men could chop, rip, tear, bag, install, hammer, and seal. Painting was left to the homeowner. I explained to Carla we should consider this job like baking a cake. Tom supplied the mix and the water. We supplied the icing.

I thought my analogy made perfect sense. Carla stared at me blankly for about five seconds, wrinkled her forehead and snapped, "What *are* you babbling about?"

At the end of their five-week job, Sal and his crew collected all of the symbols of war and piled them onto waiting trucks. It took them less than twenty minutes to gather their supplies and depart. The whole scene seemed like a whirlwind with men darting up and down stairs, tossing tools into boxes, and men inside a room passing the boxes to a colleague waiting in the hallway.

Carla and I spent the entire Saturday and Sunday straightening out the furniture and cleaning up debris.

Cleaning the rugs waited until we finished all the ancillary work: wiping down the walls to remove dust, and preparing and painting the walls.

In his poetic tome, Inferno, Dante described the underworld as being divided into nine circles where people who committed the specific sins designated for a given circle became imprisoned for eternity, absorbing the endless abuse meted out for that sin. To me painting represents yet another layer in this underworld.

The nine circles are Limbo, Lust, Gluttony, Greed, Wrath, Heresy, Violence, Fraud, and Treachery. The horrors awaiting the hapless souls relegated to these circles paled in comparison to the later discovered tenth circle: House Painting.

Some people can sweep the paintbrush effortlessly along the mating line of the wall and baseboard, leaving no paint on the baseboard. Some have the innate ability to not only put unwanted paint on the baseboard, but also on the rug. Carla and I fit in the latter category. We may have been better off allowing Elaine to do the job.

There were two elements that saved us. The builder painted the walls and ceiling the same color, eliminating cutting in at the wall-ceiling border. The builder also left a five-gallon pail of the paint he used. The drywall repair did cover a lot of area requiring us to get another five-gallon pail of paint. The paint store matched the color perfectly. Being applied to a new house the paint matched the old paint nicely.

I might as well add a third element the builder provided. As with the foyer floor with its graded sections only offered in much more expensive houses, he did something builders of developments rarely do: His crew rolled on two coats of paint instead of spraying the house. This element made matching the new sections with the original much easier.

Even with the niceties supplied by the builder, the painting still took two full weekends. Keeping several rolls of paper towels and a small bucket of water at the ready helped with removing wayward drips and splatters.

My mouth did occasionally utter a semblance of the language my father used when painting the house. Carla simply wrinkled her forehead, gave me a chiding glance and went back to her painting.

Elaine was with Carla's parents during the painting effort, both to spare us her accidentally getting into the paint and to spare her from my accidently teaching her a choice word or two as my father taught me. When she was home I made absolutely sure to say nothing more strident than golly or jeepers.

Cleaning paint splotches off a rug is annoying. The first wipe just spreads them and damp paper towels can only reduce their color density in small steps. I did manage to get the stains out, but the added time and exasperation only managed to increase the value of painting as the aforementioned tenth circle of Dante's underworld.

As novice painters we couldn't avoid the nice design touch of drip lines where roller runs mated. When I could see the ridge formation I could run the roller over it and blend it in. Somehow, no matter how hard I tried, even the re-rolling often caused further drip line ridges. Dante's cackling laugh filled the room every time this defect happened.

"Ha ha haaaa ... You will paint drip line ridges for an eternity. Ha ha haaaa ..."

"What about drips on the rug?" I cried.

"Hmmm ... I never thought of that one. That's good. Yes, that's good. Ha ha haaaa ..."

Downstairs was mostly spared. Opened test sections displayed no molds prowling behind the drywall or on the insulation.

Drilling half-inch holes made the drywall repair easy and a quick touch with a four-inch roller blended the spot nicely with the wall. Apparently Dante's description of the underworld concerned only larger touch-ups.

Someday, I may meet the builder. For my gratitude for his work I will give him a miniature dollhouse with the walls in three rooms painted one-inch thick with black mold.

"Sir, glad to meet you. Well, really I'm not, but thought you might enjoy this little gift."

"What is this? A dollhouse for my kids? They are both in college and don't play with dollhouses anymore."

"Fine. No, this is for you and the Mrs. You see, first you pour two ounces of water on this part of the roof. The water will seep inside and run down the walls releasing the spring-loaded mold. The mold will then leap out of the dollhouse and cling to your face."

"Aren't you being a little extreme for having a roof leak and a mold problem?"

"Oh, you know about those then?"

"Of course. Your neighbors must have told you by now about their house leaks. I designed those in. Kinda makes you one with your house. Like when a good friend gets sick, you get a little closer. If your house gets sick, it's the same thing."

"You are comparing a friend's sickness to roof leaks? What about the mold?"

"Oh, everyone was supposed to get the mold. I'm just lousy at gardening, so it only grew out in your house."

"Anyway, enjoy the dollhouse."

"Thanks," said the builder, "I'll put it on my mantel piece to remind me of my work."

Tom Everssold came by the following Monday to see how we were doing. Carla lavished him with praise, causing him to gush "Thank ya', Ma'am" and "Right kind of ya', Ma'am," while his stalwart steed, named Chevy, waited patiently in the driveway.

I was thinking of suggesting he add painting to his mold abatement jobs. Dante's Inferno kept ringing in my head, so I didn't dare broach the subject.

Tom departed, pleased with our praise of him and his gentlemen crew.

We hired a professional steam cleaning crew to disinfect and remove any possible mold from our rugs and curtains. The noises from the nozzle's spraying and sucking out the debris completely drowned out the screams of any spore soldiers left behind.

The cleaning company operator flashed sparks of humor. "If this cleaning effort doesn't do the job, me and Jack here will come back with tiny hammers and bash the little buggers over their heads." Carla didn't have to say a word. The wrinkles in her forehead and narrowing of her eyes spoke volumes about her seeing another version of me.

Over the coming weeks, Carla, Elaine and I showed remarkable improvement in our collective health. Runny noses stopped sprinting. Our eyes stopped conjunctivitis. Our throats stopped scratching and pustulation. In general, we were feeling fine!

Dr. Frangianelli cooed with delight at being correct about the mold.

"Sometimes doctors can only give the best guess in a situation. I am just happy I steered you right in this one. Your symptoms were just too close to a bug going around at the time, but you all had a high immunoglobulin E and white cell count, tipping me off to a likely allergy. That all three of you had it at the same time convinced me I was right."

This was a salient feature of Dr. Frangianelli: explaining things to us! He wasn't afraid to give us the straight scoop. Leaving pertinent information out does not make us feel better either as parents or as patients.

In the medical profession there is the belief the patient can't handle bad news. It goes something like this.

"Mr. Timkin, you are in good health. I just want you to take platinol once a day. Just use this little needle and inject it into your arm. You won't feel a thing."

"Why, doctor, should I take this drug and what is it for?"

"Don't worry, Mr. Timkin. Just start the drug and see me in two weeks – if you are still alive."

"Wh-wh-what? Still alive?"

"No, I meant if you still drive. Platinol may make you a little dizzy. Not to worry, though. That side effect will go away."

"How long do I have to wait for the side effect to go away?"

"About a year."

"A year?"

"No. I didn't say that. I said, it depends, dear."

"You now call me 'dear'?"

In short, Carla and I would much rather have the news laid out in black and white and the doctor answering all of our questions. To us the proper approach is a truthful and knowledgeable doctor.

"Doctor, why did my right arm fall off?"

"Sorry, Mr. Timkin, but you have Jumping Palegra and over time all of your arms and legs will fall off and then your head will fall off."

"H-h-how l-l-long will it t-t-take?"

"At the most, you have only three months if the disease is left untreated."

"How do I treat it?"

"Well, Mr. Timkin, the treatment is having one part vinegar and one part chocolate ice cream five times a day. You need to take a quarter cup at a time. Continue this for two months."

"That's ghastly, but will I die if I don't do that?"

"Yes you will. So it is either puking over ice cream with vinegar or dying. And you also have to take 150 milligrams of splotzoglotzamide twelve times a day for one month. This drug will make all of your hair fall out and your eyeballs tingle. Your hair will grow back in about a year, but the eyeball tingle is permanent."

"But will I be cured?"

"Yes, definitely."

Now *that's* a good doctor.

We also gave high kudos to Dr. Frangianelli for his suggestion of Tom Everssold.

Years from now, late into the evening, new owners of this house will hear the lowly cries from the ghosts of billions of mold spores. The rattling of their tiny chains will echo through the walls. But try as they might, they will fail to chase a single nose, junk up a single eye or scratch up a single throat.

CHAPTER TEN

The Handwriting on the Wall

Beyond the drywall work done by Tom Everssold's Environmental Services, the house grew its own drywall defects: drywall tape separations, nail pops, and even screw pops.

The drywall was advertised as screwed and glued and not nailed. But there were numerous nails used and they brought forth their share of the pops. Why the screws popped out came as a mystery. The screws have to twist out or, under great duress, be squeezed out. As I said, a mystery, but there were a few dozen of these.

My father gave me some nice tips on resetting the nails and screws and re-taping the separated tape. Basically, he said, "Son, let me come over and help you." The "help you" part involved his taking charge of resetting the screws and nails and the re-taping.

"Well, Son, looks like your builder had a love for wet wood. It is wet wood that shrinks with age and allows nails to pop and screws to twist out as well."

Ah, yes. Wet wood causing nail pops, screw pops, and mold!

The screws were easy: just re-screw them using a screwdriver until they went even deeper than their original placement.

The nails proved more resistant to treatment. The trick was to nail another one next to the popped nail, making sure the second nail fitted tightly against the first. With my frustration showing – hammering without bending the nail proved to be another talent I lacked – I found it easier to use pliers to yank out the nail and then screw a drywall screw into the hole the nail had occupied.

All of these efforts ended up requiring drywall repair and touch-up painting. When my dad could not be present, Carla and I tackled feathering drywall joint compound, just the way Dad taught us, to blend the many patches into their surroundings. We then armed ourselves with sand paper labeled "for drywall."

Someday I will use the drywall sand paper on wood, probably causing a chemical reaction creating a puff of dense smoke, opening a portal for armies of trolls to finally make it through. For now, Dad and I performed ritual sandings. Why "ritual sandings"?

"Son, when you sand joint compound, you have to do the same strokes the same way on every patch. It's like performing a ritual."

I thought it was different strokes for different folks. My dad demanded we different folks stick to the same strokes. After an hour of failing, I finally grasped the concept. Dad and I sanded away for an entire weekend, while Carla scurried around us using a vacuum cleaner, grappling with every grain of dust.

It took many weeks before Carla, my father, and I restored the walls and ceilings of our house to their original form – or at least a reasonable facsimile of their former selves.

The replacement can of the house paint the builder left was nearly used up and I brought it to the local hardware store, returning with four one-gallon cans of perfectly matched paint.

With careful roller technique, the patched areas could be coerced into matching the rest of the wall or ceiling. My dad galloped to the rescue again, waving a golden roller in the air as fire roared out of his steed's nostrils.

"Here is the mighty Excalibur! The magic roller that painted Camelot: two coats, one weekend." His great white steed whinnied in agreement.

Carla, my dad, and I gowned up in old clothes. Dad and I spread the drop clothes, while Carla mixed the first can of paint.

Armed with paint pans, rollers, corner tools and sheer guts, we attacked the walls with a bravado not seen, since a John Wayne World War II movie.

One weekend sufficed for conquering the downstairs. The following two weekends were dedicated to the upstairs and stairwell. Why two weekends? For one thing working in the stairwell required setting up a horizontal scaffolding across the steps to a step ladder and setting up a taller ladder on the scaffolding.

If climbing an outdoor ladder to the roof confirmed my fear of ladders, scaling a ladder set up on a rickety scaffolding proved an insurmountable obstacle. This job – nails, screws, drywall, and painting – was left to my father. His mountain goat skills on roofs were an invaluable asset.

Strangely, the entire painting experience transpired without any catastrophes or war stories. No open paint cans flipped over. No rollers jettisoned out of anyone's hands and careened across exposed furniture or rugs. None of us had people-to-people collisions while armed and dangerous. Nobody fell off of or tripped over a ladder.

Finally, the walls gleamed back at us, no longer displaying the blemishes from Tom Everssold's triumph over the mold or the defects spawned from nail and screw pops and drywall tape releases.

Too bad the tale of this glorious experience couldn't be showcased on national television news channels, in home repair magazines, over internet chat rooms across the world. So much pride and accomplishment bottled up among so few.

I had just Carla and my dad for sharing. At least Carla could share her experience beyond just the family unit. She had a delightful friend named Janet.

Carla and Janet were close friends in middle and high school. After graduation, Janet married, moved, divorced, moved back, remarried, and re-stoked the flames of the friendship previously shared with Carla. The re-ignition was extraordinarily successful and when together, the two became morphed into one.

Her friend's name exuded simplicity, normalcy: Janet. Living with moles, molds, wall and ceiling pops and sinkholes placed a special premium on normalcy, though Janet's came with some disclaimers.

Janet sported a lithe body fashioned from endless hours at the local gym and a diet bordering on starvation. Her pretty face always beamed a friendly smile. She was a very nice, kind person, but harbored a quirky personality that complemented Carla's sense of order and propriety.

For example, one day Janet conned Carla into buying an oval throw rug for the living room. The rug blended Early American with Manic Depressive: a brown, cross-woven fabric cluttered with stars of varying sizes and colors. Small splashes of pastels took on the shape of small cottages – the type that might appear on a Monopoly board. In size the rug only occupied a six-foot-by-four-foot area, but the design. Oh, the *design*. Let's just leave it that neighbors inside their houses, facing away and with their eyes tightly closed couldn't miss it!

"A rug on a rug?" I asked with surprise. "Is this a new trend?"

Janet giggled, "Doesn't it look great? This room has nothing but white walls and plain furniture. It needs a little spiffing up."

Spiffing up? Can one spiffy down? Or straight ahead? Does spiffing imply insanity?

"It only cost $20.00," Carla beamed.

"$20.00? How much would the garbage collector charge to retrieve it?"

"Oh, come on! Since when did *you* start becoming a fuddy duddy?"

Fuddy duddy? Carla never used that term. My grandma used to call my grandpa an old fuddy duddy. Carla took me by surprise. A few months with Janet and a woman never before known to me emerged. Invasion of the Body Snatchers! Of course. It was not just a movie. Here was Janet: so kind, generous, and friendly. Clearly an alien.

The rug remained in the living room until Elaine spilled hot chocolate on it. Carla cleaned it and it faded. She relegated the monstrosity to the attic along with the spiders, mummified insects, and household relics we hadn't used for 3,900 years – and likely will never use.

At that moment I loved Elaine more than ever! How could she have done something so *wonderful?*

But not all of Elaine's exploits filled me with wonder. Sometimes she filled me with anger, sometimes rage. On a rare occasion she filled me with dread settling into hopelessness.

About a month after charming me with her resourcefulness with hot chocolate, my little wonder found the grease crayons I used at work to draw flipcharts.

Why were the crayons at home? Why is the sky blue? Why do wolves howl at the moon? Why do whales beach themselves?

The crayons came in five colors: red, blue, orange, green, and black. And, of course, all of these colors were represented in my desk drawer.

Remember those beautifully patched and painted walls? Remember the welling of pride within Carla, my dad, and me as we stood admiring our success? Remember the three rooms needing a complete makeover?

Elaine's room, the spare bedroom and the main bathroom walls displayed magnificent scrawls. Had we left them, thousands of years from now archeologists would regard them as a system of recording history.

"See the scrawl there? Clearly it represents a condition endemic to the human species at that time."

"Ah, yes, Cogsworth. It postures a dilemma needing further elaboration. Shillingsly, what can you make of it?"

"Ahem, harrumph. Ahem. I discern a brutal society wherein a smallish race of, say, no more than three feet in stature clashed culturally with a larger race, somehow completely controlling it."

"And this larger race? What do you make of *it*?"

"They are clearly representative of the Pre-Clandestine period, just before their civilization disappeared from this planet."

"What, again, caused this demise, Shillingsly?"

"What again, indeed, Cogsworth. The larger race succumbed to feelings of dread settling into hopelessness. It was this hopelessness that caused the larger race to fail. With their societal extinction, for whatever reason, the smaller race could not forage properly and its social structure, too, perished."

Yes. Elaine's scrawlings were sowing the seeds for the total collapse of human civilization, possibly even the extinction of us all.

I stood silently as Elaine, face glowing with pride, ran over to me screaming, "Daaadeeee! Look what I drew!"

Carla's comfortable position on the couch in the living room placed her within earshot. "What did Elaine draw, Hon?"

"Do you really want to know? I mean truly really want to know?" Carla sprung off the couch and raced upstairs, gulping two steps at a time with her gait.

"What .. *happened* .. here?"

I find no need to explain her mood, when she resorted to her staccato delivery. She and I stood in total silence, our jaws dropped open sufficiently to receive a football. We passed rapidly through dread into hopelessness.

We were not spanking parents; nor did we spare the rod. Carla and I believed only lessons concerning extreme danger required reinforcement with a whap on the fanny. Besides, this event definitely was not Elaine's fault. She had only turned three and I supplied the temptation.

The first step, remove the weapons. "Come here, Sweetie. Give Daddy the crayons."

Elaine winced with confusion. "Why, Daddy?"

"You are not supposed to draw on the walls. It makes a big mess and Mommy and Daddy have to spend lots and lots of time cleaning it up." And boy-o-boy did she make a mess. The scribblings formed wave patterns reaching about as high as her little arms could extend – 930 feet!

Elaine stood her ground, clutching three of the crayons. Dread began returning as images of the fate of those missing crayons flowed through my stunned brain.

"Come on, Sweetie. Daddy isn't angry. I need those crayons for work, so let me have them."

Elaine and I could have played out a scene from a 1930's gangster movie.

"Okay, Scarface. Put down your weapons and come out with your hands up. Nobody out here wants to hurt you."

"Take this, Copper!" Blam! Blam! Blam!

"Scarface, we are going to count to ten and then we are coming in after you."

"Stay back Coppers. I mean it. I'll write all over the living room and dining room walls. I'm warnin' ya'!"

"Oh, come on," Carla grumbled. She walked over to Elaine and took away the crayons. The little tyke began crying. I thought, "Crying? Now *there's* an idea. Maybe if I sob uncontrollably for the rest of the day I'll feel better."

Carla wrapped her arms around Elaine, comforting our daughter. When Elaine regained her composure I asked her for the other two crayons.

"I trew dem away. They didn't work anymore."

By the progression of the pattern, the red and blue crayons failed first.

Carla and I tried alcohol, water, soap, alcohol with water and soap, plastic scrub pads, paint thinner, nail polish remover. The stains penetrated deeply into the paint and only smeared.

Being Sunday – wasn't it obvious? – there was nobody to call for advice.

"Oh, no," cried Carla. "Janet is coming over for dinner tonight! I completely forgot. We had shot the whole day."

She scampered around the kitchen tossing pots, pans, canned purees, and boxes of powders. Soon the delicious aroma of her cooking began pervading through the house.

At 6:30 the doorbell rang. "I'll get it," Carla shouted, rushing to the door. There Janet stood, beaming her usual friendly smile, unaware of the chaos preceding her visit.

"Uh, come in. Yes, come in," Carla blurted nervously.

"You all right? You seem *tense*."

"Tense? Maybe strung out? Or perhaps totally over the edge?" Carla retorted.

I interceded and took Janet on the grand tour of Elaine's museum of contemporary art.

"Oh, my. Ohhhhhh, my. And you two are trying to have another kid?"

"Well, I think we have this burned into our brains when the next one begins toddling around."

"I hate to tell you, but some of this is pretty clever. I mean some of it is kinda smeared all over, but ..."

"The smearing was our futile attempt to get our walls back."

"But look. This is kinda like a surreal ocean liner over the waves. And here are, I don't know, maybe sheets blowing in the wind."

Janet was right. Carla and I were far too distraught to make out any logical shapes and patterns. After all, Elaine was only three, but her art reflected a sense of proportion and design. This was not the scribblings of a three-year old. No. These drawings did not come from malice. Elaine had made a serious attempt at art. I vowed to bring home a large drawing pad and a set of regular crayons on Monday, affording Elaine a proper venue for her creativity.

I could see an amazing future for our budding artist. After all, didn't Michelangelo paint a ceiling and become one of history's most revered artists? Perhaps Elaine could toddle into homes across America and discharge great swaths of wall art, transfixing homeowners with the wonder of her creations.

"Look, Carla," I'd exclaim seeing Elaine on TV surrounded by reporters and starry eyed neighbors desiring her artwork in their homes. "Look ... It's our daughter on national television capturing the imagination of an entire nation."

Back to reality, Carla exclaimed, "Oh, she has certainly captured our imagination. I'm trying to imagine how we will ever clean up her work."

"No, Carla ... no. The idea is to allow her to cover our entire wall and ceiling areas in order to present our house as a showroom to her talent. You say you want a living room design? Here is what I suggest. The kitchen is too boring? Try these designs." Carla just stood motionless.

Some parents look for angles to live off their children. If only their little tyke could play basketball in the NBA, his parents would live on easy street. Why can't their child play pro football? After all he was twenty six pounds and thirty inches long at birth. If they can parlay his tremendous size into a tremendous NFL contract, they can live on easy street.

Carla and I are like most parents. Whatever our children choose to do, it will be fine with us. We just want them to live their dreams and be happy. We want our children to grow up to be independent and secure in their lives.

Carla, Janet, Elaine, and I proceeded to the kitchen and sat down to Carla's sumptuous dinner offering.

"You know, Carla, Elaine has the makings of a real artist." Janet's words did not elevate Carla's spirits.

"How would you like my little darling to do a mural at your house?"

The two bantered for a few minutes until the conversation settled on the issue of how to fix the mess.

"Well, you can't really paint it again. That crayon stuff will only bleed through," Janet advised. "Paneling will do the trick."

Ugh! Paneling. Both of us grew up in paneled houses and we really enjoyed the light, airy appearance paint provided.

Paneling fits the true love-it-or-hate-it syndrome. Nobody is neutral about it. Some homes, especially older homes, can look elegant with paneling. Somehow, to Carla and me, if the living room is huge, paneling makes it look like an office. If the room is small the paneling exudes a feeling of claustrophobia. A paneled kitchen projects a feeling of living in a dormitory or a motel. Now, a finished basement makes a good candidate for a paneled wall display.

I am not against paneling in general, just for Carla and me.

"I have it," Janet exclaimed. The look on her face started my dread cycle again. "Wallpaper."

My sense of dread was justified. I remember my Aunt and Uncle on my mom's side testing the very fiber of their thirty-five year marriage by wallpapering their house. They stayed married – barely. Some days no conversation passed their lips. They exchanged only grunts and growls.

"I think paneling makes a much better choice than despair." My words drew frowns from both Janet and Carla. I couldn't fathom why Carla was even considering wallpaper. Maybe she has a divorce lawyer uncle who can come to her aid in a pinch.

"That's a very good idea," Carla replied excitedly, turning her gaze from me back to Janet.

"Good idea? Hon? You going batty on me? Janet, you've dragged my wife into some pretty nutty things. But, wallpaper?"

"Hey, watch the nutty thing stuff. Besides, wallpapering is not nutty. Lots of people do it just fine. Today's materials and patterns make it so easy."

"Honey? Let's try it. It will be fun. We'll work together." Carla's expression was unsettlingly like Elaine's during her elation at showing me her wall work. Somehow, I felt the end result of our effort would make Elaine's a masterpiece by comparison.

"Ohhh Kayyy," I whimpered, bearing the facial expression normally reserved for people who have just lost a million dollars.

On Tuesday Carla convinced Ruth to baby-sit, allowing us time to romp through stores selling wall furnishings. When Ruth saw Elaine's display, her reaction was surprisingly muted.

"Oh. That's *it?* I thought the wall had been sledge hammered or something. Wallpaper will take care of that."

Now my mother-in-law began testing the strength and depth of our great relationship.

Ignoring Ruth's comment allowed me to keep peace with my wife as we embarked on the greatest adventure of our young lives: agreeing on colors and patterns.

We arrived at Our House Wall Furnishings, chosen as our first stop based on the power of the name, combined with a half-page ad in the phone book's business listings.

A Mr. Gadfly greeted us. Of course, Gadfly was not his name, but the way he pranced around the store, accepting then rejecting catalogs and brochures from his shelves, reminded me of a gadfly.

"Ahhhh, here we are." His eyes sparkled as he spread an ideas book before us. "Just browse through these pages. You've got plenty of time. We don't close for another three hours."

His sing-song speaking style charmed us. Carla smiled every time he passed by. "He's just so great," she purred. "He's just so perfect for this store."

Interestingly, Mr. Gadfly was not an owner or even a manager. The Mr. Perfect who owned this store also owned two dance clubs outside of town. I tried to imagine the wallpaper and blinds he had chosen for the dance clubs.

Husband and wife bonded for more than two hours. Our selections dwindled to seven choices. With three rooms to do, clearly four more had to go.

The selection of textures, color schemes and materials boggled my mind. There was vinyl coated wallpaper, fabric backed vinyl, paper backed vinyl, foil wallpaper, flocked wallpaper, and fiberglass weaves. Add in the endless patterns and assortment of colors and three hours did not offer nearly enough time.

The key with any overwhelming design project is to swallow hard and go with basic colors and patterns. Stripes? Too much like an institution. Weave? Too much like a preschool. Flowers? Okay. Everyone likes flowers – even my great-grandmother. But some flower patterns flow nicely and airily and some look like a mangled field scape.

As for basic colors, as with paint, just getting red, brown, green is impossible. Cherry loft signature springtime for red. Meadow summer flow teal for green. Soft chocolate love embrace for brown. Of course, I'm making those colors up, but the real names were no better.

We actually chose Tuscan sand for brown.

"Oh, Mr. Gadfly!" Carla exclaimed, eyes sparkling. He trotted over, clasped his hands together and prepared to mediate.

"We really can't decide among these seven choices. Can we take samples home so we can compare them in the proper surroundings?" Her face took on a cute pleading demeanor: lips lightly pursed, forehead wrinkled, eyes wide.

"Tell you what," he began, clearly beguiled by Carla's face, "I can let you have the book if you promise to have it back to me no later than tomorrow by 6:00 PM."

Sacrifices like this occur once in a lifetime. These are great moments in history: the soldier who gives his life to save his buddies, the mother who starves in order to feed her children, the entrepreneur who gives up his fortune in order to clothe the poor, and Mr. Gadfly's giving up his book until six o'clock the next evening.

What was the significance of six o'clock? The store opened at ten o'clock in the morning and closed at 9:00 PM. To keep the order of the universe intact, I decided not to find out.

We agreed, scooped up the precious book and took it home, realizing this tome possessed the power to transform our house, our sanity, and our marriage.

Back at the homestead, Ruth, having demonstrated her child management skills with Elaine, now turned to her home design skills.

"Oooo, nice. You have an ideas book. I love those. That's how Jack and I chose our kitchen and bathroom designs." No doubt, Jack, Carla's dad, offered little more than "Yes, Dear" and "Yes, Dear," with an occasional "Yes, Dear." I was soon to discover the value in this approach.

Within fifteen minutes, Carla's and my seven choices had swelled to fourteen, including only three of the originals.

"Look, Hon. Aren't these designs so quaint?" Carla's use of quaint somehow meant the design was compatible with Janet's latest throw rug.

About three hundred excellent responses sizzled within my brain, but all the filtering process would allow through was, "Yes, Dear."

"And look at *this* one. Stars over light pastel waves."

"Yes, Dear." Carla probably chose stars to memorialize the rug and waves to honor Elaine, assuring her a scarless memory of her deed.

"See? Janet will simply fall in love with these stars. They'll so remind her of her rug." Carla stopped short of saluting the waves, but her echoing my thoughts only unsettled me more.

"Yes, Dear," I gulped.

"Come on, Hon. You had an opinion in the store. Help us out here."

An opinion is the store? Indeed, I had many. Husband and wife stood on equal footing, thrashing through the pages of designs. Here, mother and daughter assembled a monumental unity no husband could overcome. Ruth's daughter's happiness came far ahead of anything else. Compromise was not an option. Stars and waves took first place for Elaine's room. Hopefully, all of her teenage friends would come equipped with extremely short attention spans and color blindness.

Carla and Ruth now turned their consideration to the spare bedroom and main bathroom. By now none of the original choices survived.

"Hon? What do you think about this one for the spare bedroom?"

Carla's phrasing prevented my answering, "Yes, Dear." Now I had to actually cast an opinion!

"Oh, I don't know, Dear. It seems so bleak. You know, kinda stark."

"Bleak? Stark? What are you, color blind? This is such a nice pattern, I think Carla and I will go with it." Ruth asserted her authority.

Ruth and I did have such a nice bonding, such a nice connection with each other. For some reason the "Carla and I will go with it" part didn't fit within the definition of bonding. Most in-law interactions have points of disjuncture – irritations. Ruth and I rarely disagreed and when relating to Carla's needs, I always demurred to Ruth's position. Now a stance seemed in order.

"Hold it. Carla and I live here and she and I have to both live with the choice. And I don't like it."

Ruth shot a look that could have halted a charging rhino. "I don't think you understand your wife's happiness. She has her heart set on this pattern."

"Do you, Hon?"

Carla, ever the diplomat, simply replied, "I really think the two of you need to come to an understanding."

"An understanding of what? We are going to challenge the basis of our marriage by wallpapering. I would at least like to have a say in what we are going to finally divorce over." My reply drew a rare set of sparks from Ruth's eyes.

"Well, I never!" Ruth drew her wagons in a circle and glared with a look that could have dropped a B-52 out of the sky from 30,000 feet. "I think it is time for me to go home." She departed, leaving a jagged ice trail in her wake.

Carla was surprisingly submissive. "Don't worry. She'll come around. My mom had run my life for so long she can't seem to stop."

Her face even appeared placid, projecting relief somebody had finally stood up to Ruth. I loved Ruth and certainly did not want animosity wedged into our relationship. The next morning I telephoned her with an apology and an offer to buy her dinner. She accepted both proposals – even insisting on paying for dinner.

Carla maintained her diplomatic air. "Let's keep the design she chose for Elaine's room. It'll keep peace in the family."

I added, "We'll just have to convince Elaine to always keep her door closed."

My lovely wife tossed back a look of resignation, "Let's get on with it. Okay?"

We quickly returned to three of the designs from the previous day and just as quickly reduced them to two. One pattern had soft pastel flowers and delicate leaves cast onto a light green background.

"This one has bathroom written all over it," we exclaimed in unison. Our eyes met and we laughed. By default, the other pattern whispered spare bedroom. The hour was late; we retired for the night with visions of wallpaper patterns dancing in our heads.

The following day, my workload prevented my normal departure and I arrived with barely a moment to spare to meet Mr. Gadfly's time demand. Carla swept Elaine into her arms; I grabbed the ideas book. We dashed into the car and headed to Our House Wall Furnishings. The witching hour was near: six o'clock and the space-time continuum faced total annihilation!

Mr. Gadfly pranced over to the door to greet us. "Have we chosen our patterns?" *Our* patterns? In Ruth's absence, had he assumed her ownership share of our choices?

Showing true discretion, Mr. Gadfly purred approval of all of our selections, including the stars and waves. At least he had sense enough to not break into hoots and hollers at this selection for Elaine's room.

"We are out of this pattern," he said, pressing his right hand index finger onto our bathroom choice. "It will be in Saturday afternoon, but I suggest you call before coming to make sure."

Good. It will arrive just in time to interfere with the Sabbath.

Gadfly led us through the travails awaiting us. He also laid out the weapons we would need to conquer our walls. He helped us load our booty into the car: brushes to tamp the paper against the wall, cutters, metal rulers and cutting edges, levels, rolls of wallpaper, ninety fifty-pound bags of powdered paste, paste applicator brushes, 3,000 bottles of antacids, and the name of a top divorce lawyer.

We stored the loot in the spare bedroom, locking the door to prevent Elaine's preempting us with her own ideas for the paste and paper.

Saturday arrived and so did my panic attack. "We are actually going to wallpaper!" My voice reached to the outer fringes of Heaven and the angels trembled in fear.

"Stop being so melodramatic," Carla chided me. "Let's set up the two card tables your dad loaned us."

We clamped the two tables together and spread heavy gage plastic sheeting over the top, fastening it underneath the table with duct tape. We strategically placed an old bed sheet under the table, to catch any paste droppings.

"Let's start in the bathroom," I offered, my voice trembling in anticipation of the horrors ahead. "It's the smallest room and the plastic-coated wallpaper is the most forgiving."

"Forgiving what?" Carla snickered, "You haven't done anything yet."

Remembering what Gadfly and the Encyclopedia of Wallpapering Nightmares had informed us, we cut the paper about an inch too long to allow trimming at the top and bottom for proper fitting. A professional probably measures to the closest 1/100,000th of an inch. I needed to overestimate by one full inch.

Removing moldings was not an option. When this job ended, I did not want to re-set moldings. These moldings had a fancy curled-over edge, just inviting destruction through errant hammer blows.

With the first sheet of wallpaper lying in state on the plastic sheeting, Carla mixed up a batch of paste. In my foggy recollection, the formulation included two parts powder, three parts water, four parts cognac, and fifty parts luck.

"Does this look like the recommended consistency?" she asked.

In the Old West cowboys prepared coffee out in the desert. The sign the coffee was done was when a horseshoe could stand up straight in the middle of the pot. This folk lore may have been only legend, but somehow it seemed pertinent to wallpaper paste preparation.

The applicator brush stood straight up, when jabbed into the mix. "I think it needs a bit more luck," I said, "but let's try it."

Carla swept the bristles along the back surface of the sheet. The brush seemed to readily move the sheet with this action, scattering small paste balls across the surface. We lifted the sheet into place and I stood on a ladder, holding the sheet by the top, while Carla pushed a large brush over it, trying to fix it in place.

Even against the wall, the wallpaper moved with the brush strokes. Great wrinkles attested to the battle.

"This isn't going right," I complained. "The paste must be way too thick."

After about two hours, the ringside referees had the wallpaper ahead on points, with a knockout by the paper not out of the question.

"It seems the tag team of husband and wife is so far no match for the hand speed and unbalanced style of the wallpaper," the booth announcer called into the microphone. "Let's go to Chris over at ringside for a corner update. Chris?"

"Yes, Harry. The couple is dazed, but certainly not out. The wallpaper jabbed and stepped in for some nice overhand blows, but no blood was drawn. Back to you, Harry."

"Thanks, Chris. Now we are ready for Round Two."

Another sheet of wallpaper took its position on the table. This time Carla had added more water and mixing time. She slopped the paste on and I lifted the sheet into place. Her brush strokes pushed the sheet around again, leaving wrinkles and a small puddle of loose paste on the floor.

"Ohhh kayyy. I think we have it way too thin now."

"Then *you* mix it," Carla demanded.

We tried the first batch and it was too thick. We tried the second batch and it was too thin. But the third batch was just right and Carlalocks brushed over the surface placing the paper where it belonged.

Standing back to admire our work, Carla noticed the wallpaper hung at an angle. "Quick, let's straighten it out!" She grabbed the paper and pulled it, precipitating several nice wrinkles and stretch marks. We had waited too long.

"Chris, give us an update from ringside."

"Right, Harry. The couple was really taken by surprise. I thought they had the wallpaper against the wall there, but it wiggled out and landed a staggering blow to the hubby's chin. Dazed he tagged Carla and she threw a volley of her own, but most of them missed and the ones that landed had no ginger behind them."

"Thanks, Chris. With three rounds packed away, the wallpaper shows no signs of fatigue. We can't say as much for the tag team. How do you have it scored up to now, George?"

"Well, Harry, with two against one I thought this wouldn't go the distance. But it seems to be a no-show for the tag team! I have it scored all three rounds for the wallpaper – 30 to 27. This team is gonna need a knockout to pull this one out."

"Thanks, George. All right, ready for Round Four."

Carla and I suffered a combination of fatigue and self-doubt. Going to bed made the most sense. The fight met a delay because of darkness. We put away our toys, tightly covered the paste bucket and withdrew for the evening, wounded but not defeated.

"We'll get it, Hon. Don't worry." Carla's words carried more truth than she knew: we were definitely going to get it.

The next morning in church, my eyes darted over the walls, looking for signs of angels with wallpaper brushes. None appeared. We were on our own and the wallpaper led on points. The outcome seemed grim.

Gratefully, Ruth and Jack took Elaine for the day, leaving us alone with the wallpaper.

"This one *has* to work," I cried and cried and cried.

Carla mustered a wince, paused for a moment to burn it into my brain, then said, "Hon, let's just relax. Elaine inherited her artistic talent from one of us. Let's just find out which one."

If Elaine had inherited any art talent from my side it had to have skipped at least two generations. Nobody in my family could even draw a straight line without the comforting guidance from a team of art therapists.

No doubt one of my long lost ancestors meddled in the design of the Leaning Tower of Pisa.

"No, no, no, no, no," he would have screamed. "That line is way too straight. The image for Pisa will be nobody has any imagination. Put the tower line a little more to the right. That's it."

"Giovanni, we can't tip the tower this much. She'll fall over."

"Nonsense. Notice how the tower gets smaller towards the top? That's intentional. My family has been designing buildings for centuries and nobody has ever drawn anything close to a straight let alone vertical line."

And on to today, nobody in my family has ever drawn an unaided straight line and there is no reason to believe I was to be the first. If Elaine had major art talent it would have to come from Carla's side.

Round 4 started.

The paste from the previous evening had thickened a little, so I applied a splash of water. What is a splash of water? It is the wallpaper counterpart of a pinch of salt.

However much water the splash comprised, it did the trick.

"Before we move on, why don't we draw vertical lines with a pen so we have something to guide against?" My idea contained the same level of brilliance and insight as Einstein's Theory of Relativity. I doubted the master of scientists could have properly laid wallpaper.

Memories of my dad fitting straight vertical moldings and straight vertical runs of pipes seeped into my mind. He had used a plumb bob!

Yes! Let gravity find the true verticals. I hopped into my car, zipped over to Dad's house and absconded with my treasure: his splendid plumb bob.

"Okay, George. How do you see it as Round 4 shapes up?"

"Well, Harry, the husband is beginning to fight smart. When you have an opponent as tough as wallpaper, a little street smarts couldn't hurt."

"Thanks, George. Chris?"

"Thanks, Harry. The corner team likes this new tactic. They don't know where the idea came from, but down three rounds to zip the tag team has nothing to lose."

I took up my position near the ceiling, pinching the top of the bob tightly between my thumb and index finger. Carla marked off dots along the string length. Using a metal straight edge, we drew a vertical straight line. A vertical straight line! I was witnessing something two generations of my family had never seen – a straight line.

My dad used the plumb bob to locate tops and bottoms and had never connected the dots. Elaine's children and her children's children will fashion sweeping bard songs, praising this wondrous feat. Legends about me will grow to mythological proportion.

"Are you still awake up there?" Carla's sharp rebuke snapped me back to the present.

This time, we muscled the paper into place. Carla swept the brush over the surface until the sheet lay there helplessly, submitting to our will. An edge tool flattened the paper into the seam between the ceiling and wall, allowing easy trimming.

We stood back, admiring our conquering one sheet of wallpaper. It lay perfectly along the vertical line. Maybe we will still be talking to each other at the end of this odyssey.

Amazingly, the second sheet willingly submitted to our dominion. The third sheet, witnessing the defeat of its brothers, also obeyed our will.

"Back to you, Chris. How does the team's corner feel about this turnaround?"

"They're delighted, Harry. But, you know, this isn't over until it's over and there are still a lot of rounds left. The wallpaper's seconds won't let us in, so we don't know what they're planning."

"Thanks, Chris. George? How do you have it after five?"

"I have it 48-47 with the wallpaper still on top, Harry. This turnaround is nothin' but the old rope-a-dope. You know, the type of stuff Muhammad Ali pulled. He'd sucker his opponent into punching himself out, then come out swinging. I think this tag team is showin' too much confidence."

"We'll see. Thanks, George and Chris. Let's get back to Round 6 action."

We stared at the towel rod and heat vent. The next sheet had to incorporate the entire rod and half of the vent. I trotted into the basement and returned with a small hammer and a set of straight-edged screwdrivers.

The vent yielded fairly easily, though some wall paint tore along the edge. Towel racks have a special assembly: a decorative cover concealing an ugly rusting screw and mounting plate. Removing one of the covers exposed a sleeping spider that sprung to life sending me quickly backwards, kicking over the paste bucket.

I returned to the basement in search of a trowel to scoop up the gooey paste.

Carla said nothing throughout this diversion. She simply took in the conflict as a bystander.

Some of the paste had run under a molding. I retrieved a blank sheet of paper from Elaine's drawing pad and tore it into strips, sliding them under the molding to draw out the paste. The edge of the bed sheet had become soaked and required a replacement. This stream of excitement kept us away from any danger of overconfidence spawned from setting three wallpaper sheets in a row.

"Let's break for dinner," I said, my voice laden with resignation. It was only three o'clock in the afternoon, but dinner seemed like just the right thing to do.

After dinner and a short walk, we returned to the bathroom and discovered white, dried paste streaks over the spill area. After another series of wet and then dry wipes, the floor gave up its hoard of paste.

After placing the fourth sheet of wallpaper, I grabbed a utility knife and quickly swiped away around the metal support brackets for the towel rod, attempting to expose them to receive the towel rod again. My swordsmanship had been too aggressive, removing wallpaper too far beyond the mounting brackets. Replacing the bracket cover left the wall surrounding it exposed.

By now, the paste was setting up, allowing the wallpaper to resist removal. Luckily the plastic coating afforded enough material strength to permit removing the sheet in one piece.

We swabbed down the paste remaining on the wall with wet cloths.

Our second attempt proved more successful. First I cut an "X" across the wallpaper surface covering the brackets. This cut allowed me to force the paper around the bracket, exposing a seam for trimming. The bracket cover offered generous coverage, hiding any extended knife cuts. No doubt this cover was designed by an engineer who had wallpapered his bathroom!

With the paper firmly in place, trimming the vent opening posed no problem. Imagine reading that statement from a novice wallpaperer: "Posed no problem"? Carla and I could even flash an occasional smile.

Could victory be ours?

The corner loomed ahead of us.

"So, George, how did the tag team fare in Round 6?"

"Harry, they did real well. They seem to be catching onto their opponent's style. Wallpaper jabbed nicely with that bracket cover. I thought it scored points. But the "X" cut came straight outta nowhere. I gave the round to the team and now have it even at 57-57."

"You, Chris?"

"Thanks, Harry. The team's corner is real pleased with that round. They think their guys can pull this one out. By the looks in the opposing corner, wallpaper seems to have lost some confidence."

"Thanks, George. Thanks, Chris. Now to Round 7 action."

The room corner didn't cooperate. On our first attempt, I tried pressing the paper into the corner. This tactic pulled the edge of the sheet away from the mating sheet already installed.

A second attempt had the same result.

"We have to cut this to fit." My voice reflected trepidation. Making a full length cut did not please me. Trying to also match the corner flustered me more.

"Hon," Carla pleaded, "can't we try once more? I have an idea."

We muscled another sheet into place, aligning the edges. Carla brushed the surface flat and placed several pieces of two-inch wide masking tape along the mated edges. She then pushed the brush up and down, slowly working it towards the corner. Soon only about an inch of width needed pressing into the corner angle.

I took a straight edge and worked the sheet into a crease that would have evoked resounding cheers from the most critical tailors.

"That *crease*," they would shout in astonishment, "if only pants would cooperate so!"

Carla finished laying the sheet with the brush.

"We *did* it," Carla and I shouted together, exchanging a series of high five hand slaps.

The bathroom came equipped with a double basin sink. A complex of mirrors and cabinets filled the wall space above the sink, leaving only a one-foot high section requiring papering. A full-height shower stall filled the opposite corner with a two-foot high exposed wall strip.

The strips proved to be no contest. Our exalted spirits thrust us ever forward, reducing the most daunting challenge to a simple series of measurements, knife cuts, paste swaths, brush strokes, and creases. We were invincible!

"George, how do you have it after eight?"

"Harry, that vertical crease was a work of art. It was a bold take-two, give-one Marciano tactic and it worked. With two knockdowns I have the team up 77-73. With two rounds to go and wallpaper hanging on the ropes, I think the team has this one."

"Chris?"

"Thanks, Harry. You know, there's a lot of controversy over allowing women in this sport. Frankly, Harry, I don't see how this team could be where it is without Carla. She doesn't pack KO power, but she can keep you up against the wall with her persistence."

Rounds 9 and 10 went for Carla and me. Wallpaper had no chance. Above the doorway another narrow strip awaited our muscling. The wall opposite the shower stall presented only one of the problems already encountered: a towel rod. With its extra length, the rod sprawled across two sheets, forcing only one "X" cut per sheet.

I floated like a butterfly and stung like a cobra. The bathroom, consuming two full days of our young lives, finally succumbed to Carla's relentless jabs and my overhand lefts and right crosses.

Ruth and Jack returned about 8:30 at night with our little Elaine.

"Absolutely marvelous," Ruth cooed. "Didn't I tell you it was easy?"

I formed a weak smile and pretended to agree by squeezing a small nod out of my exhausted neck muscles. Carla squinted her eyes slightly and looked at me for signs of antagonism. None were to be found; I was simply too tired to argue.

Wallpapering the two bedrooms swept up four more Sabbaths.

For the first of these lost weekends, we toiled helplessly with the uncoated paper. Its flimsiness in comparison with the bathroom stock caused us many handling problems. At least, the dimensions of the bathroom allowed us to use entire sheets; we didn't incur pattern mismatching. Well, on the main walls we didn't incur pattern mismatching. Two of the above the doorway strips did meet a little strangely. For instance, one half of a flower had a leaf for its mating half.

In our favor, the bathroom light switches were in the hall – some electrical code requirement – with electric outlets mounted within the cabinet-mirror complex. Not acceding to the whims of electric outlets and light switches lulled us into a false sense of security. I was soon to learn with any false sense comes a true blunder.

The bedroom patterns displayed a series of lines, stars, waves and stripes, demanding proper matching. Elaine's room included wall switches, wall sockets, heat vents, air returns, closet door frames, two windows, an alcove, and two built-in bookcases with scrolled tops. In short: Nightmare on Oakridge Lane!

Carla removed switch and socket covers. I removed the two heat vent and the air return grids.

"Hon," Carla whimpered, "maybe we should tackle the back wall first."

"Why? It took us all last weekend to complete a straight run along the side wall."

"Well, I was thinking if we do the hardest task it'll encourage us."

My lovely wife began displaying signs of frayed nerves. Her hair frizzed a bit and circles appeared below her eyes. Saying "I told you so" would only unhinge her more.

For whatever reason I was now the rock of the team.

We stared at the back wall – the wall with the everything topping: vents, wall switch, wall socket, built-in bookcases, and the alcove.

By employing the techniques learned from wallpapering the bathroom, we completed the alcove, including the bend onto the main wall.

The big problem in the bedroom was the same with painting: the rugs. Luckily, wallpaper paste doesn't grip rug material the way paint does. Paint spreads and the more it spreads the quicker it dries, making it very difficult to yank off a rug.

Wallpaper paste presents less resistance. The thinner it is spread, the easier it is to wipe up. Even if it dries, a little water – a wet sponge or paper towel – forces it to yield its hold on the rug.

Paste drips came in small waves. Once we let a paste-coated sheet of paper fall paste-side down onto the rug. The paper folded on itself, minimizing the paste contact surface, but the clean-up still took almost an hour.

With painting, Carla saw a less tolerant side of me. "That dratted paint …" "Frazzle dazzle paint …"

The wallpaper paste allowed me a more relaxed tirade. "Gee whiskers that paste …" "Rooty kazooty paste …"

Confidence had started to well up inside me, starting with my toes and reaching to the top of my little brain. The lesson of what spawns from false security was now ready to be instilled.

The next sheet coverage included our first outlets: a switch and a socket.

"We are going to handle these the way we did the towel rod brackets," I said with the authority reserved for experts. Yes, compared to the common ground slug I was an expert on the fine art of wall coverings.

The sheet was measured, cut and slopped with paste. Carla and I hauled it into position and she brushed it flat against the wall. I poked the switch through the paper and trimmed around the electric box. So far so good.

My surgeon's hands wielded the utility knife skillfully around the electric box holding the sockets. Suddenly a crackling sound snapped out of the box; a surge of electricity knocked my hand back, temporarily numbing my arm. The ceiling light and the lights in the hall went dark.

"You dummy!" Carla scolded me. "You didn't turn off the breakers for this room?"

"Duhhh," I replied, demonstrating my clearly superior intelligence. "You saw the lights on. Obviously the breakers were on. Why didn't *you* remind me?"

"Duhhh," Carla shot back, matching me IQ points for IQ points. "The overhead light was on. I assumed you had enough sense to not cover an open live socket with a wet coating of wallpaper paste. It's lucky we didn't have a fire!"

She was right, of course. Remember some chapters back when I said I once heard that a man gets married because now and then he'll be confronted by an event he can't blame on the Government? Whoever thought that one up did not know a wife like my Carla. She was not put on earth to be a foil for an insolent husband.

After my meek apology, she sent me on a trip to the circuit box. Upon arriving at my subterranean destination, I discovered breaker number three guarded the back bedroom switches, front porch light and upstairs bathroom lights. Breaker number four protected the back bedroom wall sockets and overhead light, the garage lights and the upstairs hall lights. Number four prevented the fire. The current knocked me back and the paste pushed in by the knife threw the breaker.

I recognize electricians do not load all circuits in a room onto one breaker. Why? Because ... Well, because ... Anyway they don't. Somehow collecting circuits from distant sites makes even less sense. Why should the garage lights be included with an upstairs bedroom and hall? Do electricians decide a circuit layout in some manner similar to the way Bingo is played?

"Front Hall on six."

"Garbage Disposal on three."

"Next call, Basement Front Light on six."

"Living Room Front Socket on six."

"Garage Door Openers on four."

"Neighbor's Light Over Their Kitchen Sink on six."

"Bingo! I got Bingo! Now I can finish my site wiring job!"

Carla collected two standing lamps and scrounged up extension cords. Let there be light! Or the job wasn't going to be completed!

The built-in bookcases with the fancy scroll headers loomed before us. To me these cases thrust upwards thousands of feet. I needed mountain climbing gear. The wooden sides taunted me, daring me to launch my assault.

We threw three sheets of wallpaper against the face. The edges matched. I even managed to trim flush against the bookcase's leading edge.

It was the scrolls that knocked me back to earth each time. No matter how many thrusts and slashes arrived from my little sword, the scrollwork fought back with the finesse of the Count of Monte Cristo. The cutting job always appeared as though a team of mice did the final trimming.

Carla cleaned up the room, while I used a toothbrush and tissues to remove wallpaper paste from the intricacies of the scrollwork.

In the end, we had lost three good sheets of wallpaper and six hours of the Sabbath waging war against the bookcases. They had arisen splattered with paste, but victorious.

Somehow, I felt if I told my neighbors about this struggle they would have found a way to place the blame on the builder.

"Oh, come on. He knew somebody was going to try wallpapering and he knew those built-in shelves would make them cry."

"Now, now. I know we have had problems with his construction, but the built-ins are unique in normal developments and they are quite pretty."

"Oh, stop apologizing for him. Pretty nothing. He just made them look good to give you a false sense of security and then, blam! He hit you with an object impossible to wallpaper around."

"That makes no sense."

"Oh, yeah? If he's so nice how come he planted mold in your walls? Huh?"

I perused the bookshelves each day and could find no way to work around the scroll design. It was complex and it would take an artist's talent with an Exacto knife to trim the wallpaper properly.

Midweek Larry joined us for a walk through the neighborhood. Carla and I told him about the running saga in Elaine's room.

"Oh, you have the built-ins? So do I," Larry informed us. "I think you are making way too much out of this."

We are making way too much out of this? How about the wallpaper? And the bookcases? Didn't they play a part? If only they would cooperate, the papering would be finished by now.

Larry paused long enough to mount his shining armor and grab his gleaming sword. Living so close to us he left his glorious white steed home and walked to our house. Imagine a knight in shining armor walking to work?

Larry spent only about thirty seconds examining the foe before he retorted, "Here is your solution. See these four wooden plugs? They cover mounting screws. Just pop out these plugs and unscrew the headers and you'll have a square section to paper. Easy."

Now Larry became a promulgator of the "It's Easy" school of wallpapering. Having witnessed his magnificent repair of my roof leak, I could not imagine wallpapering posed any challenge to him at all.

"Could you remove those plugs?" I pleaded, knowing my attempts would result in large missing sections of the header and tourniquets to stanch my bleeding.

With one hand he held a thick piece of cardboard next to a plug. With his other hand he placed the tip of a straight-edged screwdriver flush against the plug and pushed forward and upward with a wrist movement perfected from his years gutting fish during his many camping outings.

One by one, the plugs willingly yielded to Larry's wrist action, exposing four gleaming screws requiring a Philips head screwdriver. Of course! I stood two floors away from my Philips head set, while looking at a scattering of straight-edged screwdrivers.

Why didn't I bring the Philips head set with me as well? Why didn't I turn off the circuit breakers?

Why is the sky blue? Why do wolves howl at the moon? Why do whales beach themselves?

With Larry's guidance, the scrollwork fell from its roost, exposing a nice square edge. We repeated the process for the second header.

"Just push these plugs back in place when you are done. Luckily, the guys who installed this didn't use glue," Larry told us.

I couldn't imagine the omission of the glue spawned from some foresight, some realization that perhaps it would be nice to leave the headers easily removable in case some idiot tried to paper around them. More likely, the workers simply didn't want to take the time. A simple push was orders of magnitude faster than the drudgery of reaching for a glue bottle, removing the cover, squeezing glue around the plug stem, pushing the plug into place, replacing the cover on the glue bottle, and, ugh, putting the bottle back down.

No, foresight did not have a part in this. Sloth? Yes. Foresight? Hah!

Larry stayed to help us finish the back wall. This time we knocked him out, tied him to a kitchen chair and forced him to share dinner with us. Carla went to his house, kidnapped his wife and tied her to the chair next to her husband.

These were truly wonderful people who had brightened our lives in many ways. This time we gave something in return: Carla's fabulous roast chicken with turnips and garlic mashed potatoes. Turnips rarely elicit praise, but Carla's seasoning and preparation propelled them to the status of great side dishes of the universe.

That weekend we finished Elaine's room. Our daughter actually beamed at the pattern. I still refused to show it to guests with weak stomachs, but at least Elaine was happy.

With only the spare room ahead of us, Carla and I began to relax. The Wootsie-the-cat's frozen look of fear started fading from her face.

For the final weekend of wallpapering, Carla invited Janet's participation. We wanted to show her how easy this job *really* was. After all, Carla and I embarked on this odyssey at her instigation.

Interestingly, Janet immediately responded to the calling. Within three hours, one complete wall had been finished, including sockets, switches, doorway, and the two bends onto the adjoining walls.

Janet's finesse at wallpapering should not have been a surprise. She harbored many strange talents, showing proficiency with all of them. Why wouldn't wallpapering – that most bizarre of human endeavors – fit neatly into her treasure trove of abilities.

My imagination flowed over with images of her failures. I saw her knocking over buckets of paste. I heard Carla's cries for help after being trapped under a sheet of wallpaper. I envisioned cross patterns of misaligned edges.

None of these tragedies emerged. Janet had the task under her full control. My unsaid howls of "I told you so" receded back into my head.

Carla simply cooed, "Thanks, Jan. You are such a good friend."

Let's see. Perhaps once Janet had assured us about the joy and ease of wallpapering, we should have conned her into giving us a demonstration.

"Uhhh ... Janet?" I would start. "Could you please give us a little guidance on how exactly to wallpaper?"

"Sure. I'd be glad to give you a few pointers."

"Uhhh ... Could you show us by setting in one sheet of wallpaper?"

"One sheet? Sure, why not? Be done in a jiffy."

"Uhhh ... Could you now show us the secret to matching two pieces of wallpaper together?"

"Okay."

The test of wits would come from just how much she could be convinced to do before catching on to my act.

"I get it. You two really aren't up to this, are you?" she finally would have said. The next step had two possible directions.

She might have offered to just do the job, saving Carla and me 500 hours of frustration and mental dystrophy. Then again she might have simply slopped me with a pail of paste and wrapped me several times in wallpaper.

Maybe the original progression was the best approach after all.

In any event, with Janet finally at the helm, we quickly wallpapered the spare bedroom, finishing the room early in the afternoon on Sunday.

This time all of us were going to rescue part of the Sabbath.

CHAPTER ELEVEN

Solomon also Made all the Furnishings that were in the Lord's Temple

Scaling the ramparts and proclaiming glorious victories over moles, ants, mold, wallpaper, and paint leave only a fleeting sense of accomplishment. Owning a home opens a great vista of satisfying opportunities for wasting money and time – and the Sabbath.

One of those moments arose the day Ruth suggested we needed a new living room set.

"Elaine and Eric are now at the age where you can own a nice set of furniture," she proclaimed.

Elaine had reached the tender age of seven and Eric, four. Ruth meant leaking diapers, food spills and crayon attacks had passed into folklore and we could now confidently replace our stained, worn living room furniture.

Eric didn't display Elaine's rambunctiousness and seemed to listen when told not to bring the fifty-gallon glass of punch into the living room. At least, his hearing acuity improved enormously after my ranting and raving following an epic spill.

He was two then and now at four showed glimpses into the man-of-the-world he will someday become. He was quickly learning the position of the oppressed under the rule of the oppressor.

For now, the oppressors were his parents, a roll parents seem to inherit against all their better wishes. The ready-for-the-world demeanor – hunched shoulders, forward bent head with eyes glued to the ground just in front of his feet – will form in due time. This posture of submission will do him well as he slouches under the weight of tax forms, credit card bills, and ogre bosses.

He will wander the world with this universally accepted working male posture until he rescues an errant stapler or catches some overlord in a compromising position. He will then learn a second great lesson: a bird in hand is worth two in the bush.

Elaine, on the other hand, travels a totally opposite path. She is more athletic than Eric and definitely less oriented toward education. She also challenges every rule, demonstrating a remarkable acuity for horse-trading to get her way.

"Young lady, your curfew is eight o'clock on school nights. Period." Carla's adamance came with the stern expression of a parent in charge: a firm gaze, head tipped forward but with the chin jutting out.

"But Mom, I'll vacuum the house on Saturday if you let me go to the party tonight." Carla faced one of the great dilemmas of parenthood versus homemaker: how to weigh compromising on a rule against a day without vacuuming. Also, how can a parent retain the stern look of authority while facing the misty-eyed, longing expression of a child?

Usually the first child obediently moves in tandem with the household, while the second child rebels, seeing such obedience as a challenge to independence. We developed a reverse pecking order.

Eric started reading simple books at three and asked endless questions about how things worked, but didn't walk until over one year of age. Elaine, on the other hand, didn't begin reading until nearly five, asked endlessly for a horse and walked on her own at eight months.

Elaine's shoulders will never bend under any weight. Woe be unto the ogre who tries to suppress her or, worse, makes any untoward advances. Someday in the future far distant to this book, Elaine will run the corporation that hires Eric.

Redecorating the living room sparked an adventurous thought: why not build in a built-in bookshelf and cabinet combination? After all, the living room contained all the necessities for entertainment: TV, DVR, stereo, reclining chairs, bookstands, and end tables. A built-in shelf system would untangle the clutter of CD's, DVD's, magazines, and books, organizing them into neat compartments.

"Are you nuts?" Carla shouted. "After the wallpaper experience you want to take on a project like *that?*"

Her words did not dissuade me. Wallpapering was a group effort. The responsibility for the built-in shelf fell completely to me. I intended to address all complaints to the man in the mirror. He undoubtedly would respond most obediently.

Carla and Ruth combined their individual senses of order and design and shopped for the living room set without me. After voicing my opinion on the wallpaper choices, I thought better than to repeat the same mistake with the furniture.

I gave Carla and Ruth thirty "Yes, Dears" in advance and went to work on my bookshelf project.

The home megacenter stocked a small treasure trove of books about building just about anything: enclosed porches, fireplaces, patios, sunrooms, decks, inside hidden sliding doors, and built-in bookcases and cabinets.

I bought four books containing various approaches. The one constant throughout was the dire warning to plan ahead. Planning ahead. To me that was definitely a novel thought.

First, I took an accounting of all of the requirements. Carla had her novels and magazines. Elaine had her books, CD's, and movies. Eric owned books, movies, and toys. I hoarded my own supply of books, movies, and magazines.

"Don't forget my knitting," Carla cautioned. Ah, yes, her knitting. Not only did knitting provide her with comfort, it also supplied sweaters, hats, mittens, and outfits for our children when they were toddlers. Sweaters, hats, and scarves comprised her current output.

Okay. So, the shelving must be deep enough to accommodate the widest magazines, it must also have a caddy portion for the knitting needles, tape measures, and balls of yarn. There must be a section to hold Eric's toys. The books and CD's posed no problem, since the house already contained many examples of the proper shelving dimensions for these items.

"Don't forget the knick-knacks. We have some nice knick-knacks that I want to put out." Carla didn't overwhelm the house with nonsense items; she made her choices prudently and she did have some very nice articles packed away.

"Let's look them over to see how best to position them," I said. She furrowed her brow, looked at me intensely and then retorted, "This isn't really all that big a deal. Just dedicate the top shelf for my knick-knacks."

Carla turned and started walking away. I called after her, "Should I place sconce lighting at the top to highlight them?"

"It's your project. Do what you want. Just leave room for my knick-knacks."

The four books displayed a variety of projects, allowing me to mix and match to tailor one to fit the household's needs. I tore out a couple of sheets from Elaine's sketch pad and began scribbling out ideas.

"Hon, how does this one look?"

"How can I tell from some pencil scrawls on paper?"

"Can't you use some imagination?" Carla was too practical to project concepts into reality. Somehow my brain allowed me to process images this way. I could visualize how the final product would look and Carla could not. She and Ruth continued their onslaught on the local furniture outlets, testing every available variety of fixed position and reclining chair and sofa. They intended the outcome as their surprise for me. It now seemed fair my wall work project should be my surprise for them.

They were seeking furniture with dark oak trim; therefore, my creation had to be stained dark oak. At least, we had agreement on the color.

"We want dark oak," Ruth bellowed, her eyes flashing fire, her dragon talons piercing my chest. "Yes, Dear," I whimpered, beads of sweat across my forehead pulsing into torrents. "Yes, yes, yesss." I collapsed into a throbbing heap of sobs. "Carla? Let's leave this heaving wimp excuse of a man and scour this town for *my* living room furniture."

The reality, of course, played out far milder. I simply inquired about the color schemes under consideration. They replied with some prattling about fabric types, patterns, and color schemes, but the key words penetrating my conscience were “dark oak.” I understood dark oak. I didn’t understand salmon, mauve, earth tones, chenille, and brushed twill.

For people like me who find contemporary color naming bizarre, wood color naming seemed natural. After all oak, dark oak, natural pine, cherry, mahogany, and a host of other designations really are wood tones found in a forest. Early spring mauve bisque is not.

That weekend I immersed my attention into the four books, sketching several schemes.

On Monday, I purchased a seventeen inch by fourteen inch pad of gridded paper in order to accurately lay out my schematic. Lined paper presented a marked advantage to my line drawing: it already had vertical and horizontal lines I could lay a ruler against. Moreover, I could assign values to the squares. In this case each square equaled four inches vertically and four inches horizontally. Ah, something even my feeble mind could grasp.

With the help of gridded paper, I was well on the way to becoming my family’s first ever member to draw truly straight vertical and horizontal lines. This time my endeavor placed me into family history books, wherein historians might look back to determine this break with my family lineage.

My masterpiece started taking form – at least as coherent pencil lines. It would span a width of six feet and a height of six feet eight inches. Somehow feet and inches seemed such inadequate terms; cubits produced a much higher impact. I doubted the home megacenter carried wood lengths based on cubits.

“Do you need help, sir?”

“Uh, yes. I want four one-fifth cubit pieces of pine, five and one-half cubits long.”

“Ummm, do you need help, sir?”

“I told you. I want four one-fifth cubit pieces of pine, five and one-half cubits long.”

“Manager to aisle seven, we have an unruly customer.”

“Okay. Forget the wood. Do you have any burning bushes in the garden section?”

I scouted the living room for the most practical location, taking under consideration any supporting walls. That novel concept – planning ahead – may actually prevent a partial collapse of my house. Note the qualifier: *may*.

After huddling with Carla, we concluded the common wall with the garage had the most promise. The side mudroom entrance offered sufficient support to allow me to interrupt the stud structure; all of the key family activity occurred parallel to it.

I spent two more weekends completing my plans, though nervous anticipation encouraged part of my delay. The wall breaking commenced the following Saturday.

Learning from the wallpapering episode, I decided to draw the case outline on the living room wall. Elaine found my wall writing comical, the recollection of her artwork still impressed on her mind.

"Are we going to end up wallpapering *this* room, Daddy?"

My stiff smile countered her giggling. My mind flashed images of covering my eventual fiasco with several layers of heavy weight wallpaper.

"Noooo, don't lean on that wall! Noooooo!" Scccchhhhlunk! The wallpaper gave way, sucking the unwitting victim through the wall into the garage.

Would my fiasco require a wall covering made from stainless steel with a cast iron backing to hide the damage done?

Those imaginings of failure did little to support my already shaky spirit. If I suffered such self-doubt, why did I insist on taking on building projects like this?

Why is the sky blue? Why do wolves howl at the moon? Why do whales ...

Anyway, my male pride – that overwhelming force stopping any man from asking directions while driving, no matter how obviously lost – prevented my backing out.

No. Turning back could not be considered. It could not even be a fleeting notion. All of my strength, pig-headedness and ineptitude required my utmost coordination and focus. A mini version of Jericho's collapsing walls was soon to play out. And a few more Sabbaths were to fall victim to this foray into insanity.

For my first task, I called an impromptu game of hide-and-seek with wall studs. As any victim of construction knows, all wall studs are sixteen inches on center, except for those that are not. I really had my heart set on displacing as few studs as possible.

All I required was the location of the two outermost studs. The six-foot width fit nicely within the space vacated by four studs. In all there would be seventy eight and one-half inches to fit seventy two inches. Vertical studs are two-by-fours which are actually one and one-half inches thick and half of that times two – head starting to hurt – gives one and one-half inches – subtracted from eighty equals seventy eight and one half inches.

Page 34 warned: "Be sure to locate all wall fixtures – sockets, switches, and light fixtures – on *both* sides of the wall. Be sure no water lines or heat ducts pass through the spacing between any of the studs."

Here I was practicing planning *behind*. I had diligently scrawled the crayon markings *before* locating the studs and *before* reading about the paraphernalia noted on page 34 of the epic tome, "How to Completely Destroy Your House in Thirty Hours."

Pages 55 through 9,124 contained all of the techniques known for locating studs. I tapped with the middle knuckle of my right hand index finger back and forth over small sections of the wall around each crayon marked side of the bookcase. Why the right hand index finger? This was the suggestion on page 3,786. Apparently the left hand index finger produced the wrong knock resonance.

The pitch changed over a three-inch width, which I dutifully marked with a pencil. Studs are supposed to be one-and-a- half inches wide. The site required more sleuthing.

My mind raced back to the builder planning my house.

"Chuck, can we have special made wall sections with studs set anywhere from nine to eighteen inches apart?" he asked the site foreman.

"Why would you want that, sir?"

"Some bozo is bound to try and hang a shelf or, even funnier, cut into the wall to build something into it and I want them to go crazy trying to locate the studs."

"Okay, sir. Makes sense to me. I'll get right on it."

Next, I tapped a small ball peen hammer over the same path and discovered a two-inch width that did not include any of the original findings.

I darted to the basement in search of two-inch wire brad nails – suggested on page 5,997.

Aha! My wire brads stretched a full quarter of an inch longer. Did I dare violate such ancient dictates? My hand trembled as my fingers curled around three wire brad nails. Distant thunder and sinister organ music pervaded the air. Slowly, ever so slowly, my wobbly legs bore my slumping frame towards its ultimate goal – the fearsome wall.

I tapped a total of nineteen small holes, fully mapping the width of both studs framing the bookcase.

Sometimes the local demons of home vengeance take a contract mandated break or sometimes they are simply not paying attention. It is times like these, when a home owner pursuing a building project actually has something go his way. In short, the vertical crayon markings were nearly directly centered between the outer studs!

"What are you doing?" Carla asked, coming into the room after hearing all of the low hammering sounds.

"Oh, nothing. Just checking something." That pure luck had just saved me did not seem an appropriate morsel of information to share with her.

Of course, the switches, sockets, light fixtures, water pipes, heat ducts, and hidden stash of gold bullion still confronted me.

Nothing on the garage side presented a problem. All heat vents traveled through the center walls, so they were okay. No water supplies fed into the garage. My wall mural missed the living room air return vent by two feet. All switches had been placed along the doorways. So far so good.

The builder and his foreman, no doubt watched me from the bushes.

"He found the studs, sir. He found the studs."

"Don't look so happy," the builder told his foreman, "He hasn't found the wall socket yet. In case you failed at your job, I was sure the electric contractor would come through."

Ah! One socket sat smugly about one foot into the condemned zone. Why didn't I see that while placing my wall drawing? Luckily, two of the books described how to move an obstinate wall socket, including the warning to shut off the applicable circuit breakers. Carla ordered me to swipe over that statement with a yellow highlighter marker.

"Commit those words to memory. I will test you on them every night for the rest of your life," she admonished.

The next three hundred steps involved removing the drywall. Janet had arrived at some point during this process and was now peering into the room, assessing the extent of the damage.

"Oh, by the way. Before you go after the drywall, you had better get ready for a lot of dust. Don't use a saw. Use a utility knife. That drywall is only a half-inch thick if the builder was generous." Janet's words countered the great wisdom cited in my four books.

"It says here to use a jig saw." My words bore the collective authority of four world-renowned experts in house destruction.

"Do it your way. I don't care. Carla and I are going to the mall."

I went to the basement and retrieved the jig saw and accessories and pretended to assemble the components into some meaningful order, while actually waiting for Janet to leave.

"Bye, Hon!" Carla shouted as she and Janet headed off to the mall.

As soon as Janet's car veered out of sight, I darted back to the wall and started slashing away with the utility knife.

Amazingly, I even thought of using the long metal straight edge as a guide for the outline cuts to minimize filling in after the shelving had been installed. And none of the thousands of pages of instructions and hints mentioned this approach. I outsmarted four world-renowned experts. Each will devote a full chapter to my cunning in upcoming editions.

Janet and Carla returned as the last chunks of drywall found temporary rest in the metal garbage cans in the garage.

"So you used the utility knife after all," Janet said with a little hint of smugness.

"What makes you say that?"

"For one thing, I didn't get hit with a cloud of dust, when I came in." A sarcastic smile now accompanied her growing smugness.

"I'm good at cleaning up. Having two kids does that for you."

She only replied with an expression normally reserved for parents listening to their teenager deny having drunk alcohol. After a disapproving flip of her head, she spun around and left the room. Wearing a vampire's black cape and abruptly flipping it over one shoulder as she turned would have enhanced her exit.

Removing the drywall exposed insulation and wiring – more wiring than expected from one double gang socket. A bundle of wires snaked halfway through the cut away section, turned ninety degrees and headed to parts unknown upstairs. Had I pursued the jig saw approach, the saw likely would have severed these wires. Why did the wire nest travel through this particular studding?

Sometime later, Larry surmised the builder, facing a budget crunch, called off the electricians, while neglecting to stop the drywallers who continued forging ahead. The site foreman must have caught the mistake before the downstairs was inadvertently completed, leaving the electricians only this wall for the upstairs feeds on this side of the house.

"Isn't this against some kind of local or county code?" I asked with concern.

"The inspectors normally don't follow a house every step of the way. This clown had several houses going up with yours. I watched the circus, totally amazed the roofs ended up on the outside." Larry's humor did not quell my surging apprehension about what great discoveries awaited me in future projects.

"What's with all of those wires?" Carla asked, a touch of wonder spicing her voice. I did not reply, assuming her question was rhetorical.

"Let's leave Mr. Fix-It to his wiles," Janet commented, her voice having not lost any of its edge.

The wires passed through holes in the studs about a foot below the top of the cut out. Four of the studs were destined for extinction anyway, allowing my hacking them up to free the wires.

Someday the travel paths the wires took to parts unknown upstairs will frustrate a future home project. For now, their neat bundling eased my relocation effort.

Before proceeding, Carla's nightly quiz popped into my mind: turn off the applicable breakers! This meant casting the upstairs into total darkness.

Elaine took advantage of the situation, frightening Eric with tales of ghosts and monsters slithering out of the closets in his room and out from under his bed. As punishment, Elaine slept in Eric's room that night, comforting her brother by keeping the fiends at bay.

The wire bundle passed through holes in four of the studs. While Elaine spun her yarns, I freed the wires with the jig saw by carefully notching into the holes by angling in from above and below. And nothing bad happened!

Another section of drywall needed removing to expose a pathway above the top of the shelving. I notched out four channels for the new wiring passageway. The extra excised drywall piece found a temporary home in the garage for safe storage until it could be reset at the end of the project – assuming a logical terminal point existed.

Now fully competent with the jigsaw, cutting notches in the studs above the bookshelf top line proved easy. At one point Janet came over for a quick look. She examined my hands to be sure, in her words, all of my fingers were still there.

Saturday passed without calamity. But Sunday loomed before me.

The double socket presented an opportunity. I removed it, feeding the wires into a junction box for the future power supply for my planned sconce lighting.

"I really *really* hope you know what you are doing," Carla said, concern clearly evident in her voice.

Did I really *really* know what I was doing? I didn't really know what I was doing. In fact, I am not now sure I was ever sure of what I was doing. After rereading the section on moving a socket, the answer was obvious: no. I originally turned off the breaker, but now the wires sat exposed, gleefully waiting for pliers, a wrench, or just my bare skin.

The text described a fascinating invention – the wire cap. This truly amazing device contained a metal thread encased in plastic, providing permanent insulation for dangling wires left by blockheaded home improvement amateurs.

I sped off to the home megacenter in search of wire caps, accompanied by my book with the page describing the caps tagged. The author supplied a photograph of a typical wire cap, warning these buggers came in different sizes and colors.

"Do you need help, sir?" The voice swept over me from Count Clerkula. I had arrived in this aisle alone and there were no clerks in sight. Suddenly a tall man with sallow cheeks stood next to me. I quickly felt my neck to assure no exposed shaving cuts existed and no blood – wet or dry – was evident.

I showed him the picture in my book. A picture is worth a thousand words, except when they raise a thousand questions.

"What size wire do you have and is it stranded or solid?"

"Duhhh ... Gee ... Hmmm ... Wires?" I wanted to ask if wire measurements were in cubits, deflecting the shame of knowing so little back on him. "What?" I could have remarked, "You don't know what a cubit is? And you call yourself knowledgeable? Hah!"

Instead, my blank expression led him to ask a simpler question. "What are the wires for?"

"A house wall socket."

"Okay. Likely fourteen gauge, though twelve is used in many houses. Contractors usually install solid wire. Where do you live?"

A vampire wanted me to divulge my house location? Didn't vampires just somehow know these things?

"246 Oakridge Lane," I answered dryly.

"Oh, *that* development. Here's what you need."

What did I hear: "Oh, *that* development"? Fear prevented my asking what he meant. No doubt all will be revealed in due time, but for now querying him seemed like finding out exactly when and how I will die. Some things are better left unknown!

I grabbed a bag from him and streaked home to install wire caps.

Back at the wall the copper wires stared at me in defiance, but the caps fit them nicely. One foe vanquished. Nonetheless, there were more battles to come.

Carla stood silently in the doorway watching me.

"Are you *sure* you know what you are doing?" Her voice startled me.

"How long have you been watching me?"

"Long enough to cause me to ask." Her intense look sapped a vital portion of my strength. My shoulders slumped and my head bent forward as I stared at the floor in front of my feet.

In a movie she would don a police commander's outfit and bark commands.

"Assume the position. Spread 'em. Farther." Her hands patted me down as I leaned unbalanced against the wall with my legs spread uncomfortably wide.

"What's this?"

"A screwdriver, Officer."

"And *this?*"

"A pliers, Officer."

"You are under arrest for impersonating a handyman. You have the right to remain silent – and I certainly hope you do – and everything you have done to this house *will* be held against you."

"Why don't we take the kids to a movie? It's Sunday." Her request seemed inspired more by her need to rescue her sanity – and possibly the living room – than to salvage the remains of the Sabbath.

The movie and a dinner out as a family did wonders for us, but little to advance my project.

Why did I feel a semblance of guilt enjoying the Sabbath? How could my psyche have so degraded, since the wondrous times Carla and I had experienced during the early part of our marriage? Was I genuinely becoming my father? Was I doomed to wander the land seeking projects and reasons to obliterate any possibility for rest and quiet on the weekend? Had the Sabbath become a shibboleth for me?

Unnnhhh! The wall waited within, calling me with its raspy voice. "You are in my power! Come back. Come baaack."

I returned to the wall with my shoulders slumped and my head bent forward. My glazed eyes stared at the floor in front of my shuffling feet.

Upon arriving at my destination, the wall offered no condolences or appreciation. All it said was "Get to work. We have a long way to go. You won't get there whimpering."

For the rest of the evening, I cleaned up the work area, smoothed out the cut-out, reviewed my plans, and assembled tools – in general, wimped out.

The following weekend, armed with a vicious reciprocating saw rented from the local Chamber of Torture, I re-launched the shelving project.

"No more talking," I sternly warned the wall. "Only action from now on. I am yours until the bitter end. We shall see victory together."

"Now you are General Patton?" Carla asked with amusement.

"Was I talking out loud?"

"More mumbling, but I heard something about you and the wall seeing victory together. I think we'll both soon be seeing a professional."

Her eyes rolled upward and as she turned to leave her hand waved downward toward me as though she were pushing me away. By "professional," I could assume she was not referring to my hiring a contractor.

The wall and I charged immediately into action. Wielding Carla's oversized fabric scissors, I cut the insulation blankets and pulled them out, rolling them together for disposal. The back of the mating garage drywall now stood exposed.

Next, with the studs temporarily secured with a one-by-four cross piece, in one smooth flawless operation the reciprocating saw slashed through the four expendable studs, leaving perfectly straight and perfectly aligned cuts without breaking through the garage drywall. A correctly cut and perpendicularly mounted two-by-four permanently secured the hanging stud stubs, leaving an opening of exactly the prescribed height.

These events did occur, but the tools and wood yielded to my father's demands, not mine. Had I performed the tasks, the mating garage drywall would have been in shreds and I on life support.

My mom and dad visited for an afternoon with Elaine and Eric. When Dad saw my wrestling with the wall, he took charge, wrangling the reciprocating saw. Over the years, he had framed, sheathed, and painted three rooms in his basement. Taming four wall studs posed little difficulty. Amazingly, his saw cuts extended through the studs and only about an eighth of an inch into the drywall.

Fathers always seem to know how to do these things, teaching sons self-sufficiency in tax preparation, home repairs, car repairs, and handling life's little bumps and twists.

Tribal cultures hand down lessons from father to son: important lessons, such as how to attack a tiger, what vegetation to eat and what to avoid, and how to protect a family. But those fathers had fathers who learned these same lessons from their fathers – all the way back to when the argument about the chicken and the egg began.

Neither my mom's nor my dad's parents owned homes nor built anything more complex than a birdhouse or a doghouse. Fathers just seem to know.

As Eric travels through life, he will come to me to cut through studs without harming the opposite wall, to help him prepare his taxes, and to buy a house. And I will somehow rise to the occasion, exerting my influence with all the authority vested in fathers over the centuries. I will just know.

The Chamber of Torture closed in forty-five minutes. The reciprocating saw, having completed its service, needed to be returned. At this moment, out in the county, another amateur handyman craving violence against his house could be on his way to the Chamber. I had to get there before him in order maintain continuity and cohesion between him and me and with all of those clueless husbands who had come before us.

I saw myself wrestling and jousting with the wall for another 100 years, about the same time duration as the average State road project.

Three of the how-to books presented the projects in line drawings. One book used only photographs. The diagrams in the project books displayed such cleanly cut and even shelf runs. Captions under the diagrams affirmed the great simplicity involved in the assembly.

The book with the photographs contained more descriptive captions because the photographs couldn't show blow-up views very well. The photographs always had just enough blur to make the assemblies look good, without discerning the details – the details such as errant saw cuts, misfitted and puttied shelf-to-sidewall assemblies, and wood cracks splaying away from screw holes. The authors learned well by studying the ever blurry photos of Bigfoot and the Loch Ness Monster!

In one book, the line drawing showed a circular saw cutting through a perfectly flat two-by-twelve board. The caption warned that the board needed to be firmly clamped before cutting. After making five attempts at cutting two boards, I realized the clamping prevented the saw from hurling the board out the front door.

I did manage to harvest two properly trimmed, but far from flat shelf pieces.

Okay. Cutting the shelving proved less simple than the line drawings and captions led me to believe. Why was I surprised? Clearly, the books were written by people who had lost countless Sabbaths and wanted to spread their misery.

"Let's see how I can ruin someone else's weekends," one author probably said as he began writing his book.

"Dear, are you going to give false hopes and unrealistic advice on building something?" his cheery wife might have chimed in.

"Yes, Dear. Remember my book on performing your own appendectomy? And how it sent thousands of people to the hospital, writhing in agony? Well, this is going to be a self-help book on building your own built-in bookshelves and cabinets."

"Oh, my. Oh, my. I can just imagine how many people will be hospitalized and in the throes of insurmountable pain after trying your suggestions."

"Yes, Dear, I am always glad to help my fellow man."

Let me digress for a moment to make a point.

On occasion, a television commercial comes along demonstrating the activity of a medication on the body. The sponsor's medicine is compared in action to the leading competitor who is never identified. Instead, both products are represented by little capital letters flowing into the body through eating, spraying, skin absorption, or shotgun blasts. Cartoon drawings of body torsos form the background with the medicine shown as little capital letters – normally A's and B's – traveling along moving dotted lines with arrowheads.

These types of commercials, covering a number of products, have been aired for many years and just to make sure the consumer doesn't collapse into a state of blubbering confusion, a warning caption normally accompanies the commercial stating, "This is a dramatization."

Until that vital caveat was entered on the screen I used to scout around for loose A's and B's, whisk broom and dust pan in my hands. Having never found any always left me in a state of near terminal confusion. How wise of the commercial makers to keep my and other viewers' sanity in mind.

I have often wondered how many people or, for that matter, what type of people find themselves confused by seeing little letters flowing into a cartoon torso. Perhaps the manufacturer simply wants to avoid a lawsuit.

"Your Honor, my client was misled by the product commercial. I offer Exhibit A to be placed into court record."

"Objection. The defense has not had a chance to review this exhibit."

"Objection overruled, you knucklehead. This exhibit is a screen shot of your commercial."

"May I continue, Your Honor?"

"Proceed."

"I call the plaintiff to the stand – Mr. Joseph Clueless."

The judge bellows, "Sargent-at-Arms, please escort the witness to the stand."

"Mr. Clueless, in your own words please tell the court what happened, when you took the medicine."

"Well, I took the medicine. You see, it was kinda a nice day and the sun was shining. The dog needed to go out."

"The witness is reminded to answer the question."

"Sorry, Your Honorness. You see that little picture over there? The one with all the writing? Well, when I swallowed, rubbed in, sprayed on, and shotgunned that stuff into my body, there were *no* letters bouncing around. Now that's false and misleading advertising."

The jury leaps to attention and roars out in unison, "Your Honor, we've heard enough. We find in favor of the plaintiff and award him two million dollars and thirty three cents."

Now we return to the line drawings.

Here in blown-up view were three shelves, a top, a bottom and two sides. All seven pieces fit together perfectly in the next drawing. Nowhere on any page of any of the books did that necessary warning appear: "This is a dramatization." I was lulled into the false belief a flat piece of wood could be obtained and straight, square cuts with a circular saw were possible and at exactly the premeasured places on the board.

"You Honor, may I bring to the court's attention Exhibit C – the pile of wood in the corner?"

"The plaintiff will identify the Exhibit for the court."

"Your Honor, that's *it!* That mess is twenty-six attempts at trying to make wood cuts look like this drawing."

"Will plaintiff's council please show the court the drawing in question?"

"Your Honor, I present this overhead slide to the jury. In it the drawing is clearly displayed."

The jury breaks into shouts of anger. "Cannot be done!" shouts one juror. "This is pure heresy!" shouts another. "That is the same book that landed my father in the hospital with chest pains!" "Lynch the author!"

"Order! Order in the court!" With mighty gavel strikes the judge brings the jury back to its senses. "I may as well hear the jury's decision. What say you?"

In unison, with teeth bared, the jurors chant, "Guilty! Guilty! Guilty!"

"You have been heard," the judge growls. "My own father used this book and I didn't believe his ranting and raving until now. The defendant will please rise. You are sentenced to life in prison without any chance of parole and you will be assigned to cabinet making using your own books until death releases you. Court is dismissed."

My cut boards had slanted edges and clearly visible warpage. Each board required careful post-operative treatment to fit the proper shelving dimensions. I filed, planed, sanded, remeasured, refiled, re-planed, re-sanded, re-remeasured, re-refiled ...

In frustration, I moved on to the cabinet. The books dutifully explained how to form a cabinet door, leading to the court's applying consecutive life sentences to the author's life sentence already administered.

Over the next few weeks, Carla noticed the lack of progress despite the high level of activity.

"Everything okay, Honey?" she asked.

"Uh-huh," I grunted. The grunt conveyed to Carla the need to review our home insurance policy to see if it covered damage from well-intentioned, but deranged, husbands.

I want to spare the reader a painful blow-by-blow exposé of my next sequence of traumas and failures and fast forward to the end of the project. The scene had Carla standing by my side expressing her disbelief at the professional appearance displayed by the shelving and casework.

"I guess you did know what you were doing. Though I admit I had my doubts until five minutes ago." She laughed; I forced a tired smile that looked more like a grimace.

Janet joined us, standing between us, placing her arms over our shoulders.

"I'm absolutely speechless. I really am." She squeezed us together against her, demonstrating her affection. "How did you ever do it?"

It is true that all do-it-yourself books attempt to present an organized step-by-step approach with drawings and descriptions seldom connecting with reality. It is also true the authors mate each step with an illustration showing an ideal result. More adventurous experts display photographs at key stages, ending with a shot of a perfectly assembled and beautifully finished project.

I must be fair. We know there are people who can wrestle giant alligators, people who remain uninjured while lying on a bed of sharpened spikes while cement slabs are smashed on their chests with sledge hammers, people who can safely dive into shallow water from cliffs hundreds of feet high, and people who can chew and swallow light bulbs without sustaining injury.

Most surely history must have spawned at least one individual who successfully fabricated a built-in shelving/cabinet unit at home that matched the description in the books. I cannot prove it, but by applying the laws of statistics, we see there is the likelihood such a person exists. He or she probably lives with Bigfoot and swims with the Loch Ness monster; but at least that person enjoys a sturdy place for storage.

The number of exuberant amateurs who finally hire a professional carpenter or the number who take an axe to their failed creations are not known. I cannot imagine truthful responses to an interview on this subject.

"Hello, this is Paul Paulson of Dynamic Question Askers. We are taking a survey of people who have bought do-it-yourself books and attempted a project. Do you fit this category?'

"Yeah, I guess."

"What book did you buy?"

"You name it, I bought it."

"What project did you undertake?"

"A dumb built-in bookcase and cabinet combo."

"Were the instructions clear?"

"Sure, to a journeyman cabinet maker with thirty years' experience."

"Did you come across any problems?"

"Yeah! Nuthin' worked."

"Could you elaborate?"

"Yeah. They showed perfectly flat boards. When was the last time you saw a perfectly flat piece of wood?"

"And?"

"They somehow could cut a perfect edge and within one-thirty-second of an inch with a circular saw. The blade alone is an eight-inch thick. I think they had a mechanized cabinet shop make their pieces. I couldn't get it within a quarter-inch."

"And?"

"They never make mistakes, so you don't know how to correct one. I used a lot of wood fill."

"How did it turn out?"

"Crummy. It looked like some hack amateur went after it with meat cleavers."

"Would you attempt another project after this experience?"

"Oh, yeah. Of course. But I'd rather have open heart surgery without anesthesia first."

"Thank you for your time, sir. I'll put you down as satisfied."

My experience contained too many of these elements.

Installing a half-inch thick urethane insulation board against the back of the garage drywall went well: it would be hidden. Installing the side support two-by-fours also went well: they, too, would be hidden.

Anything exposed challenged the limits of my ability. I eventually assumed the authors who resorted to illustrations did so because the final product only existed in their minds. Those authors using photographs? They had devoted friends in the furniture industry spiriting out espionage photographs of their employer's production.

After four weekends, the work in progress required a supreme imagination combined with tightly squinted eyes to present any semblance of a built-in shelf unit.

Carla took little notice of my efforts. So long as no excruciating screams emanated from my side of the room and so long as no ambulances raced to 246 Oakridge Lane, she left me to my wiles. Alas, progress needed a boost from the professionals.

During the following week, I scoured phone books from several counties and made about two dozen phone calls searching for an outlet specializing in unfinished furniture. Subterfuge was to win the day!

I succeeded in locating a one-month old store two counties over. That Sunday I spent about four-and-a-half hours at the outlet, measuring, sketching, and comparing with the available space. I purchased a four-foot wide by thirty-two inch high cabinet, a four-foot square bookshelf, and a pair of two-foot wide by forty-inch high book shelves with shelving spaced eight inches apart. These last two units would become the long-sought CD shelves. Amazingly, all of the dimensions added up.

The bookshelf came with lots of shelves and vertical pieces that allowed for dividing some of the shelves into smaller sections. Carla had plenty of space. The cabinet came with doors – a major battle averted. I could use some of the extra shelving from the bookshelf inside the cabinet. Carla would have plenty of space for her knitting and I would look like a champion.

Let's see, third grade math at work again. I left an opening six feet eight inches high by six feet wide. In non-cubit terminology that's eighty inches high. The cabinet is thirty-two and the bookshelf forty eight and that adds up to eighty inches. The two CD shelves. They are forty inches each and that also makes eighty inches. Ohhh, head hurting again. The cabinet, bookshelf, and CD shelves added up to six feet wide. Brain turning to liquid! Knees beginning to wobble.

What *did* add up is once again my life was saved by pure luck.

So in the end when Janet asked, "How did you ever do it?" I replied with a wink and a smile and then quickly changed the subject.

Finishing off proved almost effortless. I stained and clear-coated the cabinets in the garage and waited several days for the odor to dissipate.

A pair of two-by-fours on each side of the opening in the wall filled the extra space in the width, leaving one-half inch to spare to fit the cabinetry. The two-by-fours were screwed into place behind the drywall using four-inch screws deep-set into the wood.

These side supporting studs needed a slight coaxing with a two-pound sledge hammer in order to accommodate the assembled units. Once the stud supports were firmly in place, the assembled cabinet/shelving unit was slid neatly into place. Remounting and blending the drywall sections required techniques already learned during the attack of the mold.

No doubt many readers are shaking their heads. "Come on. No way had you got all that stuff at just the right size," some of you may be thinking. And I didn't. The bookshelf and cabinet were fifteen inches deep and the CD cases were twelve.

Oh, let's see. Third grade math again. By gluing two-by-fours to the back of the CD shelves and by using one-half inch insulation board everything came to sixteen inches deep.

One thing always comes to my mind. Two-by-fours never exist as two-inch by four-inch boards. They are always a half of an inch smaller in both directions. What if we applied that everywhere? Two-inch long screws were really one and one-half inches long. One-inch screws were a half of an inch long. One-half inch screws really came in an empty package.

Some people rant and rave how useless math in school is to learn. Had I skipped the third grade this cabinet/shelving project would have been impossible.

The project still needed another full weekend to complete.

For stability I had to screw the cabinets and shelving units together. Screws, however, would have been ugly. Instead, I drilled holes all over the place and pushed a wooden dowel through each hole pair. I had applied glue first for extra strength.

Okay. I cheated. Two of the books described how to handle this task. But I accomplished it, without destruction to either the shelving or my body and mind – and without tearing pages out of the books. And I didn't even need my dad.

Dowels didn't work everywhere. Screwing the bookcase and cabinet into the side supporting studs was necessary for strength. My dad helped me set all of the assembly screws and finished them off with properly stained wood plugs.

My dad also cut wide molding strips that passed completely around the framing to hide the open space between the drywall and the cabinetry. These last efforts comprised more of a challenge than one might surmise and absorbed a good portion of a Sunday. But *this* time at least, father and son shared the time, reclaiming some measure of the value of the Sabbath and reinforcing the adage dads just seem to know how to do things.

Yes, luck – and only the most powerful and purest luck – had definitely saved me again! Luck helped along with Carla's and Janet's ignoring me through most of the job. To this day I still don't understand how I dragged the shelving and cabinets into the garage, stained them and set them in place without Janet noticing. Carla saw them but didn't make the connection until they were set into place.

Had Janet noticed, I fear I would have never heard the end of it.

Carla later told me, "I thought you had bought some cabinets and shelves for the basement and I didn't even recognize them when you put them in. With everything else, I never would have guessed you could buy the right sized units and mount them."

"Well, how *did* you figure I got everything done?" I asked, hoping for a positive response, something championing my clearly superior skills in woodworking.

"Dumb luck, I guess. Dumb luck and some well-placed nudges from your dad," she replied.

Instead of eloquent praise I had to settle for raw truth.

There was my secret of success: fail so many times that when I finally get it right I can do it right in front of everyone's noses without anyone noticing. Sometimes going to work and working at home are too closely related.

Carla and I sealed a verbal pact to never let Janet know what I did.

"I love your friend. She is lovely. She is great. But if she ever finds out, she will flay me down to my bones." We agreed the secret must remain as securely as that of a blood bond.

With miles of open shelf space, Carla rounded up a variety of accessories to augment the shelves to store her knitting supplies and to provide dedicated zones for each family member. Her knick-knacks claimed the top shelf.

And the sconce lighting? I left the wires dead capped in the junction box. My luck had already been stretched beyond all reasonable limits. Well, the truth? I had forgotten about the junction box while assembling the cabinets. To reach the wires now required slicing up the drywall on the left side of the built-in assembly.

Carla asked me in passing about the lighting. "Where is the sconce lighting to highlight the knick-knacks?"

"Sconce lighting? What sconce lighting?"

"The one you were supposed to place next to the shelving." Carla's forehead began to narrow and her eyes attained a noticeable squint.

"Oh, *that* sconce lighting," I replied, feigning a look of surprise. "Oh, yeah. It just didn't seem to fit into the overall look."

Carla said nothing either then or any time thereafter. She didn't have to. My reputation hid in plain view.

Once upon a time I replaced the radiator on my jalopy during our dating days. Carla came by from time-to-time, observing the progress. I did very well. I broke no hoses, punched no holes in the new radiator, properly reconnected the transmission cooling lines, and even left all of my skin and body parts intact.

She rushed over to me upon hearing a series of oaths bubbling out of my mouth.

"What happened, Honey? Cut yourself? I thought you were done."

She then said no more. Her eyes followed my glances as I first glared at the radiator and then at the driveway – back and forth, my head swinging like a clock pendulum. She noticed the radiator sat in its proper place with all hoses, lines and bolts connected.

What attracted our eyes to the driveway?

Sitting in a small pile near my feet were the four shiny hose clamps that were required to secure the hoses from the engine block to the radiator.

She gave me a little hug, a kiss and gently patted my shoulder as she walked away. I continued repeating the words my father passed down to me from his days of painting the house. The words flowed quietly as I removed the radiator hoses and connectors. Each clamp received a special name as I thrust it over a hose.

My poor wife witnessed my glower at other times. For example, she endured me as I tore open newly sealed envelopes after discovering their intended contents still residing on the kitchen table.

Her silence said it all: okay, so you forgot to run the wires before placing the cabinetry.

In all, millions of pages of do-it-yourself instructions can be reduced to a few words: if you want professional results, buy professionally made components.

Had I pursued this philosophy from the beginning, my final cost would have been lower and at least four Sabbaths saved.

CHAPTER TWELVE

Rule Over the Fish of the Sea and the Birds of the Air and Over Every Living Creature that Moves on the Ground

Some of you readers may take offense at my whining and ranting in this chapter. Fear not. Owning a pet can be, in a word, idyllic. But owning a pet quickly dissolves into the realization dogs and cats have their own personalities, moods, idiosyncrasies, and foibles. Once a pet enters your home it becomes an inseparable part of the family and this is how it should be, and it is in my home.

We often think of animals as dumb creatures that can be bent to our will. Maybe that is true for stuffed animals we buy for our children when they are babies. But the flesh and blood, breathing, plotting, and scheming animals we get as pets are another thing. They bring joy, but the terms they bargain for can be daunting.

Let me illustrate.

The day has been long and tiresome. Your bed beckons you with soft coos like doves settling into a night of rest.

"Hey, move over. I am taking my share of this bed, buster, so move it." Your pet has figuratively spoken as he or she jumps up and nestles into your space.

My question: How does a ten-pound cat take up the space equivalent to a two hundred-pound person? Oh, you have a large dog? Then your choice is simple: nestle on the living room couch or don't sleep at all.

Anyone who believes humans are granted domain over the beasts in the world doesn't own a finicky pet. Of course, most pet lovers claim their pets corner the market on being finicky.

Doctors, medical and psychology magazines, television news programs, and pet store owners all elaborate on the many benefits accrued to pet ownership: inner peace, tension relief, companionship, and fur layer to hide defects on furniture and floors and walls.

Strangely, the benefit list excludes the physical therapy rewards. Bad backs snap immediately into place from the owner's reaction upon discovering animal droppings on a $5,000 white Angora rug. Observation skills improve from searching for all the items your pet hides. Memory enhancements come from trying to decide if a furniture piece always had that stain.

The cardiovascular benefits are the most generous advantage of pet ownership. Running along hallways, around furniture obstacles and up and down stairs, shouting and wildly flailing one's arms while chasing a cat who just pulled down a curtain, afford a greater workout than one can get at the most well-stocked health clubs.

So it came to pass the day 246 Oakridge Lane was invaded by Fluffy the cat. Just the name alone – Fluffy – expressed our lack of understanding of the nature of cats. Anyone versed in ways of catdom uses more meaningful names, like Ravage, Fury, Tiger, Scarface, Claws of Iron, or In You Face Buster. Certainly not Fluffy, a name born from misguided notions of cats being purring subservient fur balls of delight.

Fluffy was a gentle Maltese variety – at age five weeks. The pet store proprietor furnished the title, Maltese, probably to gather in more dollars.

"Here is a lovely pet you and your children will cherish. This variety is a very special breed. It is called a Maltese."

"Maltese? Is that good? I mean is there something really extraordinary about a Maltese cat?"

"Of course not. Who knows? I may even have just made that name up."

"Why on earth would you *do* such a thing?"

"Hey, buddy, which would you pay more for: a cat or a Maltese cat? You know, Humphrey Bogart starred in a movie called 'The Maltese Falcon.' He wouldn't touch the script when it was simply 'The Falcon.'"

"You just made that up, too, didn't you?"

"Sure. Now hand me five hundred dollars and this fur ball is yours."

"Gee, Honey, this man seems so honest. How can we go wrong?"

Obviously, the conversation didn't play out that way. That approach would have been too simple.

With children in tow, pet purchasing is a completely different endeavor. Elaine was nine and Eric on the verge of six when we scouted for our first pet. Elaine had horseback riding to occupy her early animal ownership needs. The stables offered a reduced price plan in which the rider "adopted" a particular steed and participated in the upkeep and grooming.

Elaine loved the visits. My car hated the one mile gravel road access. Elaine dubbed her steed Rocky. Interestingly, that was also my name choice for the road.

By age nine, grooming and exercising Rocky began losing its luster. Elaine wanted a smaller, more manageable pet – one closer to home. A cat seemed the right family fit.

Cats didn't wake owners at six in the morning for a walk. A cat's bathroom needs were all met indoors. Thunderstorms and snow, the bane of dog owners, didn't impact cat owners. Cats self-groomed and didn't pick up odors requiring bathing. Cats didn't need constant attention. A cat was just the right choice.

Eric showed no overt desire for pet companionship until Elaine expressed her needs. Of course, if sister wanted a cat, brother wanted a dog.

At the pet store a twenty-something female clerk caught us at the door.

"Looking for a pet?"

Many answers flashed into my mind. How could I resist such an opening? Before I could whip out my book, Classic Insults to Ruin Every Occasion, Elaine rushed over to a bin of cats. Eric headed to the dog cages.

Eric's choices varied from a husky to a Saint Bernard.

"Son, we don't need a pet the size of our refrigerator."

"Awww, Daaaad. This one is so cute. I'll take care of him. I *promise!*"

Never have any parents heard a more fearful promise. A simple perusing of any suburban neighborhood before seven o'clock in the morning will reveal a small army of tired parents – some in bath robes and slippers – being hauled behind gargantuan animals. Each animal was seeking the proper location to "do his business."

I have always loved that term: do his business. Did dogs franchise? Did the type of business depend on demographic studies performed by national dog marketing associations? Was there a federally established minimum hourly rate?

On occasion, I converse with these hapless denizens. Invariably, the discussions lead in the same direction.

"My kid wanted a dog. He promised he'd take care of it."

"Didn't you know what you were getting into?"

"How could I? Rufus was so small and cute. How could I deny my kid?"

"But this animal is larger than a Clydesdale. Didn't you get a hint as a puppy? Like maybe its paws were a foot in diameter?"

I refused to fall into this trap. The dogs' names on the cages supplied sufficient information: Mammoth, Paul Bunyan, and Godzilla.

"Eric. I *know* you mean well. But you have school and all and taking care of a big dog is a big responsibility."

"But Daaaad. But Daaaad. But Daaaad. But Daaaad. But Daaaad."

"Let's see what Elaine is doing."

Elaine had scooped up a lovely fluff ball and was scrunching it against her chin.

"Can we have this one, Daddy? Please, Daddy? Please? Please? Please?"

"What's your opinion, Carla?"

"Elaine is so good with pets and I know Eric will love a cat," she offered.

On what did Carla base her reply? She somehow drew an analogy between once a week horse grooming and daily pet care. She also assumed Eric would do everything to outperform his sister in pet loving. Eric's dark expression projected a scowl that countered Carla's glowing appraisal of his motivation.

"What do you say, Son? Tell you what. Why don't you name him?"

Eric stood for a moment, staring at the kitten. He glared back at me and then shot a fire bolt towards Carla.

"What do you say, Honey?" Carla quizzed him, her beaming smile appearing more born from anxiety than joy.

Eric had to buy into this decision. We didn't want a competition between him and Elaine. We certainly didn't want the cat stuffed into an envelope and mailed to a distant part of the world.

Eric stared back at me, then his face softened as he stared at the fur ball cuddled in Elaine's arms. The fur ball gazed directly into Eric's eyes and with a tilt of the head seemed determined to win him over.

I broke the silence. "Elaine. Why don't you let Eric hold him?"

Elaine unfurled the kitten and handed him to Eric. The kitty looked up at Eric and started to quietly purr. Eric even broke out a little smile.

"He loves you, Honey," Carla sung out. "What name do you want for him?"

Luckily Eric was under ten, eliminating any names specifying gross references to body parts or body functions.

"Fluffy. I want to name him Fluffy, 'cause he is so fluffy."

So it came to pass and Fluffy joined the family unit.

Cats are nocturnal predators, performing most of their antics at night. Domestic cats seem to sleep about twenty two hours a day.

Fluffy proved consistent with these traits and does to this day. Still, I am convinced Fluffy will outlive me, for he will be the death of me!

As a kitten, Fluffy furnished enough love and delight to keep the children from killing him. Elaine discovered the centuries old cat trait of chasing balls of yarn.

I always suspected this trait derived from an innate need to attack sheep. After all, lions and tigers chase furry animals. The domesticated cat only confronts goats, cows, horses, and sheep. Antelopes stay out of the neighborhood. Goats have horns and can be ornery critters. Cows are big and would likely clumsily step on an attacking cat as run from it. A horse? I think the domestic cat would rather stick to the small and furry, which leads us back to sheep.

Do cats that live on a farm chase sheep? I don't know anyone who runs a farm and if I did I couldn't imagine how I would broach the subject.

"Excuse me, sir. I just happen to be driving by your farm and I noticed you have plenty of sheep and a bunch of cats. I was wondering, do you notice the need to replace your sheep from time to time?"

"What are ya' driving at, mister?"

"I mean, do your cats feed off mice and rats?"

"No. I give them a steady diet of monitor lizards. You know, a full grown cat has quite an appetite."

"Okay. I'll get to the point. I am going to buy a cat for my kids and I was wondering if it would chase sheep?"

"What? Why on earth would your cat chase sheep? You plan on dropping it off here?"

"Forget it. I'll settle for a timber wolf. They are less trouble."

Now where was I? Oh, yes. The process of elimination leads us to house cats and sheep. Most neighborhoods have zoning ordinances against owning farm animals and farms are all too often, sadly, a long way away, so Fluffy would have to settle for attacking a product that comes *from* a sheep: wool yarn.

Why else would cats chase yarn? And what about yarn not made from wool? I will elaborate.

The well-heeled cat still has the need to now and then bring down something large and furry. A cat bringing down a mouse is, in relative size, like a lion the size of an elephant attacking a dog – an insult to the cat's integrity. The horse and cow aren't furry enough in addition to being oversized, and the goat's horns get in the way. As noted before, by process of elimination the cat must bring down a sheep.

Also as noted, most domestic cats do not have access to sheep. Therefore, as a surrogate, the domestic cat turns to the yarn ball. Originally, yarn balls were made from wool – from sheep. The turn to synthetic materials does not deter the domestic cat. It is the thought that counts.

This discussion is for cat owners who take offense at guests and family members who comment negatively on a cat's desire to chase yarn balls. It is a sign of resignation to an inherent need that has been denied and not a lack of intelligence.

And, yes. Cats are intelligent and do think – in a most sinister way. Stare endlessly into the eyes of a cat someday. Besides having a cold feeling grow around your heart, you may also find yourself serving as a scratching post for an irate cat.

For her part, Elaine found a ball of yarn provided hours of fun for Fluffy, without her expending much energy while watching plenty of television.

Eric preferred dragging the yarn ball around the house with Fluffy in hot pursuit.

Fluffy performed as an ideal pet for about six months. Elaine and Carla shared litter box detail. Fluffy and I formed a relationship based on tolerance. So long as I kept my distance, he tolerated me.

Basically, cats form attachments to various family members. For Carla and Elaine, that attachment was cozying up to them and lovingly purring while sitting with them. Fluffy's attachment to me was more physical: claws attached to me if I got too close.

The day came Fluffy gained sufficient complacence and security that he began asserting his rights as a cat: attacking furniture, hurling fur balls, annoyingly placing droppings in obscure places in the house, and giving me a well-placed chomp when I attempted to pet him, alerting me he was in one of his moods.

First came the furniture attack.

Going back three years Carla and Ruth purchased a beautiful living room set. The color was ... Well, was one of those new terms that confuse me. I don't know when paint and furnishings lost simplicity. Once upon a time paint was blue and not blueberry and light blue and not morning mist. To me the furniture was green with dark oak wood trim. Carla corrected me, "It's morning teal, Honey. Not green."

To Fluffy the color was that of a green traffic light, giving him the go ahead to attack.

"Honnneyyyyyyyy! Come quick." Carla's beckoning wail declared another calamity to ruin my Sunday. "Honnneyyyyyyyy!"

I rushed into the living room and saw Carla frantically pointing to the corner of the sofa. "Look at that tear! That cat!"

Fluffy stood in the doorway, evaluating the alliances. So far Carla stood against him; I hadn't stated my position. First I glanced at Fluffy. Next my eyes swept over the striated tears on the sofa corner. Finally, moving over to Carla, I said, "He needs to scratch. We should get him a scratching post. Fluffy's outgrown the small scratch pads."

Fluffy couldn't believe it. He had an ally he had been chomping on for four months. How could this be? His little cat brain tried to reconcile action and reaction. "I chomp. He supports. Maybe if I chomp harder, he'll be my friend for life!"

We spent Sunday traveling to pet stores and home centers searching for a cat scratching post. A return visit to the home megacenter saved the day. Why didn't we go there first? Because a special place in the human brain took over – that special sub cranial region making one go last to the place most likely to have what one needs.

Carla instinctively went to the pet section. The clerk informed us scratching posts were in the sporting goods section. Of course. How obvious! How could we have gotten that one wrong?

At sporting goods the clerk told us scratching posts were in the pet section.

"Who sent you to sporting goods?" He paused, apparently waiting for a precise response.

"I don't know," I replied. "Maybe if you get the employees' records we can identify him from a mug shot."

His scowl denoted his dissatisfaction with my answer. "Well, anyway, we don't have scratching posts in sporting goods. Why would scratching posts qualify for any sport? Can you name one?" He then turned and swooshed off.

Back at the pet center, a new clerk waited on us.

"We were previously told here the scratching posts are in sporting goods," I said to her with just a hint of annoyance.

"Who told you that?"

"That guy over there." My finger snapped erect, lining up with the poor sap standing about twenty feet away. The distance was far enough to assign blame without the expected repercussions, such as his rushing over and accusing *me* of insisting scratching posts *had* to be in sporting goods, because only a good sport would buy a cat in the first place.

"Oh, him. He couldn't find his head if it weren't tied on."

Carla and I just learned the minimum requirement for employment.

"Come in. How do you do? My name is Mr. Mutter. Please have a seat and we can go through the interview."

Nestling into the chair next to Mr. Mutter's desk, I fumbled with my umbrella.

"Oh? Is it raining out?"

"No, no. The umbrella is just in case, you know. Must be prepared. That's my motto."

"Hmmm. Uh, let's see." His eyes lingered on a stack of documents scattered on his lap. My squirming went unnoticed.

"Ah, yes. Can you locate your head?"

"Right here, sir. Right where I left it last night!" I emphasized my answer with solid, loudly audible whacks on top of my head with the palm of my hand.

"Good. Good. Yes, very good. Not only can you locate your head, you have enthusiasm. Much more than we can ask for in an employee. When can you start?"

That the assistant clerk in the pet center can now not normally find his head indicated the store did not have a retesting program.

The kindly woman in pet supplies showered us with sympathy. "Oh, come on. Follow me. I'll show you where they are."

She trotted off with Carla and me in tow.

In a very loud voice she proclaimed, "Here they are. Right where they have always been."

The other clerk in the Pet Center now stood about four feet away. He glowered at her, then at us, then quickly looked away and trundled off – no doubt in search of his head.

Fluffy deserved the latest design with all the bells and whistles, unless, of course, the whistles would scare him while he whacked away at the bells.

The clerk continued, "This model comes in two configurations. One is free standing allowing you to place the unit where it is most convenient for the cat."

"Convenient for the cat?" I responded. "That would place it on one of the couch cushions."

"That's pretty funny," the clerk replied. "Your cat must love you." Yes, loves me to pieces, I thought to myself.

"The other configuration requires the accessory bracket for securely attaching it to a wall for use when space is at a premium."

"We'll go with the free-standing configuration," Carla chirped happily.

Prudence kept me from voicing my opinion. Yes, free standing, I thought, to allow me to stick it in the garage the next time Fluffy gnaws on me.

The scratching contraption was a resounding success, allowing Fluffy ample exercise as he scurried over its arms, platforms and posts. The carpeting was extra durable, strengthening and sharpening his claws to carry out his further war plans.

Oh, did I mention cats do have war plans? First, a cat chooses sides. Fluffy seemed to prefer females to males. He would purr contentedly when either Elaine or Carla picked him up. My attempting to pick him up would only elicit a low growl followed by a short hiss and the mandatory swat. As for Eric, he wasn't interested in Scruffy, so his skin surface remained intact.

On to the fur balls.

One of the salient features of a cat versus a dog is the pet odor. Cats just don't seem to have an odor. The potty box – my name for it – can be odor controlled using modern technology: baking soda impregnated litter, multiple 3,000 cubic feet per minute fans, and scooping the bowel movement out of mid-air before it has a chance to hit the litter.

Back to fur balls. The way a cat stays odor free is by licking all exposed fur areas profusely, an act we humans have lovingly dubbed the cat's giving itself a bath. I will always be bemused by the odor free technique a cat can employ despite eating some of the most fowl smelling food possible: fish of unknown origin, liver, kidney, sasquatch, and space alien.

Every good side has a bad side. We all know that. You win the lottery but break your leg falling off the sidewalk in front of the lottery office. So it is with cat baths. The downside is the fur ball: a delectable mixture of fur, stomach contents, and mucous.

The first time Fluffy regurgitated a fur ball I thought he was dying. I went white as a sheet hearing his choking sounds, a sound a bit like yelling "hoopla" while gargling. This spectacle continued until he delivered a one-inch slimy, sloppy creation. It wasn't really one inch as a compacted specimen, but it covered that much territory on the rug.

Fluffy still delivers these gifts despite our trying every recommended cure. We brush him. Well, Carla brushes him – I don't have enough retained skin on my hands and arms for this task. Carla even occasionally bathes him. I had suggested she use her tongue the way he does, but her expression let me know never to broach that subject again.

Now, fur balls are annoying, but not a disaster. Clean-up is relatively easy. Relative to what, you are probably asking. That is the next subject: litter box droppings away from the litter box.

Another salient feature of cats is the ease of care one must give to their urinating and bowel movements. During heavy rains, snow storms, and bitter cold windy days, the cat just trundles over to the litter box and makes a deposit. No muss, no fuss, no bother.

Well, some muss, some fuss, and much bother.

The litter box must be kept in near unused condition. When the box becomes too dirty – a decision the cat makes spontaneously based on a set of rules only he or she knows and refuses to share – the cat will then seek another venue for this deposit. Often, this new location is behind furniture. Now keep in mind cats dig and bury their bodily deposits, so why use a rug? The litter box is a natural digging venue. But a rug? It is in the cat rule book somewhere under a chapter dedicated to harassment of one's owner.

To this day nobody has ever determined how dirty dirty is. Sometimes a single bowel movement will elicit the need to go behind a couch or chair. Sometimes three bowel movements can be given a pass – rarely, but it has happened.

Normally, the discovery comes in the living room during a show we all want to watch. One of us, starting with me because my nose is the most sensitive, will begin to sniff the air.

"Carla, do you smell that?"

"Smell what, Hon?"

"Did Fluffy do something in here again?"

"I don't know, Hon, can you locate it?"

Of course, locate it means I will also clean it up. Latrine duty just seems to have become a way of life for me since Fluffy joined our family.

Now, before you cat lovers out there rip up this book and send it to me with a hefty dose of poison, Fluffy is a very well cared for and deeply loved member of my family. Thanks to Carla, he jumps into bed with us and curls up purring me to sleep. There is probably no sound more comforting than the purr of a contented cat. Just so long as I don't make the deadly mistake of petting him.

Before I move on from this chapter, dog lovers are about to get their chance to rip up these pages, because one year after getting Fluffy, Eric drove us to getting a dog.

"Please! Please! Please, Dad! You got Fluffy for Elaine. I want a dog. I don't like cats."

This gentle coaxing continued for a few months until Carla broke down and started appealing to me.

"Honey, Eric needs a pet, too. You know how it is: a boy and his dog are inseparable."

"Carla, I grew up with dogs and my mom and dad had the lion's share of walking and cleaning up after so-called 'accidents.'" You can see where this was going. Accidents are a euphemism for Poochy did his business on the rug.

Back at the pet store we were met by the same man who sold us Fluffy.

"Remember us?" I queried.

"Should I," he retorted.

"You should. You told us a pack of lies about cat ownership and you did such a wonderful job of misleading us, we figured we would give you another chance, only this time with a dog."

"Of course. Now I remember. I sold you the Maltese cat. Glad to get rid of it. They grow to five feet long and often weigh past fifty pounds. So let me show you this Saint Bernard puppy. Isn't it cute? It was named after the patron saint of very small people. Saint Bernard was barely a foot tall and so these teensy dogs carry on his name."

Of course, this conversation never happened, though I would have expected it.

Eric went over to a cage with the cutest puppy he could find.

"Eric, leave that one alone. It is a mastiff and they grow to huge sizes, sometimes over two hundred pounds."

"But Dad, he is so cute as a puppy. Let me have him? Please? Please? Oh, please?"

The mastiff thing was not going to happen. I know very little about dogs. The tag on the cage told me all I needed to know: grows to twenty feet at the shoulder and weighs in excess of two elephants and in the Cretaceous Period guarded triceratops against tyrannosaurus attacks.

"Here is one you will definitely like," I said. "It is a Labrador retriever and everyone just loves these dogs."

Eric was not impressed. "Dad, there are like a zillion of these in our neighborhood."

"So just think of all the friends he will have. Besides, just get a unique color, like blue."

"Dad, you can't get a blue dog."

"We can just paint him when he grows up."

"Daaaaaaad."

So a Labrador retriever is what we bought.

On the way home I reminded Eric he had yet to name his new dog.

"Let me," Elaine chimed in. "Eric named my cat so I want to name his dog."

"Daaaaaaad! No, don't let Elaine name my dog. She'll just make fun of me."

"Elaine, what name did you have in mind," I asked.

"Well, something that reminds me of Eric, like Bonehead."

"Just to get back at you that's the name we'll use and every time one of our friends asks where the name came from, I'll tell them you named it after yourself," Eric chided Elaine, squinting his eyes at her.

Little did I know Eric at nearly seven was a born diplomat.

So it went. We now had two pets: a cat named Fluffy and a Labrador retriever named Bonehead.

Nobody thought of the obvious: Don't cats and dogs fight like cats and dogs?

When we arrived home, we let Bonehead out of his carrier and he ran over to Fluffy. Fluffy, as noted, grew rather large and at one year old was pretty much fully grown and did not see the tiny Bonehead as a threat. One swat and a swallow would have ended it right there.

The two pets immediately grew very fond of each other. As Bonehead grew, he knew Fluffy from the start – six weeks old when we got him – and Fluffy never saw Bonehead as a threat, even after he grew to full size. They are still the best of friends.

Sometimes I have seen the dog lick the cat. Of course the result is a smelly cat, but it is so cute nobody wants to intercede.

We got a dog during the springtime, so walks were a pleasure. My doctor had often said if you want to lose weight get a dog. It'll force you to walk and the pounds will melt away.

If that were true my streets would be flowing with liquid fat. Instead, there are endless lines of over upholstered dog owners walking their over upholstered pets.

One owner had three pugs. Yes, three pugs being walked at once. Anyone who has ever witnessed a pug walk finds it irresistibly cute. The pug has to mark every bush, leaf, twig, and even atom of air along the path. With three pugs she was constantly tugging and yanking the leashes to keep the dogs moving.

Now, Bonehead was a walking pleasure. He just strode by Eric's, Elaine's, Carla's, or my side depending on who was holding the leash.

In the early days Eric and Elaine would fight for who had the right to walk the dog.

"Mom, tell Elaine to let go of the leash. He is *my* dog and she has a pet at home. Let her walk Fluffy."

That image has stuck in my mind: Fluffy creeping along the ground while tugging against a leash. We never tried it, but the looks on the neighbors' faces could have been worth the attempt.

Now, dog ownership is wide spread. Nobody needs polls or studies to determine the breadth of dog ownership.

I don't know what the studies show – some 60% of households have dogs or 60% of dogs belong to a household or sixty million people own six dogs each.

I offer my own study. Just get up at 7:00 AM, harness your pet and go out walking.

There are more dogs than people here. There have to be. The number of people walking two, three, four, seventy, three hundred dogs at once is a preposterous number.

Add to the tally the dogs with their noses pressed up against windows staring at you as you walk by. Sometimes their mouths are yapping silently, with the sound blocked by the windows.

Another treat are the menacing looking dogs who snarl, growl and snap at the air while they roar towards you, lurching hard against the end of the leash run in their yard.

Of course there are the hidden animals who bark furiously as you pass by, but are hidden by fences or trees and bushes.

Yes, sixty million people with six dogs each has to be a ridiculously low estimate.

Hold it. I almost forgot the most treasured neighbors: the ones who have dogs they just know you want to meet. Let me wax prophetic into another set of scenarios.

"Whoa! Please restrain you dog; he is licking my pants leg getting it all soppy."

"Oh, don't worry. Whoopsie is such a friendly dog. He just loves people. You must be someone special because she doesn't take to just anyone."

Okay. You want to bop her over the head with Whoopsie. After all, the dog is a schmatza schmootza or whatever she said. In short, she is a little dog.

But you are restrained by her compliment. But then another neighbor is walking some fifty feet behind you as Whoopsie returns her visit upon him, slathering up his pant leg as you hear the owner chirping, "Oh, don't worry. Whoopsie is such a friendly dog. He just loves people. You must be someone speci …" And her voice fades away across our widening distance.

Then there is the owner of a Great Dane, that can stand fourteen feet from the bottom of his rear paws to the tips of his raised front paws, who just knows you want a dog jumping on you,.

"Yow. Please call him off. He is writing his name on top of my head with his toe claws."

"Oh, don't be silly. Brutus couldn't hurt a fly. He just wants to show you how friendly he is."

"Couldn't hurt a fly? He could hurt a horse if he stepped on it."

And, of course, we love the neighbor who has an electric fence – or so you hope – and doesn't react when Spike rushes to the edge of his property, spitting through menacing snarls, snaps and growls as he follows you to the end of his property run.

Owning a pet, however, leaves you wide open to the Friday Night Effect. No pet gets sick Thursday afternoon, for example. It is only when you have settled down for a restful Sunday that your child comes running into the living room crying, "Dad! Dad! Dad! something has happened to Bonehead. He is just lying around and not wanting to play and he is breathing hard. Dad! Dad!"

The phone book pages are full of veterinarians and animal hospitals and clinics. But who is open on a Sunday? The first step is to see what is wrong with Bonehead. Yes, he is listless and doesn't want to play – sort of like me after any day at work.

Manning the phone I called every one of the listings. Now, human nature forced me to go in a random order that seemed logical based on who I thought most likely to be in business on a Sunday or at least on call.

"Let's see. Bartholomew's Pet House and Clinic. With a name like that, it is unlikely anyone is there after 5:00 PM on Friday. Ready Clinic and Animal Hospital. Now there is a place likely to be at the ready."

Of course Ready's not only didn't answer they didn't have an answering service or even a machine. Neither did The Wellness Animal Hospital or The Pet Kindness Clinic. After fourteen calls, who answered and set an emergency time for us to bring in our pet? Of course it was Bartholomew's Pet House and Clinic. Mr. Bartholomew, no less, answered the phone and told us he would wait there until we arrived.

A quick initial examination led to the discovery poor Bonehead had simple stomach distress caused by a large piece of pepperoni and sausage pizza fed to him by Eric.

"Eric. We feed Bonehead a quality dog food and limit table scraps to baked or potted chicken and meat. Why on earth did you think he should have pizza?"

"Dad. If pizza was no good for him, why did he eat it?"

How does one explain this logic to a child? Food may taste good but can be somehow bad for you.

"It's this way. Just because something tastes good doesn't mean it is good for pets as well as people. Maybe, if you just gave him a tiny piece of the piece – like a one-inch square."

"I tried that Dad, tearing off a small piece to see if he would eat it. He then rushed forward, knocked me over and ate the whole piece."

Well, a pet doesn't have to be sick to remove a chunk of a Sunday. Just as Fluffy migrated to his favorite spot behind the furniture to go when his litter box was anything but perfect, Bonehead would make his own deposit if you missed taking him out for, say, twelve seconds.

"Honnneyyyyyyyy!" Carla's now familiar cry set my autonomous nervous system in motion. Touching a hot surface sends a signal to the spine where a return signal pulls your hand away before the pain signal reaches the brain, squeezing out the nerve crushing scream a burn can elicit. In the same manner Carla's "Honey" scream sends a signal directly to my legs from my ears, without ever reaching the brain for interpretation. Her scream springs my legs into motion and I am carried along by them in her direction.

So it went with Carla's clarion call. I was off to her rescue without even realizing what foreboding task faced me.

"Bonehead did his business behind the couch."

"What? He can't even be original? He has to go where Fluffy goes?"

"This .. is .. not .. funny."

That bone-chilling staccato voice always settled me down in a hurry. "What do you want me to do?" I pleaded with her.

"Well, for starters you can take him out."

This logic never made sense to me. If the pet has already gone in the house and it is fresh, what is to be gained by taking him out? Maybe putting the couch on the lawn would inspire further bowel function?

"Okay, I will take him out. C'mon, Boney, let's go outside."

"I wish you would stop calling him Boney," Carla would admonish me. "His name is Bonehead. Bonehead, not Boney. Bonehead."

Normally, this would bring someone to side-splitting laughter, but not when bonehead did his business on the rug and it was fresh.

On more than one occasion Bonehead had a strong semblance of diarrhea – perhaps creating the urgency that led to his going in the house. Of course, diarrhea is no easy cleanup, requiring a lot of dry then damp wiping and finally an attack from a steam cleaner. We happen to own a steam cleaner because of previous accidents. No matter, this whole process can take most of the steam out of a Sabbath.

Regardless of the illogic of now taking the dog out, I never argued because even walking him in a blinding snowstorm with slicing ice pelting my skin was better than cleaning up even one more mess from the rug.

We had formed a team: the cleaner and the walker. Where was Eric when this would happen?

"Gee, why blame me. If Bonehead would like give me a signal or something, maybe I could walk him in time."

Somehow, prancing around by the front door while whimpering didn't signal "I want to go out" to Eric.

Of course, many pets are fair weather friends, meaning they willingly go out to do their business on fair weather days. When the wind was blowing and the temperature dipped to single digits and sleet was coming down, it could take Bonehead an hour to go. On a nice day? Five minutes or less.

What could possibly enter a pet's mind that says, "I feel warm and comfy so I'll go right away so I can get back inside"? But on a bad weather day say, "Today I feel chilled to the bone, shaking until my teeth rattle, with ice building up on my eyelids and nose. Seems to make sense to sit this one out outside, facing the brunt of the storm."

No amount of cajoling and pleading could get the desired result. The worse the weather, the more stubborn the pet. Meanwhile, Fluffy was sitting on an end table, looking out the window laughing at us.

Cleanliness has always been important to Carla and me and, therefore, we liked to have clean animals.

Consider this aspect: clean animals. The cleanliness of cats has already been discussed. Dogs normally come with a natural odor most dog owners find acceptable. After going out in the rain the odor becomes amplified a bit and we try to keep Bonehead off the furniture until he dries off. A toweling gets most of the job done and good old fashioned air drying does the rest.

Now, there comes a time when both Fluffy and Bonehead need baths. What determines this need? Usually a foray into a garbage pile or the discovery of a dead animal leaves enough of a residue that Bonehead must have a bath.

Fluffy's bathing needs are very rare and usually occur after his fur becomes too knotted or tangled for his licking to accomplish its job and Carla cannot brush out the problem hairs without eliciting angry growls and hisses.

Fluffy seems to lick tangled parts less, allowing them to also become somewhat matted.

Let us first visit bath day for Fluffy. What usually determines the down time between bathes is how long it takes for skin grafts to knit together, resurfacing Carla's and my arms and hands.

The first step in bathing a cat is to don long rubber gloves. The gloves serve three purposes: protection against skin dryness, enabling the holding of a slippery soapy wet cat, and protection against teeth and claws.

The bathing must take place in a tub with extremely high sides – like maybe four feet or higher. The cat also must be placed into the tub with both the cat and tub bone dry. Any hint of water at this juncture would cause the cat to erupt into a blinding flurry of flailing claws.

One advantage of bathing a cat is the anger portion causes the fur to fluff out and the tail to grow four-fold, allowing complete washing of the fur.

Once Fluffy is in the tub, Carla and I then position ourselves somewhat along the lines of a Quarterback and Center in football. I place a firm hold around Fluffy's body and neck. No, not the complete neck! I am not a fiend. My left hand presses down on his back, while my right hand is placed around half his neck just behind the ears. The hope is to hold him in place while Carla administers the cleansing.

As I have said, bathing Fluffy is a rare event.

Carla brings a small one-gallon bucket into the tub to aid in the washing and rinsing.

We tried using the shower head, but a cat's strength can increase exponentially when he is perturbed to the extreme. Once the shower began spraying, all four of Fluffy's paws went out to the side, the growl turned into a steady siren of "reeowwws," his eyes went saucer wide and he escaped my hold only to place a death grip on my arm with his teeth.

I certainly could not blame the poor critter. The goal is to keep all motion steady and calm. Any sudden moves only lead to sudden death.

We move Fluffy to the far end of the tub away from the faucet, while Carla turns on the water slowly and runs it until it warms up. Carla uses the elbow approach used for testing baby bottles before a feeding. She would repeatedly place her elbow into the stream until it felt just right. Cold water? Prepare for a life-threatening thrust from the cat every time.

As I have said, bathing Fluffy is a rare event.

Carla then fills the one-gallon bucket in preparation for soaking down Fluffy.

When all the preparations have been made, we slide Fluffy over to the faucet until his paws get wet. At this point he has already begun fussing. Touching the water with his paws focuses his attention on his feet – and not on my hands.

Carla then pours the entire bucket contents over Fluffy, adds soap, mixes thoroughly until all bubbles have been smoothed out, pours him into a greased baking pan, and bakes at 350 degrees for thirty minutes.

No, that's when I help Carla preparing cakes for Thanksgiving and Christmas.

For Fluffy, Carla uses long, gentle strokes with her fingers, unknotting hair with each stroke.

After a couple of minutes, Carla refills the bucket and pours it over Fluffy, repeating for a total of five bucketfuls. We are ever so careful to *not* get Fluffy's head wet. We want him clean. We are not suicidal.

Once he has been rinsed, Carla and I count to three and simultaneously let go of Fluffy and jump back, while he shakes off excess water.

Carla then picks him up with a bath towel and gently wipes him off, while he purrs at the attention.

After an official bath, Fluffy will spend upwards of thirty minutes giving himself a complete head-to-toe cat bath.

How long this whole ritual lasts I don't know. I keep meaning to time it, but once the bathing commences Carla and my attention is too fixed on staying alive during the bathing process to keep track of time.

And as I have said, bathing Fluffy is a rare event.

Now on to Bonehead.

Dogs love to disguise their odor when they can. It is a protection thing from their days in the wild.

Dead animals really appeal to dogs, especially the smellier they are.

We don't let Bonehead run loose on his own, but in the early days, Eric seemed to not hold fast enough and Bonehead would occasionally run off. On some of these forays, he would come back with the smell of a rotting animal on his fur.

Labrador retrievers are still about the right size for bathtub bathing, but a dog smelling of rotting flesh will not be let into the house.

Rolling in garbage or dead animals is a spring and summer thing and bathing outdoors is the only choice. Dogs still need baths in the fall and winter, but those can be given in the bathtub.

Carla had inherited an old gray-metal wash tub from her grandmother. This is the type of wash tub that wash boards – those corrugated metal relics of the past – were used in.

The process with Bonehead was a bit different, due to its being outdoors and the fact that dogs usually actually love water. Bonehead is an excellent swimmer and can't get enough of our trips to the lake in the summer.

First, I fill the wash tub with water and then call to Bonehead. Luckily, he obliges and jumps into the tub. I could not imagine how long I would be retching after having to pick him up and place him in the tub.

The rest of the bath is uneventful. I hold Bonehead by his collar while I run water over him with a hose.

Once he has been bathed all he has to do is shake off the excess water and then submit to my toweling him off.

Strange. A fourteen-pound cat? Baths are murder, with total human destruction coming at any moment one's guard is let down for even a second. A sixty-pound dog? Gentle as a summer breeze to give a bath.

Pet stores and breeders must give caveats with the sale. They may go something like this.

"Well, Fluffy is such a beautiful cat I cannot imagine having any trouble with him."

"Oh, you won't. You will be so glad you made this purchase you will have years of boundless joy ahead of you."

Then as we pack up the kitten and head for the door we hear an "Ahem."

"One little tidbit to remember. Cats are very independent."

"I know. My mother has seventeen cats and they all have their own personality. One is snippy, one is callous, one is punctilious, one is diffident, one is sleepy, one is haughty, one is …"

"Alright! I didn't mean that. Cats usually hate water and the time will come when you may have to bath them. Be aware you may need a skin graft afterwards."

"Why on earth would one ever have to bath a cat?"

Switch to the dog purchase.

"Well, Bonehead is such a beautiful dog I cannot imagine having any trouble with him."

"Oh, you won't. You will be so glad you made this purchase you will have years of boundless joy ahead of you."

Then as we pack up the puppy and head for the door we hear an "Ahem."

"One little tidbit to remember. Dogs can be very loyal and friendly."

"Of course, we know that. My mother has seventeen dogs and their names are Trustworthy, Loyal, Helpful, Friendly, Courteous, Kind, Obedient, Cheerful, Thrifty, Brave, Clean, Reverent ..."

"Alright! I didn't mean that. Dogs usually love water, a fact that will come in handy every time he rolls in something dead or in a garbage pile. The stinkier they become, the better they like it. Be aware: They love to show up at dinner time after rolling around in something hideous."

Pets are not all work. Fluffy has his moments of tolerance of me, such as when I entertain him with a ball of yarn. Only in this case *he* tosses the yarn ball while I chase it. His purring in bed at night still lulls me to a peaceful sleep.

Bonehead is great for walks around the neighborhood and he loves to sleep stretched out on the floor near my feet.

As expected, the pets have become more and more Carla's and my responsibility as time has gone by and our children have taken on more interests.

But we knew that going into pet ownership and really find it all very enjoyable.

Before leaving this subject, the idea pets are excellent for exercise has to be covered.

Yes, walking a dog can be good exercise, especially in good weather. When the temperature scoots along the zero degree mark or rain just doesn't seem to want to stop or snow and biting sleet rules the day, the exercise quotient can run close to zero.

"C'mon, Bonehead. Let's do your business. I'm freezing."

So why wasn't Eric walking his dog? In *this* weather? Somehow children aren't waterproof. When the weather is bad all I get are moans, groans, and "aww gees." But have a party or an outing take place? They can't be held down.

"The weather is horrible, Eric. How can you stand being at an outdoor party in this weather?"

"Daaaad, this is a party. I'll be having fun. All kids have fun no matter what the weather."

"But this is exactly the kind of weather you refuse to walk your dog in."

"Daaaad, that's different. That's work."

Work? I seem to remember those fateful words spoken by a nearly seven year old Eric: "Awww, Daaaad, this one is so cute. I'll take care of him. I *promise!*"

Did I ever remind Eric of this promise? Of course! Perhaps three hundred times. And Eric's response? He just grunted and walked away three hundred times.

So Carla and I were left with an exercise that sometimes included torture waiting for a dog to do his business in bad weather.

Labrador retrievers aren't especially active dogs, but they need workouts in order to sleep indoors. Luckily, dogs love to chase sticks and balls. There are just two problems involved here: getting the dog to chase the stick or ball and then getting the dog to bring the stick or ball back to me.

Getting the chase aspect down just requires persistence.

"Get the ball, Bonehead. Get the ball."

A dog just stares at you while the ball sails over his head and rolls some fifty feet away.

The next step required my trotting past Bonehead and fetching the ball.

"Maybe you should run out on all fours and bring the ball back in your teeth to show Bonehead what to do." Carla rarely played the sarcasm card on me, but when she did, she hit her target.

Somehow, magically, every dog seems to get the idea of chasing the ball and holding it in his or her teeth. Bringing the ball back and then letting it go so I can throw it again make two more mountain peaks to climb.

"Bring it back, Bonehead, bring it back. C'mon, boy. C'mon."

The blank stare as he sat down and watched me gesture spoke either of a higher intelligence knowing he can make *me* do the exercise or he just didn't understand.

One day he came trotting back to me and looked up while holding onto the ball. Grasping the ball with my hand I called to him to let go. Instead, he turned and ran back out into the yard, ball in teeth, waiting for my next move.

"Show persistence. Pull the ball out of his mouth," Carla called to me.

"Easier said than done," I called back.

Eventually Bonehead got the idea of dropping the ball at my feet and running as I threw it again.

The exercise rapidly dwindled to throwing a ball, letting the dog do most of the work. Walks got shorter and ball throwing time got longer.

As for Fluffy, cats exercise somewhere between midnight and 2:00 AM. The sound of low "mrrrows" along with the patter of little feet chasing something around downstairs indicated Fluffy was going to be active for about fifteen to thirty minutes. People who own pianos tell tales of ghostly notes emanating from the piano as their cat or cats run across the keys. A low "mrrrow" or "mrrrip" call separates cat from a specter. To my knowledge, nobody ever declared his or her cat broke out into a session of Bach fugues or Beethoven sonatas – just plain old kitten on the keys performances.

We don't own a piano, so the sounds of cat play are generally quiet, minimally interrupting sleep.

Of course, during waking hours Fluffy could be coerced into chasing a ball of yarn. With age his yarn chasing has slowed down, but interestingly has never stopped.

I have often wondered if Fluffy played with the yarn to entertain us and not himself. I can almost hear his inner voice at work.

"Look at those idiots. Tossing a ball of yarn at me as though I can find interest in it. Well, they do keep me fed and my litter box ready. Might as well entertain them. Come on, throw the thing already."

CHAPTER THIRTEEN

The Story of Noah – Part Two

After the roof leak, I would have thought the story of Noah would have been satisfied. But there are events that take place inside a house as well. These events can be summed up in one word: plumbing.

Unfortunately, as with other events, plumbing is beholden to the Friday Night Effect. A completely intact pipe that has had water coursing through it for years will break and leak catastrophically just after five o'clock on a Friday. A toilet that has flushed thousands of times without any errant discharge problems or leaks will crack spontaneously and need to be decommissioned after the first flush post five o'clock on Friday.

Classic comedies – movies and cartoons – show scenes where people try to sleep while a faucet drips in the bathroom. In their minds the dripping grows louder and louder until the sound becomes cymbal crashes. If the hapless victim were drunk, the dripping brought out beads of sweat on the forehead and cacophonous sounds obliterating all ability to think.

My bathroom faucet was a builder installed central gooseneck spout faucet. There was a faucet handle on each side of the spout.

The sound was loud because the spout position remained fixed by design, aimed directly over the sink drain, with the water discharged from a height of twelve inches. Kersplat … Kersplat … Kersplat …

The dripping intruded into Carla's and my sleep.

"Honey, let's call a plumber and get that faucet fixed. That sound is starting to get on my nerves." Carla's nerves had only started to fray. Mine were already unraveling.

Kersplat … Kersplat … Kersplat …

I could swear the "ker" was beginning to form an audible "wake" and the "splat" an audible "up."

"Don't worry, Carla. I can fix those faucets in a jiffy. They have replaceable cartridges that make the job easy."

"That make the job easy." Those words were surely going to haunt me and sooner rather than later.

Saturday was a catch-up work day, meaning I had to go to work to straighten out the nonsense mistakes other people had caused, leaving Sunday for the faucet repair.

My boss had appealed to my better nature.

How did he ask me? Did he offer an extra day's pay? Certainly not. My employment status was called salary exempt, meaning I was exempt from any additional pay.

Did he offer me compensatory time off? Certainly not. My employment status was called salary exempt, meaning I was also exempt from any additional time off.

He approached my desk around five minutes to 5:00 and said the following: "Uhhh, we have a problem. Some of the folios and reports somehow got mixed up and we need them to be correct for presentation to the Board of Directors on Monday. I was really hoping you could come in tomorrow and help us out of this quandary."

My hope rested on his noticing his stapler gone again, giving me four minutes to retrieve it, leaving one minute for him to forgive my needing to come in Saturday. But his stapler held tight to his desk. He stood fast waiting for my response.

My wishful response centered on finding out who caused the problem and if they were going to be present to help straighten it out, though they might actually make it worse. My actual response? "Of course I can come in. Anything to help the team."

On Sunday I tackled the faucet project.

First order of business: Find the manual. Of course! The builder had all the manuals thrown out. Why would home owners want manuals on their refrigerator? Their built-in oven? Their dishwasher? Their lighting fixtures? Their built-in microwave? Their ragglelapoodilla smattabinga? Okay. I made the last one up, but no doubt if I had broached the subject with the builder he would have replied. "I threw that manual out – I save nothing."

Next step: Go online to find the manual. By matching the product manufacturer with the goofy pictures of their faucet offerings I found my specific model.

Now locate the part number for the cartridge. And, there is no cartridge. The builder found one of the models that use old-fashioned washers. Why did he install this model? Builders often use close-outs to fill their orders in order to install items as cheaply as possible. By purchasing a couple hundred items or even all the manufacturer has left, a builder can save a large amount of money.

Now the logical step: Off to the home megacenter.

At the megacenter, I went to the plumbing section in the hope against hope of finding the appropriate accessories for my faucet.

"Can I help you?" A new voice punched through my thoughts. I had never seen this fellow before. Having broken in most department service people, I looked forward to the challenge presented by a new service employee.

"Have you worked here long?" I asked him. "And what's your name?"

"Depends on what you call long and I am Alfred."

"Somehow I expected that answer. In any event, I hope you can help me."

"That's what management claims I am here for. Now what is your problem?"

I then went into a description of the dripping, the washers and why anyone would be stupid enough to use washers these days.

"Oh, you'd be surprised. There are many upscale faucets still using washers. These are not the old rubber washers that deform with use and then leak. These new materials last years and years, outlasting even many of the good cartridges." His eloquent presentation was impressive. I thought maybe he should negotiate my Saturdays with my boss.

"Next question: Do you have washers for my unit?"

"Where is you faucet? I will have to see it to see what size washer it needs."

"What? There are different sized washers?" Why should I be surprised? There are probably different shapes as well.

"Of course washers come in different sizes. They come in different shapes as well. Some are conical. Some are flat. Some are rounded. So you need to have the washer in hand so I can match it."

"Why can't we just go on the Internet and look up the part?"

"Even if you could find a parts list, you can't be sure the washer didn't change. Again, we need to have the part in hand,"

After driving home, retrieving the washer and returning to the store, I was met by another new person.

"Where is Alfred?" Had he moved on in only forty five minutes?

"I'm Todd and Alfred's shift ended at three o'clock."

My project had taken on such weight, it had already moved through two shifts of employees.

I explained the situation to Todd and he brought me over to the washers and other plumbing accessories. I didn't like having the washers categorized as accessories. Accessories come and go. Accessories can be special ordered, but delivery can take three lifetimes of a Galapagos tortoise.

Of course, the washers in question were not only not in stock, but special ordering required their delivery from Eastern Europe – could be several months.

"Several months? What if I offer my first born plus a rookie to be named later?"

"You're funny. We can try to see if there is a USA distributer that stocks the washer."

Todd scooted over to his computer and went on the Internet. Going on the Internet always reminds me of the movie, "Tron." Someday the event of ending up *in* the Internet seems all too plausible considering my experiences so far.

"Amazing. Found a supplier on the first try," Todd beamed. "And here they are showing that washer in stock. I'll order one for you."

One? Is he kidding? With only one washer I am bound to tear it into thirty pieces. Get me ten and I will install it trouble free.

"Why not order me at least five so I can have them to replace the washers in my other bathroom."

"Good thinking," Todd replied.

Good thinking? I wonder how that statement applies to life.

"Officer, I was going forty-five in a thirty-five mile per hour zone because the extra ten miles an hour allowed me to cool my car off better in this hot weather."

"Right, sir. Good thinking. Be on your way and be sure to keep your speed under fifty-five for your safety."

"Good thinking, officer," I shouted as I drove away.

"Here is your bill," the waiter caught my attention at the end of my meal.

"Sorry, I don't have my wallet with me."

"How could you go out to eat without your wallet?" the waiter complained. "I need to get the manager."

"Hello, I'm Mr. Snodgrass the evening manager. Now, I understand you have eaten a large meal and do not have your wallet to pay for it?"

"Yes, that is true."

"Why on earth would you go out to eat at an expensive restaurant and not bring your wallet?"

"Well, you see. It is like this. By intentionally leaving my wallet home I can plead insanity and get a free meal because it is easier for you to let me go than it is to make an issue."

"Good thinking, sir. Please go now and give my regards to the missus."

Good thinking may not work for all events in life, but having an extra dollar part for security during a repair definitely falls into the category of good thinking.

"I've placed the order," Todd chimed in, "and that will be twelve dollars even with shipping and tax. For special orders we need payment in advance."

"Good thinking," I replied.

One week later the washers came in and I was set to attack the faucet so Carla and I could finally have a peaceful night.

The builder placed shut-off faucets in the sink cabinet for the hot and cold water lines. This convenience was to be temporary. When I grabbed the faucet handle to turn it, it would not move.

"Oh boy, now I am facing my first problem and I haven't even tackled the sink faucet yet," I ruminated out loud. I would need channel locks for this effort. How did I know about channel locks? From my dad. Now, did I *have* channel locks? Of course not. Why have a tool you may not need? Not good thinking.

A trip to the megacenter had me returning with two sizes of channel locks. I got a large and a medium size not knowing which one would work best, since I was at a distance from the faucet. Yes, good thinking.

I placed the channel locks through the openings in the shut-off faucet handle and twisted to release the faucet. The handle began to move. Success, I thought. Then suddenly the handle fell off or, rather, broke off.

The valve was sweated in place using solder. Of course! Why install a faucet using threaded fittings so a homeowner could easily replace it? Sweat fit it in place so only a magician can do it.

I toddled downstairs to the basement, unsure of what I was going to find as a whole house shut-off valve. My fear was having the same type of valve used in the bathroom shut-off being used to stop flow everywhere. I imagined the builder having this facet covered as he discussed it with Brock, his foreman.

"Hey, Brock. Come here. I want to show you something."

Brock strolls over to his boss. "Yes, boss? What'd you want to show me?"

"See this valve I got over at Junky's Valve and Pipe? Look how shoddy the construction is. Look how hard it is to turn the handle. I bet anything some home owner is going to try and turn it to shut off the water and it'll break off in his hand."

"Let me see that." And Brock fiddles with the valve trying to turn the handle. "Yeah! This is really a piece of junk. It'll drive anyone nuts. Let's put them throughout each house."

"I was thinking the same thing." His boss rings out.

Whether or not this conversation ever happened in any form, the same valve was used to shut off the water main coming into the house. When I tried to turn the handle it was stuck! Of course. Why wouldn't it be? These valves were related and, for some reason, the valve family had it in for me. No doubt some ancestor of mine did something to dishonor these valves' great grandvalve, causing vengeance to be wreaked upon me.

Faced with a dilemma, I had to make a decision. The upstairs' bathroom sink on Carla's side was now out of order. If turning the valve in the basement caused the handle to break off, Carla's wrath would be tripled if not quadrupled. Her stern warnings to me to not take on projects for which I did not have sufficient knowledge usually go unheeded. In this case, a potential catastrophe loomed before me.

I thought of something clever: loosen the nut at the base of the stem where the stem enters the valve body and this may loosen up the handle enough to be turned without breaking.

Strangely, this worked. Strangely because my dad didn't see why it worked.

"These valves are really cheap," he told me afterwards, "and they get bound up at the base due to corrosion." His words didn't mean much after the fact and since the valve gave in to my superior intelligence, the reason for success was moot.

With the house water shut off my efforts gained significant importance. Every toilet could be flushed once, so there was some breathing room. But no hands could be washed, so the breathing room shortened to a breath.

Not knowing what was in store for me, I packed wrenches of every type, pliers, screwdrivers, paper towel rolls, cups to catch excess water, and the largest most complete Bible I could find and carted them all upstairs.

Sweat fittings. Here I met a real challenge, having never done sweat fittings before. The home megacenter again became my salvation. At the megacenter I met Todd again.

"Oh aren't I lucky," he declared as I walked towards him. It seemed in this place I was a straight man to every comedic sales rep and clerk in the store.

Someday, I thought, the bunch of us should pack ourselves into a bus and go on tour. We would start off modestly, just touching on small and medium towns and cities until we got our footing. We might just use fighting insects and moles for starter material and as our comedy reputation grew nationally, roof leaks and plumbing could be added.

Definitely, the home megacenter would launch my new career free from ogres and nine to five schedules.

I explained my situation and fell on his mercy.

"First, you will need this booklet."

"What is it," I asked, "twenty ways to destroy your house in one easy afternoon?"

"Ha, ha. No. It is a step-by-step guide to sweat fitting pipes and fittings."

Todd then led me through the aisles filling up my cart with acetylene torches, solder, solder flux, fine sand paper, valves – always more than one valve to assure good thinking – fittings, copper pipe, pipe cutter, hair curler, fingernail and toenail repair kits, tourniquets, slings for disabled hands and arms, and burn treatment creams.

Arriving home Carla met me at the door and began questioning everything from my knowledge base to my mental state. The look in her eyes spelled out her fear she would be spending some time at her parents' home. After all it was Sunday and why shouldn't she scavenge part of the Sabbath?

I could offer little in the way of comfort. Why would I insist on taking on a project for which I was probably totally unqualified? Why is the sky blue? Why do wolves howl at the moon? Why do whales beach themselves?

I opened the booklet to page one. Why page one, you readers are asking? Why not start at the ending to see how it all turns out?

Step One: turn off all water to the house at the faucet controlling the main water line entering the house from the street.

There was solace in that step one did not call for a prayer session led by all the Holiest of Holies in a hundred mile radius from my house.

Next, the faucets had to be opened at the bathroom and kitchen sinks to drain water away from piping. Mission accomplished. I awaited my destiny at the Battle of Bathroom. The pipes and faucet prepared their defenses.

First came unsweating the valve from the pipe extending above and below it. If all were done properly the pipe coming up from the wall and the pipe with the compression fitting coming out from the top of the errant valve could be preserved, saving probably a week of 24/7 work.

Unsweating the pipes from the valve proved surprisingly easy, surprising in that all of my fingers and all of the skin on my hands remained intact. I even checked on my toes and had Carla inspect every inch of my back to assure no damage had been done. Of course, that last sentence isn't true. Carla would never stoop to inspecting me for obvious injuries. She would assume they were there.

Thanks to my great ingenuity, a drinking straw came in handy to suck out the water standing in the pipe coming from the wall to allow open space for the soldering to take place. Having children affords many benefits from the great to the small. In this case, the smallest of small was having drinking straws available.

After prepping the pipe with sand paper and solder flux, I pushed the new valve onto the pipe and began to whimper. The next step called for using the acetylene torch to draw the solder into the space between the valve and the pipe. The idea of performing this task brought home why this was called a sweat fitting. Doing this job brings great beads of sweat to one's forehead, arms, back, legs, and between the toes.

The drawings in the booklet were very precise and, amazingly, the valve was sweated in place on the first try. No skin burns. No singe marks inside the cabinet. Only a nice, clean sweated joint. The sweat fitting on top of the valve proved just as easy. I wanted to run down the street, grab Larry, and show him the wonders of my work.

"I can't believe it," he would chortle, "you can't climb a ladder but you sure can sweat fit with the best of us."

What about the other valve under the sink, you are wondering? It turned rather easily. Sometimes, when something works as it is supposed to it just seems like pure luck.

Now to the faucet.

The washers actually fit and were easy to replace. After defeating moles, ants, built-in cabinets, and wallpaper, why wouldn't washers be easy to replace? In my experience, why *would* they!

Now it was time to turn on the water in the basement and test the new washers. Turning the valve in the basement brought the water whooshing to life. The whooshing then turned to banging – water hammer, my dad explained later. I turned on valves all around the house to fill the pipes less violently and after a minute or two, the angry water calmed down.

The washers held. I couldn't believe it. Carla certainly couldn't believe it. In fact, it wasn't long until a familiar cry of anguish permeated the house. "Honnneyyyyyyyy!" Only this time the cry had more the quality of a wail than the usual cry of panic.

I rushed into the living room and there on the ceiling was a rapidly widening circular wet mark. I knew immediately a pipe had ruptured or a fitting had separated. Somehow I had attained the level of genius to reach such a deduction.

I imagined a meeting of Mensa where new inductees were being screened for proper credentials.

"Now, all inductees. Please pay special attention, for the following example is of such a nature so as to separate the true geniuses from the smarty wannabees."

The room murmurs with activity as notebooks and pencils come to life.

"A man has attempted to fix a leaky faucet."

"By leaky, do you mean a drip-by-drip leak or a steady flow leak?" one of the hopefuls chimes in.

"Leaky. Just accept that point. This is not a fluid flow problem in the classical engineering sense. Now, upon fixing the leak and turning the water back on a loud thumping was heard. This obtrusive sound was then followed by a widening wet mark on the first floor ceiling. It is your job as potential inductees to determine what has happened."

The room fills more and more with murmuring. As the hopefuls scour their brains for a solution, I rise up, snapping my hand into the air with the confidence only born from true genius.

"Yes. You in the back," the host says sternly.

"Sir, it is in my most humble opinion, based only on my sense of true genius, the cause of the wet spot was due to a leak in the pipe resulting from water hammer, the bane of empty pipes rapidly filling with water."

"You are correct. Does anyone else have an opinion? Gremlins, perhaps?"

The room grows eerily silent as all eyes fall upon me. That day, out of a field of twelve potential inductees, only one rose to the level of genius needed for acceptance. It was only I who passed muster.

Carla's whimpering brought me quickly back to reality.

The next steps were obvious: turn off the water main and drain the water lines to all sinks below the upstairs. The leak stopped.

Next came a flurry of motion as I ran up and down stairs grabbing tools and performing an operation on the house in preparation for the assault on the pipes.

With my trusty utility knife I cut away the wet drywall, making sure to use a metal guide to assure a square cut-out for easier repair.

Once the drywall was removed, the culprit pipe was exposed. An elbow leading to the upstairs main bathroom had separated. Once again my genius level of deductive ability came to the front: what a crummy sweat job!

After the faucet battle, fixing this failure was easy. Even nicer, the elbow was suspended out in the open allowing me to position the torch without setting the house on fire – something I am sure Carla had in the back of her mind. She didn't say anything, but after years of knowing someone, facial expressions can have a way of expressing one's feelings and admonishments better than any words.

The epoch tradition – the Turning On of the Water – came next. This time, faucets throughout the house were opened before the water main was turned on. And this time, I opened the water main very slowly.

One by one the faucets were shut off, following another epoch tradition: the Turning Off of the Faucets. Just as with knights of old who made their rank by turning water on and off in the great castles, I achieved sainthood this day by fixing not one, but *two* water leaks.

The house buzzed with excitement as toilets were flushed and water was drunk out of relief spawned from the fear such events may have been unattainable for many hours.

Fixing the ceiling remained as the only thing left to accomplish. With help from my dad that, too, came to pass – and on a Sunday.

CHAPTER FOURTEEN

And the Priest Shall Burn the Whole on the Altar, as a Burnt Offering, an Offering by Fire

With small children and families living nearby, home ownership seems to naturally engender the need for family barbecues. Now, barbecues should not be Sabbath busters, but sometimes that is the result. For a case in point, let's scoot back to a lost Sabbath past: July 4th with my family and Carla's family.

Barbecues are a rite of passage for adult Americans, much like bringing down his first boar was for a caveman's son.

"Oong, today you turn thirteen and it is time for you to prove your right to be an adult caveman by bringing home your first dinner."

"Uhhh, Dad?"

"Yes, Oong?"

"How do you know we are cavemen? Aren't we the most advanced we can be?"

"I can see the future and there will be a time when people have machines and Xboxes and structures made from trees called houses. They will look back and call us cavemen."

"Dad, you're so smart. So tell me, smarty, how am I at four-feet tall supposed to kill a three-foot tall boar?"

"Well, that's part of being an adult. But don't let me 'boar' you with the details. Ha ha."

And hence, both a new adult and the world's first rotten pun came of age.

Back to my fateful July 4th.

Carla and I had held barbecues for both ourselves and small gatherings that included her or my parents. This day twelve people would be present: Carla, Elaine, Eric and myself along with her and my parents, her sister and her husband and my brother and his wife. In our family, as in most families, everyone is a critic, which made this day even more stressful.

Preparations seemed to run along smoothly. Lea, Carla's sister, and her husband, Darryl, brought the necessary potato salad and green bean casserole.

My brother, John and his wife, Carol, brought their infant son and three gallons of drinks including coffee, tea, and punch.

Now, you are probably wondering why I didn't name my infant nephew. Because as an infant he didn't have a say in the proceedings, affording me one less critic this fateful day. Okay, his name was Joshua.

Ruth and Jack – Carla's mom and dad – appended the hamburgers we had bought with an entourage of hotdogs from all beef fatties to foot-longs to cheese filled to those with fur to those that looked and barked like Dachshunds to … You get the picture – a wide variety. I never knew hotdogs came in any more than two sizes and one type. For the final touch, my parents brought marinated chicken wings and enough ears of corn on the cob to feed a medium-sized army. They also brought the required brownies, augmenting the brownies we supplied.

In preparation of this major rite of passage, Carla and I had researched barbecue grills from those using charcoal only to hybrids using some form of gas or charcoal to grills running only on gas to grills that came complete with a small chef who promised to only eat one 'burger. We had settled on the charcoal only type because if you don't have charcoal, how can you possibly be guaranteed to burn your fare to a crisp?

The day began inauspiciously. I filled the charcoal bin, poured over the necessary half-gallon of lighter fluid, reached over with the ten-inch match and watched the towering inferno. Nice black smoke began to rise indicating to all of our neighbors it was time to run indoors, lock all windows, and begin breathing through oxygen masks.

After about an hour, the mass of coal briquettes glowed a dull orange indicating the time was right to begin the sacrifice. The hamburgers played the part in place of a bull. The chicken wings would have to do instead of a goat.

For the first step, the salads and drink stations were placed on one of the myriad of tables. Amazingly, a nearby rental store that delivered came to the rescue with four tables and fourteen chairs – two extras for the firemen in case they were needed.

Paper plates and plasticware forks, spoons, and knives assured us of an easy cleanup. You probably see a pattern shaping up: all seemed just so easy, almost too easy to last.

The trash receptacles of choice were two large cans: one for general garbage and one for all the aluminum cans and glass bottles. Recycling is a must in my township and that presents no problem, except when nobody pays attention to the separation of items.

One can had a large sign on it reading "General garbage: paper, plastic, food." The other can was just as easily marked: "Recycling: cans, glass, metal."

Had we had fifty children over, there would have been no issues. Children find recycling fun. Separating items into their appropriate cans appealed to a child's fun nature.

Adults? Initially, I had to remind everyone. Then I had to move the items to their proper locations myself. And, finally, after a number of beers had been drunk, cans and bottles rarely even made it into the trash can, with a small army of them littering the lawn due to poor basketball technique. There was a toss, followed by a guttural cheer from onlookers and next a collective "Oooooo" as the toss missed its target, sometimes by several feet.

I have labored the discussion to show no serious foreboding had reared its ugly head this day. All rumbled along nicely. Everyone was friendly. We all hugged in various combinations. We prattled on and on in shifting groups about what had transpired in our lives to this point. There were no ill words and no conflicts. A wonderful July 4th was what the ghosts of Sabbaths past seemed to promise.

John offered his advice first. "Cook the hamburgers first because they take the longest."

Carol chimed in, "No, cook hamburgers on half the grill and corn on the other half. Corn should be barbecued for at least five minutes."

"Nobody cooks corn for five minutes," Jack admonished, "You cook it long enough to bring out the flavor but still leave it crisp. I say two minutes is plenty."

And so it went for about ten minutes. At least everyone agreed the corn must be wrapped in aluminum foil so it didn't burn.

The hamburgers went on first due to a consensus of opinion, meaning I had no say in the matter. The grill could hold nine patties and that meant three cooking sessions to produce the necessary beef to accommodate the lack of a bull.

The first batch of 'burgers should have gone swimmingly – the coals were the right temperature and they were placed in an even layer. The glowing embers filled the top layer of charcoal.

Then Lea spoke up. "Who wants rare, who wants medium rare, who wants medium and who wants well done 'burgers?"

A murmur passed across the crowd. My dad then called out, "Well done for everyone. Hamburger beef must be well cooked all studies show. Ground beef is loaded with bacteria and anything but well done is potentially dangerous."

"No way," Darryl called out. "I'll take my chances on medium rare." Two others likewise wanted medium rare.

"You had better make up your minds quickly because in a couple more minutes there won't be any rare anything available," I said.

The first batch of hamburgers came out without incident. Well, except there was no rare anything to eat. "What kind of cook are you," Darryl scolded. "Mine is overcooked." Jack reprimanded his son-in-law, "Oh, just eat the thing. These hamburgers are delicious." After a few glares the patties were eaten.

The foil wrapped corn was cooked for only two minutes – carefully timed by me – allowed to sit for one minute, and then unwrapped. Ruth and Lea complained, "My corn is undercooked. Put them back." With a roll of my eyes, I rewrapped their corncobs and cooked them for another five minutes. Thinking back, I often wonder if just leaving the corn to cook would have created popcorn. Probably not and probably this effort would have created a family fight.

"How could you think cooking corn for one hour made any sense?" Ruth would have cried out.

"The kernels are little shriveled hard knurled pieces stuck to the hard-as-rock cob. Great cooking job, brother-in-law, great cooking job," Lea may have retorted.

No. That experiment was better left for another day. My saner side kept me just recooking the corn cobs until all were satisfied, though even this approach led to the inevitable complaints.

"My corn is too soggy," Lea whined. My eyes then rolled downward and a small grumble emitted from my mouth. Lea and Carla passed a few words between them as Carla defended my grumble.

I should have traveled to the local zoo and returned with three bears and they could have tested each batch of corn.

"This one is too crisp," the momma bear would have protested.

"This one is too soggy," the papa bear howled.

"Where's my Xbox?" the baby bear complained. "Since when do bears eat corn on the cob?"

The hotdogs, remaining hamburgers, and corn and the chicken wings were yet to come.

I made two slits along the length of each hotdog, a most benign effort and one assured of no controversy. That is until my dad saw the slits and offered, "Just one slit would have been plenty." Darryl didn't want any slits. "When you slit the 'dogs the juices come out and they lose their plumpness."

Carol, already showing some fray marks due to the complaining, said, "Oh let them be cooked anyway he wants. This is a family get together and surely how a hotdog is cooked shouldn't matter. They taste the same no matter what."

How a hotdog is cooked now formed two opposing sides that cackled on about the pros and cons of slitting the 'dogs before cooking. During the arguing, I allowed too much time on one side and each hotdog – all twelve of them – gained a nice black streak across its length.

"Anyone want a skunk dog?" I asked hoping to break the arguing. The crowd stopped talking and all eyes turned on me and a cold silence fell over them.

"Okay, let's make more hamburgers," I said rhetorically with the understanding the "us" would really mean just me. No such luck! Darryl and John came over to offer their knowledge and each made a grab for the patty plate and the spatula.

Of course, the patty plate fell on the ground face down. This event stopped the arguing. "We'll do this my way, please?" When throwing your weight around always say "please." This magic word can often allow you to get your way without getting clonked on the head.

The day was still young and already we had two fights, a batch of hotdogs with skunk streaks and an array of wrongly prepared corn on the cob.

At this point two beers and a coffee began kicking in requiring a bathroom call. "Will someone take over the cooking, while I go to the bathroom?" John and Darryl all too willingly came to take over.

Upon my return I witnessed my brother and brother-in-law arguing over how to best tell when a hamburger is done. In the meanwhile, small flames were leaping around the patties and smoke was pouring out.

"My patties!" I screamed. "You're burning them to a crisp! Isn't anyone going to intercede here?" Jack replied, "When a barbecue is in progress, there is just too much testosterone for anyone to get in the way."

My mind went back to Oong and his son.

"Now, my boy, your great success at bringing down the boar is only part of the ritual of manhood. You now must pass the greatest test of all: the barbecue."

"But, Dad, I thought my manhood test stopped at facing down and conquering a wild boar twice my size."

"No, my boy. The true test of a man is how he fares when confronted with a communal barbecue. Now get going. You will have to wear your hair in curlers until you prove your manhood."

Yes, even cavemen knew the power of the barbecue in separating the men from the boys.

The burnt offering – uhhh, hamburgers – didn't go over as well as the ancients would have thought. Some were actually eaten and many just sat staring at their better cooked brethren.

The corn on the cob fared only slightly better. Thanks to the aluminum foil and to my refusal to take another bathroom break none were burned, though every batch had its detractors.

"My corn is too hard to eat. It needs to be cooked longer," Lea complained. I thought, "Longer? If I cook it any longer it will ooze out of its foil wrap." Of course, a simple smile was all I could muster.

"My corn is overcooked. You shouldn't have done it more than five minutes," Darryl said. "I cooked it for exactly five minutes, timed on the stopwatch portion of my wrist watch," I declared.

"You'd better get your watch looked at or get glasses," Darryl shot back.

Carol, ever the more diplomatic family member, simply added, "Perhaps you should have turned the corn more frequently making it more evenly cooked."

And so the day went from hamburgers to skunk 'dogs to some manifestation or another of barbecued corn on the cob.

The chicken wings had yet to be cooked. Ruth brought the first chicken wing loaded dish over. I asked for more barbecue sauce in case people wanted more on their chicken.

"Here it is," my mother said in a voice more of a warning than simply information. She may have been actually saying, "Here is the bottle of barbecue sauce. Keep in mind I marinated these wings overnight in this dish and woe be to the one who makes any attempt to add more. Woe be it to him, Son."

At this point it seemed prudent to add more charcoal briquettes to make the level even again. I squirted more lighter fluid causing not only more smoke, but also garnering more comments.

"Whoa, there. Be careful," my dad warned me. "Even though these lighter fluid bottles have anti-flash caps, that doesn't mean it is safe to just go about squirting fluid onto hot coals. You could get a flash fire."

Jack couldn't be left out. "No, don't worry. These caps have been thoroughly tested to prevent flash fires."

Darryl added, "Don't believe everything you read, Dad. There still is danger when adding flammable liquids to hot, glowing coals."

John couldn't be left out. "The cap design is fool proof. This means even a fool, no offense, Bro, couldn't cause a flash fire."

While this parlay continued, I prepared the chicken wings for cooking. With a basting brush I stroked each wing to remove excess sauce before placing it on the grill.

The first twenty wings were in place and cooking away.

Let's flash back to the hamburgers. One thing I didn't mention was the mini flash fires that sprung up each time a sizeable drip of fat would happen. The little fires would normally quickly fizzle out, but every once in a while a flame persisted long enough to burn the meat, requiring I take action. My action of choice was a squirt bottle of water to mist down the coals to snuff the flame.

Even this little act didn't pass without comment. I was accused of not allowing a man's barbecue to take place, because real men eat singed beef without complaint. The flavor of burnt beef did not appeal to me. So regardless of the complaints, I squirted away.

For some strange reason, it didn't occur to anyone to keep the squirt bottle around for the chicken wings. Barbecue sauce and wing juice create nice flammable splatters. And the wings splattered away. With the loss of the sauce coating I saw the need to compensate by brushing on more barbecue sauce. Brushing on more sauce only created larger drips and soon a heavy smoke rose from the grill.

As anyone who has ever barbecued knows, no matter where one stands the wind blows in *that* direction. Why? I have had engineer friends try to explain it with some even declaring it was my imagination and nothing more.

The smoke surrounded me and my eyes began tearing. Cries arose from the family members closest to the grill.

I tried using the spatula to turn the wings, but the barbecue sauce formed impenetrable glue when heated at a high temperature.

"My fellow scientists," the head scientist at the Laboratory for the Development of Impossible Glues began his sermon to his underlings. "We have seen the development of many types of strong glues, from the manmade acrylics and epoxies to the nature made slime that holds barnacles in place regardless of the forces exerted on them."

"Here, here," the audience of scientists purred its approval.

The head scientist continued. "We have spent tens of thousands, no, hundreds of thousands of man hours trying to develop the ultimate glue: one that would resist temperature, weather, time. And let me tell you of an experience that has ended our quest."

He added, "While on the moon some astronauts did the ultimate experiment: they barbecued chicken wings outdoors in temperatures approaching 250 degrees F in the daylight and minus 240 degrees F in the dark. What better test? When barbecue sauce was added, the chicken wings stuck to the grill with great force in both the daylight and darkness."

The head scientist concluded, "For a final test, a chicken wing was attached to the outside of the spaceship with barbecue sauce and it not only survived take-off, it survived the outlandish temperatures and force of re-entry into our atmosphere."

"But sir," one of the audience members queried, "didn't the wing get completely consumed by the re-entry heat?"

"Of course it did, but the ashes were still held securely in place by the barbecue sauce."

Back to barbecuing. My efforts with a spatula only had the wings fall apart with the skin sticking with great tenacity to the grill. Of course, pieces of skin fell onto the coals causing even more smoke.

In my panic, I slopped more sauce on hoping it would dissolve the existing sauce cake, allowing me to remove the wings. More smoke and now arching flames ensued.

Along with the added smoke and flames came a cacophonous chorus of complaints.

"What are you doing? Trying to choke us to death?" said one.

"What a stench. It smells like road tar mixed with burning chicken feathers!" cried another.

"Bugark! Bugark!" screamed a chicken when seeing what had become of its brethren's wings.

Strangely, this batch of wings didn't go to waste. The skin crisped nicely and the flavor was fine. The complaints stopped, but the smoke continued. Searing glances from neighbors downwind could be seen through the haze.

What happened to the remaining dozens of wings? A little family ingenuity saved the day: Carla baked them in the oven. It took an hour and a half to cook them all, but the neighbors must have appreciated it.

And the chicken? She clucked her approval.

As the grill settled down, so did the company and a better time was had by all. Except, there were the normal family complaints, such as from my mother when she noticed how many brownies Elaine and Eric were eating or how much punch they drank.

"You should control how much sweets your kids eat," she warned me. "They will rot their teeth and get themselves sick."

Ruth inserted her opinion. "Carla, how do you justify allowing your kids – my grandchildren – to eat so much junk?"

Carol added, "When little Joshy gets older we are going to keep him on a sweets-free diet. We intend to keep him healthy." And she said this while slurping down a large glass of punch.

I wisely stayed out of this discussion. The burnt offerings had placed me in a very precarious position.

The grill needed a major overhaul to clean off all the burned on material, a job that was left to me.

The family group survived the barbecue as did Carla's and my nerves. I fully expected at some point to hear her cry of "Honnneyyyyyyyy!" and upon arriving in the kitchen, the oven door would be thrust off its hinges while chicken wings flew furiously around the room.

Such an event would have topped off the day nicely. My dad may even have smiled approvingly as he saw me run around the kitchen with a spatula in one hand and a fly swatter in the other, smacking down the errant wings before they could escape out the door and window. And all because of a misuse of barbecue sauce.

Centuries later, archeologists plowing through the ruins of our society will come across the bones of thousands of chicken wings and one, just one, empty fossilized bottle of barbecue sauce.

"Look here, gentlemen. Fosselman was correct in his analysis. Some poor unfortunate soul held one barbecue too many and brought down the society at large."

"Bennilsworth, you are daft. Explain how such an unremarkable event as a barbecue could have brought down a thriving, diverse social structure."

"Well, Hammersmith, this is how it happened." And Bennilsworth would plunge into the story of that fateful July 4th, when an unsuspecting world social order came to a resounding end. Among the multitudes of bones and artifacts, only one empty bottle of barbecue sauce would stand in testimony to the events that had transpired.

Normally, Carla saw the humor at the edge of almost any event. This day, however, tested even her resolve. That night after all the guests had gone and we had retired to bed, she said to me in a quiet monotone, "Sometimes, Honey, even I see the value in living alone in a cave hundreds of miles from the nearest living anything – insect, animal, plant, bacterium. Just to be in a quiet place for just a little while."

The ghosts of Sabbaths past have this day documented in bold print, filed under Barbecues from Hades.

All of the family members from both sides did stay in touch, visited each other and even held their own family barbecues. Family ties can and should survive what ultimately are minor tribulations. Carla and I, however, never tested the family barbecue waters again.

CHAPTER FIFTEEN

And He Covered the Floor of the House with Boards of Fir

In our apartment, creaking floor boards were a small problem and one that could be ignored compared to the travesties vested upon us by Dr. Cough Plop and the 1P2 twins from Area 51. In our house, creaking floor boards gave occasional shocks to the person downstairs from someone walking upstairs.

Most noticeable creaks occurred in the bedroom and, like a dripping faucet, floor creaks amplify when one is sleeping. C-r-e-e-e-a-k! And Carla stirred in her sleep, rolling over or sometimes emitting an audible groan indicating her sleep was being interrupted.

Apparently maintenance free means the outdoor portion of the house. The builder had moved on about ten months after we had moved in so the one-year warranty shrunk to ten months. The floor creaks now became my problem and another Sabbath or two or three would fall to remediating the moans from our floors.

At the home megacenter, I found another new aisle clerk to break in – a bearded man named Hal.

"Welcome to hardware," Hal greeted me in a gruff voice.

"I have a new house and it has developed a lot of floor creaks and I want to fix them."

"First, we have to determine where the creaks are," Hal retorted.

"They're in my floor."

Hal wrinkled his forehead and then furrowed his eyebrows in response to my answer. "No kidding. It seems we already established that."

My answer suddenly seemed foolish. I wonder if anyone ever came to Hal complaining about creaky walls or ceilings. Anyway, I described the creaky spots around the house with some upstairs and some downstairs.

"Well, the downstairs ones are easier to fix. You go into the basement and apply this flooring adhesive with a caulking gun and smear it into the seam between the floor board and the joist. After the adhesive sets – give it about an hour or two – the creak will be gone."

How hard could this be? Just take a caulking gun and squirt on some adhesive, run my finger along the seam to spread the goo into the seam and the creak is history. The upstairs creaks had to be handled, but a ceiling stood between me and my caulking gun. I asked Hal how to solve the upstairs problem flooring.

"You have a real challenge there," he replied. There are kits that allow you to shoot finishing nails through the rug into the flooring, but they don't hold up well. You really are best pulling up the rug and screwing the floor down to the joists."

Let me see if I got this one right. There is an easy method to fix the upstairs floor creaks, but this method has problems. There is a really difficult method wherein I pull up the rug, the padding, screw the floor down, and somehow replace the padding and rug while staying alive and the creaks will stop forever.

"Any suggestion for which screws to use?" I asked Hal.

"A two-and-a-quarter inch coarse thread drywall screw is best. Here is a brochure on proper nailing techniques for setting flooring. Doesn't matter. Screws. Nails. Setting technique is the same."

Okay. So I am to fix the floor using drywall screws. Does that mean flooring screws are used for walls? What about ceiling screws? Somehow howling at the moon and beaching myself came into focus as positive alternatives. But Carla must sleep.

Hal helped me further by selling me the screws and a screwdriver bit to fit my electric drill.

"Why use an electric drill?" I asked him.

"I hope you weren't planning on screwing in a few hundred screws by hand," he said. "In fact, buy a couple extra bits in case you strip one during your frenzy." Somehow megacenter humor still escaped me.

So, I headed home armed with several boxes of drywall screws and three Phillips head screwdriver bits for my drill. Mr. Jorgensen had brow-beaten me into another Saturday of work catch-up, leaving me the Sabbath to labor over floor creaks.

I decided to attack the downstairs creaks first, considering the relative ease in reaching the floor boards from the basement. To locate the creaks I walked around the rooms and placed a small piece of masking tape at each location from where a noise came.

Carla stood in the doorway of the dining room watching me walk around until a moan emanated from the floor. At each point I gently hopped up and down to exactly pinpoint the creak.

"Okay, Carla. I have mapped all the creaky spots. Here is what I want you to do. Start at the far end of the room, stand on the tape and rock back and forth to make the floorboard move. I will then call out and you step off so I can fill the gap with adhesive. You can then mark the tape with a pen so we can know which ones were done."

"Why not just pick up the tape?" Carla asked.

"In case the adhesive didn't take, we can easily find that spot again." I countered. With age and experience, knowledge was actually being gained.

Sounded simple enough. Stand on the masking tape, rock back and forth, mark the tape, and move on to the next piece of tape. Repeat until all gaps had been filled. Sort of like shampoo: wet hair, apply, rinse, repeat.

The first attempt went remarkably smoothly. Roughly measuring the distance from the basement wall under the floor in question positioned me near the proper joist. Carla's rocking brought out the noise in stark relief – much louder than upstairs – and my fingertips could feel the floor move.

What surprised me most was how little the floor actually moved. I then spread the first length of adhesive, applying to both sides of the joist for security. I ran about a foot-and-a-half length of goo, squeezing it into the crevice between the floor board and the joist.

Amazingly, the creak died down almost right away. "This is going to be a snap," I thought. "With about twenty more areas to go this job should be finished in a jiffy."

"Okay, Carla. Move on to the next spot!" Carla heard my clarion call and moved deeper into enemy territory. So far, no mines had exploded and no sniper fire came from the kitchen or living room.

Two more creaks fell in battle. Carla and I were winning!

Creak number four found a place to hide. The fiberboard ductwork ran in two parallel runs with about a four-inch space between them. Number four had crawled along until it neatly fit above the center of one of the duct runs, just out of reach of my caulking gun and fingers.

To not be deterred I went outside and found some fallen branches. Breaking them up gave several sticks to reach into the space between the ducts. Or so it seemed. This creak had hidden itself well. It was camouflaged and settled inside its bunker. After about ten minutes, Carla came downstairs to find out why she hadn't heard any screams of triumph.

"I just can't get enough adhesive into this space; the ductwork is just too close together."

Carla brought her needlework skills to bear. I applied a two-inch run of adhesive and she worked her nimble needlework skills to push the adhesive along. It took another ten minutes but most of the creak had been vanquished.

"We have to move on if we want to finish this job today," Carla said. I climbed back into my tank, cranked up the engine, and moved on to the next creak bunker.

A few more creaks had found inconvenient hiding places – above light fixtures or sewer piping or side runs of ductwork feeding vents along the outer walls. But Carla's fancy needlework skills vanquished those creaks.

The dining room, living room, and half of the family room were finished in a couple of hours. Victory was in sight. With my trusty caulk gun by my side no creak soldier stood a chance.

Except, unknown to me, some creaks had found allies: nails shot into the floor boards at an angle that had been placed too close to the edge of the joist, allowing the nail point to extend beyond the joist and into my unsuspecting finger.

Carla misunderstood my yowl of pain for a signal to move on. My index fingertip now sported my first war casualty. Blood and pain flowed freely. I jumped off the ladder and began jumping around the basement. Carla ran down the stairs to find out what had happened.

"Oh, Honey. We need to get your finger cleaned up and bandaged right away."

The question flowing through my brain was how does one remove errant adhesive from an open wound without causing even more pain? The answer became clear: You can't!

The creak lieutenant now cheered his troops on.

"Men, we have attained our first real victory. He has only nine fingers left and if we work with our nail allies, final victory will be ours." The smug attitude displayed by the creaks only made me more determined to win.

In the meantime, Carla nursed my finger back to health. First she wiped away the adhesive using mineral spirits. Next she cleaned up the area with rubbing alcohol – well-named, though her rubbing was gentle. Next she used soap and water and dried my finger and finally applied a bandage. Florence Nightingale could not have done better under the circumstances.

Even the creak lieutenant was impressed. "Men, we have a new adversary, Carla Nightingale, a nurse fully capable of keeping our enemy in the battle. We will have to try harder, maybe even recruiting a few spiders to scare him off."

No spiders came along and the remaining crevices were more carefully filled, slowly moving my middle finger along the joist-floorboard line. A few minor pinches occurred and I moved on to my fourth finger before the job was finished, but victory was mine.

The next day, Monday, found all but a few creaks had retreated, probably to a neighbor's house. Those remaining were a mere shadow of their former selves and the creak lieutenant was nowhere to be found. My index finger still throbbed a little, but a job well done ameliorated the effects of the wound.

The creaks upstairs still awaited me.

Somehow, using the Sabbath for untoward efforts had become a habit, sort of like scratching when nervous or rapidly blinking the eyelids when suddenly frightened. And so, tackling the upstairs creaks fell on the Sabbath. To be fair this one Saturday was an all-day shopping affair.

Upstairs, the bedrooms, hallway, two bathrooms, and a walk-in closet called to me in creak language. Carla could retire her nurse's outfit, since she would not be needed for this effort.

With the vinyl-covered bathroom floors, any creaks there would have to remain until the day comes when the vinyl is replaced. The creak army had a camp ground out of my reach.

Through the complex decision making process of eenie-meenie-minie-moe, the bedroom of first attack was chosen.

A wrestling match ensued between me and the rug. The rug refused to let go of the tacking strip along the edge of the floor under the rug. While my battle ensued Carla's friend, Janet, came over.

"What are you trying to do?" she queried.

"I have to loosen the rug from the tacking strip so I can roll it up to screw down the floor to stop creaks."

"Carla explained this to me already. You'll never get the rug loose by hand and if you use a screwdriver and hammer you'll only tear the rug. You need a knee kicker carpet stretcher to do the job."

"A knee whater?"

"A knee kicker."

"Why on earth would I use a machine that kicks me in the knee?" My surprise only made Janet laugh. "It doesn't … Oh, never mind. Let me show you online."

Once I knew what a knee kicker was and that I used my knee to kick it and not the other way around, I called the local equipment rental shop and not only did the sales person immediately know what I meant, he had several in stock.

Just the thought of there being several in stock made me wonder how many people were right now trying to release their rugs to screw down their floors. Maybe there are social clubs of individuals who meet once a week to air their problems.

"Hello, my name is Ralph and I am a creak addict."

"Hello, Ralph," the others chime in.

"I have obsessed over floor creaks for six years now and I have a room full of knee kickers."

"You need a knee kicker/floor creak sponsor," a long-haired, bearded man spoke up. Apparently, he led the meetings and offered to be my sponsor.

"Anytime you feel the need to rent or purchase another knee kicker call me anytime, day or night. I will come over at once and help you through your crisis. The important thing is you need to know you are not alone in your addiction to floor creaks."

A trip to the rental center to procure the anointed tool gave me a rest from my attempts to pull the rug free from its moorings.

Janet met me upstairs again to admonish me I will need to remove the baseboards to free up the rug.

Let me see. The room was empty to start with so I assumed this chore would go smoothly. First, I needed a knee kicker; next, I needed to remove the baseboards – a most unenviable job.

"Okay, Janet. How do I remove the baseboards without breaking them? And please don't say, 'Very carefully.'"

"Sorry to disappoint you, but very carefully is how you have to do it." She then took me to the home megacenter where she showed me little pry bars that will allow me to pull the baseboard from the wall, loosening the finishing nails enough to pull them out.

"How come you know so much about these things?" I had to ask her.

"Look, girls aren't helpless when it comes to home repairs. I have painted my rooms and painting is much easier if you first remove the baseboards. Besides, I have a dad who made sure I wasn't helpless in this world."

"You know, maybe you should stay with me through this endeavor so I don't hurt myself." Janet laughed, but somehow that laugh didn't build my confidence.

And so I released the rug on three sides only – another bit of advice from Janet – allowing the rug to stay fastened at one end, preventing wrinkling when I replaced it. Moreover, by rolling toward the doorway there was no need to cut the rug to release it.

Rolling up the rug gave me enough room to get all the necessary floor area for screwing. The padding rolled up into a very small tube, showing me just how thin it was – no doubt another builder's special deal.

The screwing went unusually smoothly. No screws broke. I didn't strip a single screwdriver drill bit. And, most importantly, I accrued no injuries. The room grew very quiet. Hopefully, the creaks didn't scatter to other rooms.

Now, the rug replacement and resetting the baseboards faced me. And I faced them with great trepidation.

First I rolled the padding back into place. Being relatively new, the padding stayed fully intact. Stapling the padding in place went easily.

I next rolled the rug back out and, of course, it fell a few inches short of the tacking strip on the far end of the room.

"That's where you use the knee kicker, to stretch the rug back into place." Janet's voice surprised me. I hadn't known she was there.

"How long have you been watching me?"

"Long enough to know you now need help." She explained the art of replacing the rug by knee kicking towards the far ends until the rug comfortably fit back over the tacking strips. I knee kicked forward, left, right, forward again, left then right again until my knee became a little sore and the rug lay neatly over the tacking strips.

Replacing the baseboards proved easy, since the paint on the wall showed a clean edge for lining up the top of the baseboard. I even knew how to set the finishing nails with a nail punch, something that seemed to surprise Janet.

"I thought Carla and I were going to have to go out and buy a bunch of throw rugs to fix up the rooms after you were done," she cackled. My mind flew back to the oval throw rug Janet had bought Carla for the living room. I imagined a slew of rugs blending Early American with Manic Depressive.

The rooms with furniture proved strangely easier to deal with. By moving all the furniture to one side of the room the rug became pinned in place, allowing for easier stretching to the opposite side. The doorways didn't have any creaks, so this method was a sane alternative to attempting to move all the furniture out of a room.

For once, my mind did not conjure up images of Carla bringing me to the emergency room. Of course, with any home project there always exists the possibility of something going horribly and unexplainably wrong.

"What on earth happened to your husband? How did he get in this condition?"

"Well, Dr. Bonesetter, you see he was trying to fix creaks in the upstairs bedroom floors and ..."

"I get it," Dr. Bonesetter says, cutting Carla off. "He went to move a dresser and ran it over his feet, correct?"

"Yes, doctor. But that wasn't the end of it. He then ..."

"Let me guess," he continues, cutting Carla off again. "He fell backwards and bumped into the chest of drawers, causing it to fall on him. Correct?"

"Yes, doctor, but that wasn't the end of it. You see he is a typical husband so he felt there was no need to see a doctor."

"Ahhhh," Dr. Bonesetter retorts, "I see this all the time. Wives bring in husbands in all stages of ailments. The worst cases are those husbands who insist on doing home repairs themselves. I tell my married male patients to make excuses to avoid any do-it-yourself home projects. A bad back is a great excuse that works every time."

And so it went. All went well and the creaks were fixed. Carla would sleep through the night again and I would live to fight another day.

Of course, the main casualties were three Sabbaths.

CHAPTER SIXTEEN

And God Said, "Let There Be Light," and There was Light

As with all the houses in the development, mine came with the seemingly mandatory two outdoor lights by the front door – one on each side – with one light in the upper center of the garage, and one out back by the door to the outside of the garage.

"Let's install more lighting," I said to Carla one day.

"What brings this on all of a sudden?" Carla responded.

"Well, I have been thinking about this a long time and it just seems so dark out in the back yard at night and the front walk could use a row of lights to emphasize it and they would accent the house nicely."

"You know what happens whenever you take on a project?"

I thought, of course I know what happens. But why be deterred by the obvious? When has a husband backed down from a challenge? Ask a husband to do something and a litany of excuses will pour forth.

"I can't. You know how my back bothers me?" Or, "My arm still hurts from high school football." Or, "My knees, you know how bad my knees are."

"I'll get around to it. Don't worry. Since when have I ever let you down?" is one of the best feints. The frazzled wife could answer, "Only the last two hundred and twelve times I asked you to do it!"

But challenge a husband once he has gotten an idea imbedded in his head? Only major brain surgery, wherein only three brain cells remained, could even slow down his determination to do a chosen task.

"We will team up in the design and the choice of fixtures and you will oversee the project to make sure I come out alive," I added.

Carla knew I would not be dissuaded. Besides, I thought, how bad can the project be? Traveling around I could see houses with successful walk lighting. They were still standing with no signs of abuse and on occasion the home owner could be seen getting into his car on his own power without any indications of bruises or loss of mobility.

Yes! If other people could do it, why not me?

The home megacenter loomed into our present again. "We should set up a bunk bed to sleep here, since we come to this place so often." I told Carla. She didn't even smile. Why encourage me further?

In the outdoor lighting section a clerk appropriately named Gabriel approached us. I looked around for his horn and seeing none felt compelled to proceed.

"May I help you? You seem confused," Gabriel said.

My first thought went back to Alfred and his innate megacenter-born sarcasm. Will Gabriel follow the noble tradition laid out before him by the store's management?

"Remember, Gabriel," the store manager would caution him, "we have a long and noble tradition to uphold. Sarcasm and working the customer until, in frustration, he buys one of each type of item he is looking for are bulwarks of our store policy."

"Yes, Mr. Clobbersmith, I understand. I read the company policy manual from cover to cover, in fact, including the covers."

"Now as an appendix to the policy manual, here is a book of snappy one-liners to use on your first customer. Try them out. I'm sure you'll like them," Mr. Clobbersmith would assure him.

And so another new megacenter employee entered my life to test his talents.

"Yes, Gabriel. We want to install a flood light for the backyard and a lighting row to accent the front walk."

"Well, this should be easy," he exclaimed. "You don't even need to wire in a light for the backyard. We have a nice selection of solar powered flood lights that are quick to install and use the sun for its electricity source."

Now, why didn't I think of that? A solar powered light for the dark, sunless backyard at night. What else does he have to offer me? A solar powered flashlight for those really dark evenings, when light would be such a relief? How about an underwater match for lighting cigarettes for those who must smoke while scuba diving? Maybe he can sell me a car designed to only go backwards to avoid those pesky and dangerous front end collisions.

"You still seem confused," Gabriel said. "What don't you understand? Here, let me show you the items on display."

The neat row of outdoor lights came with little photos of successful installations, one for each light fixture. The photos showed no signs of bodies spewed across the yard or ambulances parked on the grass ready to scoop up hapless do-it-yourselfers, who succumbed to their struggle.

Gabriel went on to explain how the light worked on a rechargeable battery that got its charge from a solar cell and even on cloudy days there was enough sunlight to do the job. Somehow I felt like a three-year old.

This effort was not going to be a Sabbath buster. A few minutes on a ladder with a hammer and screwdriver and the job would be done. Installing the front walk lights would be even easier: just hammer them into the ground and plug them in.

Gabriel assured us many of the megacenter customers have installed their own lights. Somehow Carla was not convinced. At home the saga of the two light arrays began. For expediency, the rear flood light became the first of the projects.

"Carla, I need to find a center point to place the flood light and maybe you can see if my choice makes sense."

I then taped three broom handles together with a ball of paper towels taped to one end to emulate the light fixture.

Now, you the reader are probably wondering where I got three broom handles. I am a pack rat and save what seem to be valuable parts of warn out devices. An extra broom handle can always come in handy in case an existing handle breaks. So when a broom becomes unusable the handle is scavenged for a potential future use.

Taping the broom handles together gave me the chance to show a position about ten feet or so above the ground, a minimum height recommended in the installation guide.

The back of the house had the garage appended to the left and I thought centering the light between the extreme ends of the house and garage made the most sense.

"That looks silly, Honey. Try centering the light between the outside edges of the house and forget about the garage."

Having asked her advice in the first place made it wise for me to follow her guidance. I paced off the length of the house twice to be sure and then paced back half the distance.

"Still doesn't look right," Carla said with some consternation. "Let me think about this for a minute."

"I know," she then chimed in, "place the light above the center point of the atrium door. That way, the light will not only look right it will give the most light where it is needed."

I couldn't argue with her logic, so out came the trusty tape measure to find the exact center point of the back patio door.

The next step brought me some trepidation along with a few beads of sweat on my forehead: the raising and climbing of the ladder.

I leaned the ladder against the back of the house and slowly climbed until I could reach ten feet above the ground. There would be no roof scaling and no swan dives from twenty feet in the air. This ladder work didn't even require any separating of the two parts. Just lean the ladder against the house, climb it and, of course, forget the tools.

Larry with his trusted wisdom convinced me to purchase a tool belt. I then placed into the belt screwdrivers, hammer, the plumb bob scavenged from my dad during our halcyon days of wallpapering, a drill, drill bits, a buzz saw, a machete, a shot gun to fend off any eagles trying to carry me off, a sword, and a bag of peanuts in case the job took longer than expected.

Of course, the tool belt was totally useless sitting on my work bench in the basement, while I was perched on a ladder. Oh ghosts of home projects, why do you torture me?

One warning in the instructions was to make sure the light was seated firmly against a wall stud behind vinyl siding to assure it would not fly away to Oz during a strong storm. Of course, the stud finding took some of the greatest ingenuity known to mankind: pressing the siding tight against the house and tapping gently with a hammer. Unfortunately, between outdoor sounds – wind, dogs, buzzing insects – and the soft insulation board under the siding no definitive stud location could be found.

Now here is where the ingenuity part came into play. Go indoors and find the stud there and assume it doesn't walk around during my trip back outdoors.

The stud was about an inch off center, something I certainly expected. Why have everything on perfect centers? There has to be a universal builder's manual that gives the offsets required for all aspects of construction. Sixteen inch centers for studs? No. Sixteen plus or minus sixteen inches says the manual.

Locating the stud outdoors did pose a small problem: locating the same stud outside. After carefully measuring I drove a small diameter brad nail through the siding and completely missed the stud. With a nice sized backplate on the light fixture, I could drive several small holes until the stud width had been fully mapped, knowing the holes would be covered.

A small dab of caulking compound sealed each errant hole and the backplate installation went forward. What a Do-It-Yourselfer I had become! No pratfalls off the ladder. No slamming the hammer against my thumb. No driving screws through my palm.

With Carla's help and the use of the plumb bob and tape measure, the appropriate location ten feet above the ground was found.

Placing the light fixture actually proved surprisingly easy. The installation instructions were very clear, the manufacturer supplied all the required hardware and I only had to make one extra trip down the ladder to the basement – to get the drill bits!

Best of all, I didn't fall off the ladder! I just can't mention this enough!

I completed the whole project in a little over an hour – an all-time record for my handyman work. In fact, this job was so easy it motivated me to tackle the front walk lights the same day. Another hour or two borrowed from the Sabbath shouldn't hurt anything. The operative words: "Sabbath" and "shouldn't."

The front walk measured twenty-eight feet and I had six lights in the pack. Starting four feet from the stoop outside the front door would exactly accommodate the six lights placed four feet apart. The project was off to an amazingly easy start.

I was so sure of easy success I lay the six lights on the lawn and carefully measured the distance between each fixture, placing them exactly four feet apart. The operative words were "carefully" and "exactly."

Somehow my measuring and locating ability falls into that silly contractor joke. An interior contractor carefully measures the lumber needed to frame an alcove he is building for a customer. No matter what he does, the pieces just don't ever fit together properly. Finally, in frustration he complains to the home owner, "I don't understand it. I measured the piece once and cut it twice and it is *still* too short."

Undeterred, I plowed forward. Placing the cable across each light fixture and attaching the cable created no difficulties. A fifty-foot length of electric cable was supplied and I left about twenty feet of excess cable to attach to the power pack, trimming off the excess later. What a Do-It-Yourselfer!

With the six lights daisy-chained together and ready to install, the easy part loomed ahead of me: pushing the lights into the ground and burying the cable.

The first four lights pressed into place quite nicely. Too nicely! When something is too good to be true it probably isn't. Fixture number five hit a rock.

"This should be just a small rock blocking my way," I thought out loud. The operative words were "should" and "small."

Digging around the rock showed it to be about five inches across, certainly not an insurmountable obstacle. The light fixture, however, refused to go any deeper than a couple of inches no matter where I placed it.

By poking a small garden spade in bigger and bigger circles, the extent of the rock became evident. It was *big.* Truly, very big. The declared surface covered some three feet in diameter with all of it too shallow to successfully plant the lighting fixture. As expected the center of the rock was four feet from the previous fixture placement.

The cement walk placement just skirted the edge of the rock. Did the builder know about this beast lurking below the surface and just so happened to curve the walk enough to get around it? It didn't matter now, for this side of the walk is where the lights had to be in order for the power pack to be plugged into the outside outlet.

Geologists in the coming eons will ponder the question of rock placement in developments.

"Sondersohn, what can you make of this remnant? It looks just like a walk formation placed ever so perfectly next to this subterranean mountain."

"Dr. Michaels, I believe this is what is aptly termed walkus locatus syndrome, a common disorder wherein a person known in those times as a builder would locate any structure next to a humongous underground structure known then simply as a rock," Sondersohn replied.

"What is the significance of the term 'walkus' if the understated rock could be found anywhere, Sondersohn?"

"Oh, no. Not simply anywhere. Oh, no. The term walkus refers to the most common aspect of this syndrome: the location of the front or back walk exactly alongside of a humongous rock, leaving the rock in the way of a homeowner's attempt to plant something called a garden, place a small decorative fence or place lighting fixtures."

"Then, this subterranean beast could be found anywhere a homeowner was likely to place some ancillary object?"

"Correct, Dr. Michaels. Say, for example one was to locate the necessary spot to put a storage shed based on yard structure and local codes. Since the shed would require both securing four posts to be driven a couple of feet into the ground and a concrete base, that is precisely where the top of a twenty-foot in diameter subterranean structure would be found, completely blocking one of the posts."

Certainly, my rock didn't descend another seventeen feet into the ground, but it was large enough to completely disrupt my light fixture placement. Moving the rock could not be done, especially not without cracking the edge of the walk. Besides, I could not determine the actual shape and size of the rock.

My dad came to the rescue – in a fashion. He had what he termed a coal chisel, an oversized chisel meant for cracking small rocks. The key word here is "small."

"Well, son, I can't say I recommend doing this, but the only way you can get the light post into the ground is to chisel away until you have the proper depth or jackhammer the rock."

"Dad, isn't there some type of drill I can use?"

"You'd have to drill a four-inch diameter hole. I think that's a lot bigger than drills for placing dynamite. I don't know where you would get such a drill and how you would handle it without tearing something on your body."

Tearing something on my body – one of my least favorite pastimes! So I drove over and procured the coal chisel and combined it with my four-pound sledge hammer to get the necessary depth for placing my light.

It occurred to me to make sure the sixth light could be placed without incident. It could. Now, a simple job suddenly developed into something horrendously time consuming.

Carla just looked at me through the window. She didn't say anything, semaphore signal anything to me, blink her eyes in Morse code, mouth any words or even make any facial expressions. She didn't have to. She knew my frustration.

I proceeded to whack away at the rock. The rock resisted with all of its might. Each whack sent a jolt through my left wrist. I forgot to mention I am right-handed, meaning I grasped the chisel with my left hand.

After some thirty minutes my shoulder began to feel the effects of the sledging. Whack! Whack! Whack! I persisted and the rock resisted. The struggle developed into thirty-minute rest periods in between now twenty-minute hammer and chisel sessions.

After about three hours I made a fateful decision. Hold the chisel at an angle with the business end towards me and hammer away.

The first two blows seemed to show some progress, in that the rock didn't grow any bigger in defiance.

The next hammer blow shot a medium-sized piece of rock at my face, hitting me square on the eye. Eyelid reflex seems faster than head jerk reflex and my eyeball was spared the direct hit.

I let out a small lion's roar, grabbed my face and began rolling back-and-forth on the ground. Carla just happened to look out the window at that moment and witnessed my self-inflicted injury. She rushed out to help me.

"What on earth were you thinking? Let me see," she cried out.

Blood streamed down over my eye from a gash just below my eyebrow and Carla ran into the house, grabbed some peroxide solution, and a large piece of gauze. She ran back out and furiously applied her medical skills, honed from dealing with skinned knees, cut hands, and other sundry wounds fourth graders accrue doing what they call play and the rest of us know as pitched battle.

We are going to the hospital. This cut needs stitches. Luckily, Eric had headed over to his friend's house for a sleep over. I mention "luckily" because Elaine had the tough enough constitution to handle seeing blood. Eric would have turned white from a near faint. The trip to the hospital may have then had two victims: one from blood and one from seeing it.

At the hospital emergency room I was told to sit down and I would be called in the order I signed in. Fine. Before continuing on I want to caution the reader I am a terrible patient. I scream, kick, carry on, howl, cry, and roll on the floor pounding my fists and all of this *before* the doctor arrives. Waiting for the inevitable only heightened my sense of self-torture.

"Honey, you aren't that injured. Just a cut above the eye. It could have been much worse. You could have lost that eye." Though Carla's words flowed with reassurance, she did not allay my fears.

Finally after a quarter of a lifetime, my turn came. The check-in procedure was simple: what happened and how are you going to pay for this?

Next Carla and I were ushered into a room or, rather, a space designated as a room by sliding curtains on each side and in the front. Howls emanating from other rooms did nothing to help my fraying nerves.

All my mind could comprehend was Carla's cautionary word, "stitches." I could imagine the doctor holding a small handheld sewing machine and setting the stitch style.

"Now let's see here. Maybe a crisscross pattern would look nice over your eye. Or should I go for a zigzag pattern. Yes, zigzag pattern it is. That will flow nicely with your eyebrow."

"Now doctor," I screamed, "couldn't you just tape the wound closed or use super glue?"

"No, no, no. None of that will do. We do fancy work here. Which brings up the matter of thread color choice. Do you want blood red? Or skin orange?"

I began to audibly moan. Carla didn't have to ask what my mind had conjured up. She just patted the back of my hand and said quietly, "Just relax. This will all be okay."

After about ten minutes a young doctor came into our space. He greeted us and shook my hand.

"Hello. I am doctor Fressner and I will be attending to you this afternoon. Now, please explain to me what happened"

Somehow "I-was-chiseling-a-rock-without-safety-glasses-and-cut-myself-with-flying-rock-guts" just didn't seem noble enough to be carted into an emergency room. My mind summoned more heroic adventures.

"Well, doc, I was laying out lighting fixtures along my front walk when a giant snake rushed out from under one of the bushes and lunged at me. We had a ten minute pitched battle. He kept coming and I held him off with mighty swipes of my hands. Before he gave up he jumped up and bit me over the eye just to make a point."

"I see," the doctor answered. "Now, how did you know the snake was a he?"

"Well, doc, it was like this. I was laying out lighting fixtures along my front walk when a massive bear lumbered over to me. It was clear from his growls he was going to eat me. We had a ten minute pitched battle. He kept coming and I held him off with mighty swipes of my arms. Before he gave up he bit me over the eye just to get a taste for future reference."

"I see. Was he carrying a menu?"

"Well, doc, here is what happened. I was laying out lighting fixtures along my front walk when a giant eagle swooped down and tried to carry me off. We had a ten minute pitched battle. He kept coming and I held him off with mighty swipes of my arms and legs. Before he gave up, he pecked me over the eye just out of spite."

"I see. Was he wearing an American flag shirt?"

I actually gave in and simply told him the silly truth.

"Oh, there is nothing to be ashamed of. Accidents happen. That's what we are here for," Doctor Fressner responded.

After a one minute observation liberally punctuated with "Hmmms" and "Ahas" he decided I needed six stitches, explaining the options and why the stitching was the best choice.

"Do you use a handheld mini sewing machine?" I inquired.

"Actually you are thinking of the stapler. No this will be just sutured by hand."

Actually I wasn't thinking of a stapler and enough trepidation crossed my mind to not ask what the stapler was and what it did.

The procedure went painlessly except for the initial needle prick to administer the local anesthesia.

As a squeamish baby when it comes to blood and needles, this occasion did not go smoothly for me. My nerves kept me talking until Dr. Fressner threatened to sew my mouth shut.

Images of another doctor – Victor Frankenstein – quickly fluttered up into my mind and Dr. Fressner's countenance darkened as he cackled that hideous cackle monster makers are known for.

His nurse assistant, named Igor, slouched his way around me holding my head in a death grip as Doctor Fressnerstein worked his wonders, sewing my head closed and installing those stylish electrodes in my neck.

"Zoon you vill be whole, my monster, zoon. Yass, zoon."

Igor imitated the unsettling cackle as he tightened his grip on my head.

"There. That should do it," Dr. Fressner said. "All finished. Come back in one week and we'll remove those stitches."

My mind tried to imagine who the "we" was. He and nurse Igor? Or maybe he and I? Would I hold my own head still while he pulled the stitches from my head with pliers?

Before leaving, the good doctor gave me a sheet of instructions on caring for my new stitches. The instructions did not mention caring for my neck electrodes.

Back home, after putting away the tools and front walk lighting in the garage, I just decided to rest for the remainder of the day.

At work the age-old story of walking into a door trumped telling the truth. My boss didn't accept it, but he just shrugged his shoulders and walked away, never bringing the subject up again.

My right shoulder pained me all the next few weeks due to the odious whacking with the sledge hammer. Somehow the human shoulder design did not accommodate sledging away with big hammers.

I wonder how lumberjacks of old held up year after year of wailing away with axes at giant tree trunks. I wonder how many had to have their heads sewn back on after the ax head released from the handle, dislodging his head from his shoulders.

Regardless of Dr. Fressner's success or the stamina of legendary lumberjacks, my days of sledge hammering rocks were over.

The following Saturday I made the decision to pack all the lighting equipment into a box and store it in the attic over the garage. Too much had been done to the items to return them to the store and too much had to be done to make them work.

Carla agreed it was better to admit defeat than to stress my shoulder and wits further.

At least there was more light out in the back yard. I settled for a 500 batting average.

CHAPTER SEVENTEEN

Revelation

We now fast-forward to the present one last time.

I am back to sitting on my own front porch watching my children play in the yard.

There are yet many lessons for me to impart to Eric and Elaine and much fatherly knowledge.

No doubt a Steve Rain will enter at least once as they move to distant shores. Hopefully, both can avoid ogres with bone grinding machines. A great Gape may threaten to swallow his or her house. And certainly the Friday Night Effect will intrude on their lives from time to time. Nobody can predict the future and who would really want to know what comes next?

No. We all travel our paths with the understanding the Ghost of Sabbaths past will sweep into our lives from time to time.

Honoring the Sabbath comes with various duties depending on how serious one is about his or her religious obligations.

I once heard a rabbi speaking on the radio about keeping the Sabbath. Why a rabbi and not a minister or a priest? That day a rabbi just so happened to be on. His advice was quite prescient.

He said holding the Sabbath and honoring one's religion is the noblest of purposes. Even if one is not religious and does not see any reason to honor the Sabbath, it is a day of rest. Holding the Sabbath as a day of rest adds a measure of meaning to one's life. He added we all need one day a week to recharge our batteries and recoup our senses. Using the Sabbath as just that day – a true day of rest – adds significance to this special day and growth to our lives.

I have learned much over the years and I have much to learn. Sabbaths are still broken. I tell myself sometimes there is no choice and sometimes an emergency arises requiring my attention.

The Friday Night Effect will always be with me. My boss no longer wants to grind my bones, but he will never understand the need for a day of rest. At rare times, workloads spill over from Saturday to Sunday.

A typical conversation between Mr. Jorgensen and me always seems to follow this pattern.

"Uhhh … Can you make it Sunday? We just need to get on top of this work load. I would really appreciate it if you can make it."

"Sure, Mr. Jorgensen. I see no reason not to make it. But I do ask why we can't hire more staff. Our workload certainly justifies it."

"Uhhh … Upper management would never go for it. They see people as cost and we have to hold costs down."

"Have you ever requested more staff?"

"As I said, upper management would never go for it. I would really appreciate it if you can make it Sunday."

The operative words were always "I would really appreciate it." Translation: You can say "no" at your own peril.

"Except," I once added, "Eric's baseball game and Elaine's dance recital are taking place Sunday." That time both occasions did occur. And when work review time came around my refusal to work Sunday came to haunt me. I lost some allocation of a raise and a little disdain from my boss. But I saw Eric hit a two-run triple and Elaine dance her little feet off. Those events were priceless.

The Sabbath won that time and it lost some other times. Once I did not witness Eric's game-winning home run and vowed Mr. Jorgensen would not steal another key family event from me! Even more ironic, I only made the average salary increase. Apparently, it was time to hide my boss's stapler in some far flung corner of the building and rescue it once more.

Why did I seek so many ways to break the Sabbath? Why is the sky blue? Why do wolves howl at the moon? Why do whales beach themselves?

The answer is all of the above. Explain one and you explain them all. I am not foolish or vain enough to vow I will never again fail to hold the Sabbath dear, but I will make a mighty effort.

When the time comes for me to be put in my final resting place, nobody will stand and say how much I dedicated to my work and how much that meant to my boss. They won't declare how green my lawn was or how pretty my built-in shelving looked. They won't regale the funeral attendees with grand stories of battles won against moles and ants. No. Someone will stand and tell the bereaved how nice a family man I was. They will gush euphorically about how well my children are doing and how much time I spent with them and Carla.

Very few die wealthy and proud of the costs to their families of getting there. Very few die wealthy and proud of the deductions against family life and how much better their travels through life were versus time spent with family.

I am back to sitting on my own front porch watching my children play in the yard.

These are not the best of times or the worst of times. These are simply the most important and rewarding of times.

Mr. Jorgensen has penciled me in for next Sunday's departmental work detail. This week he is going to find out why pencils have erasers.

Attending religious services is one way to honor the Sabbath. But how much honor does a religious service create if the remainder of the day involves toiling at some task that could just as well be handled on another day?

In my own view, taking the children to a movie or planting flowers or just relaxing talking to Carla fit well into honoring the Sabbath. One does not have to sit on a chair and stare at a wall for a dozen hours. In fact, just overt sloth may not be honoring anything but overt sloth.

Piling your young family into the car and just going for a long drive to explore places not before seen or to take roads just for the sake of seeing what is there can be rewarding.

Just getting down on the floor and playing a game with your family can also be rewarding.

There are so many ways to enjoy that special day and so many ways to make it special. Plodding my way to work just to satisfy the whims of my boss does not fit honoring the Sabbath.

This book contains many other ways I chose to not honor the Sabbath and many ways in which just being a home owner chose some of those ways for me.

Hopefully, my journey has brought a smile or two to your faces and a lesson or two to your hearts.

www.ingramcontent.com/pod-product-compliance
Lightning Source LLC
LaVergne TN
LVHW041800060526
838201LV00046B/1062
* 9 7 9 8 8 8 6 4 0 4 5 1 7 *